THE NEUTERED MOTHER, THE SEXUAL FAMILY

AND OTHER TWENTIETH CENTURY TRAGEDIES

THE NEUTERED MOTHER, THE SEXUAL FAMILY

AND OTHER TWENTIETH CENTURY TRAGEDIES

MARTHA ALBERTSON FINEMAN

1995

Routledge ☐ New York   London

Published in 1995 by

Routledge
29 West 35th Street
New York, NY 10001

Published in Great Britain by

Routledge
11 New Fetter Lane
London EC4P 4EE

Printed in the United States of America on acid-free paper.

Fineman, Martha.
    The neutered mother, the sexual family, and other twentieth century
tragedies / Martha Albertson Fineman.
        p. cm.
    Includes bibliographical references and index.
    ISBN 0-415-91026-9 (acid-free paper).—ISBN 0-415-91027-7 (acid-free
paper)
    1. Domestic relations. 2. Sex and law. 3. Sociological
jurisprudence. 4. Feminist jurisprudence. 5. Mother and child.
6. Family.   I. Title.
K670.F56   1994
346.01'5—dc20
[342.615]   94-30807
                                                                  CIP

*This book is dedicated to
my mentor and friend,*

Murray Edelman,

*who showed me the power
in an eclectic approach.*

Contents

Acknowledgement   xi

1 Introduction   1
    I.   Three Vignettes   1
    II.   Family As Usual   6

Part One—Concepts and Constucts   11

2 Law, Ideology, and the Perspective of Feminist Legal Theory—Limitations
    on Imaginations   14
    I.   The Limits of Law   15
       A. Law and Imagining Society   16
       B. Classification and Residue   18
       C. Those Who Would Reform   19
    II.   The Role of Ideology   20
       A. Ideology and Discourse   21
       B. Patriarchical Ideology   22
    III. Feminist Legal Theory   24
       A. Women in Families in Feminist Legal Theory   25

3 Differences in Context—Feminist Legal Theory and Gendered Lives   34
    I.   The Evolution of Difference in Feminist Legal Thought   36
       A. The Initial Feminist Project—Women Into Law   36
       B. The Shape of the Contemporary Debate   39
       C. Questions of Representation in Feminist Legal Theory   43
          1. Differences Among Women   44
          2. Representation and Tokenism   45
    II.   Shared Position—The Concept of A Gendered Life   47
       A. Making Gender Central   47
       B. Gendered Life in Application   49
       C. Differences Among Women   51
    III. Conclusion   54

Part Two—The Neutered Mother   67

4 The Neutered Mother   70
   I.   *Mother As Symbol*   71
   II. *The Construction of Mother in Law*   75
     A. *The Law of the Mother*   76
       1. Early Law—Motherhood at Divorce   76
       2. Early Law—Never-Married Mothers   79
     B. *Modern Trends*   82
       1. Motherhood Descending—Transformations at Divorce   82
       2. Motherhood Descending—Nonmarital Motherhood   83
   III. *Conclusion*   87

5 The Deviant Mother   101
   I.   *The Construction of Maternal Deviancy in Poverty Discourses*   106
     A. *Popular Discourse*   107
     B. *Political Discourse*   110
   II. *The Construction of Maternal Deviancy in the Context of Divorce*   118
   III. *Abusive Mothers*   122
   IV. *Conclusion*   123

Part Three—The Sexual Family   143

6 The Sexual Family   145
   I.   *Structuring Intimacy*   145
   II. *The Sexual or Natural Family as Sacred*   150
     A. *The Merger of Sacred and Secular*   150
       1. Deep Structure and Metanarratives   151
     B. *Legal Challenges to the Natural Family*   155
       1. The Egalitarian Family as a Challenge   157
   III. *The Undeveloped Dependency Discourse*   161
     A. *Inevitable and Derivative Dependencies*   161
     B. *The Failure of the Family*   164

7 The Limits of Privacy—The Public Family   177
   I.   *The Discourse of Intervention*   177
   II. *Privacy and Single Mothers*   180
     A. *The Limits of Privacy—Separate Patrimonies*   180
       1. The Constitution and Individual Privacy   181
       2. The Family as "Entity" and the Common-Law Concept
         of Privacy   186

B. The Public Family   189
III. Conclusion—The Role of Law in Social Change   192

Part Four—Other Tragedies and Utopian Visions   199

8 Other Tragedies   201
I. The Discourse of Fathers' Rights   201
   A. Three Strains   201
   B. Submerged Symbolism—Father and the Masculine   205
II. Differentiating Fathers   208
   A. The "Responsible" Reproducer   209
   B. The "Irresponsible" Reproducer   211
   C. The Paternity Proceeding—Transforming Irresponsible
     Reproduction   212
III. Single Mothers and the "Costs" of Responsibility   213
IV. The Further Separation of Mother from Child   217

9 Re-Visioning   226
I. Re-Visioning Family Law   227
   A. Ending Marriage as a Legal Category   228
   B. Mother/Child Dyad   230
   C. Mother and Metaphor   233

Index   237

Acknowledgment

I would like to thank Marie Ashe, Sherry Colb, Dirk Hartog, Dorothy Roberts, and Carol Sanger for their comments on an earlier draft of this book. They greatly enriched the final version with their generous remarks. Martha Mahoney made many valuable suggestions during the two years I was engaged in the project.

I would like to extend a special note of gratitude to Joyce Davis who, as a graduate law student, took time from her own work to help me through the morass of rewriting and footnote construction that seem to inevitably accompany any writing project in law. Joyce's considerable energy and her unwavering faith in the project helped to bolster my own morale at crucial times. Isabel Karpin and Hyunah Yang provided important research, criticism, and comment. Adrienne Hiegel read and commented on the manuscript with a good editor's eye. I thank all three of these students for their contributions.

I would also like to thank my assistant, Cynthia Hewett, for her essential work on what she consistently referred to as "that darn book." We are both relieved that it is finally finished.

1

Introduction

THIS BOOK CONTAINS both a critique and a vision. The critique examines the cultural and legal processes in which the sexual-intimate connection has been designated as dominant in the construction of family—husband and wife established as the core intimate relationship around which law, politics, and policy revolve. The critique is the product of a long analytic, conceptual, intellectual, and personal struggle with the limitations of current family law that have made me reflect on the ways in which our society validates and defines appropriate intimacy. The vision is the result of a much shorter process, but it has evolved as the limitations of the traditional ways of thinking about family intimacy became clearer.

I. Three Vignettes

There are three stages to my thinking on these issues, which can be captured in three vignettes. The first has to do with my experience during the late 1970s as a Commissioner on the Madison Wisconsin Equal Opportunities Commission during the time when an Alternative Family Ordinance that would confer some benefits and protections on nontraditional families was first suggested in that city. In the process of considering the Ordinance, I wondered why "alternative" families were only conceived of by the other Commissioners in forms that mimicked marriage—unmarried, monogamous, "committed" heterosexuals or same-sex couples. I suggested that alternatives not be exclusively defined in terms of two adults with or without their children; what about plural sexual groupings or nonsexual intimate connections?

I argued that heterosexual monogamous pairings failed to reflect the situations of many groupings that functioned as families. I objected to sexually affiliated couples being valorized as the new norm. Only relationships that could be analogized to marriage stood a chance of inclusion within the protection of the Alternative Family Ordinance. The Commission had an opportunity (at least in my mind) to really rethink the concept of the family and to ensure protection for many different types of alternative formations. It failed to rise to the task, suffering instead from a collective failure of nerve and imagination.

Some Commission attention was diverted by the (politically) threatening prospect of proposed recognition of polygamy and polyandry, but even my concern with the nonsexual affiliates was not sympathetically received. I was at that time particularly concerned with the refusal to accommodate the dependencies of many "adult" children (those over the age of 18 years, in most jurisdictions). Many children older than 18 live at home with a parent or parents in "dependent" relationships, yet our alternative family model would not reflect or accommodate that dependency by ensuring they could not be dropped from family insurance coverage, for example. Furthermore, I argued that many people assume responsibility for aging parents, some of whom—though dependent in some aspects—might live separately or be able to provide substantially, though not completely, for their own support. These dependencies were also ignored in a system that assumed the nuclear family paradigm.

These nonsexual relationships would not obviously be counted as "family" under the proposed Ordinance for purposes of deciding who was entitled to benefits such as insurance coverage or tax consideration. These dependencies were not organized nor understood by the Commissioners as the functional or symbolic equivalents of marriage: they were not based on sexual affiliation and therefore were not *ipso facto* included in the conceptualization of what constitutes an appropriate "alternative."

It was at this point that it first began to be clear to me that, for even the most "progressive" among us, the "family" has at its core a sexual tie. We may not articulate our premises, but the "sexual family" has been invested by our culture and society with exclusive legitimacy—it is the foundational institution (these concepts are developed more fully in chapter 6). The sexual tie may not be one formally sanctified by marriage, or may be one that exists between members of the same sex, but even in our "modern" thinking, sexuality is central to our understanding of intimacy and family connection.

Several years later, a second event reinforced that initial insight into the nature of our societal understanding of intimacy. The sexual formulation of intimacy also determined the direction of the discussions about faculty retention at the university where I was teaching at that time. The proposed plan was to institute a spousal retention program in which other departments and schools within the university would be given financial and other "incentives" to hire the spouses of those "star" faculty who were sought to be hired or retained. Of course, this being the mid-1980s, there was pressure to expand the definition of what constituted a "spouse" along the same lines as those described above in regard to alternative families—including same-sex and nonmarried heterosexual couples.

I raised a fundamentally different question about the politics of incentives with my suggestion that the faculty-retention policy also address the need to provide and care for children. I suggested that we provide incentives to stay by granting scholarships to the university or private school tuition for the children of faculty we were in danger of losing. Given the relatively low salaries at that state school and the increasing costs of education, it seemed to me a significant way to tie someone to the institution. This suggestion was received as outlandish, a dismissal I still do not entirely understand. I would predict that there would be relatively few situations in which "parental-faculty retention" would come into play. In addition, and in contrast to a spousal retention program, a child subsidy system anticipates that the university's obligation would last only a limited time. It would also be much less costly on a yearly basis, given that tuition is typically far less than salaries.

Furthermore, I had some conceptual problems with the whole idea of spouse/faculty retention policies—those responding to faculty members' claims that if "spouses" were not appropriately accommodated within the university in some capacity, they would leave. Marriage is a relationship easily terminated. Parent-child ties, by contrast, tend to last—they are not as fragile in our contemporary society. Someone's spouse could be hired and within a year or so separate from and/or divorce the retained faculty member, thereby severing family ties but keeping their university ones. Could one assume that, in this case, the retained faculty member might also form a new relationship with another (perhaps, younger) person who would need to find local employment, thus beginning again the university's search for accommodation if the "star" faculty member was to be retained?

I was intrigued by the policy that recognized only sexual affiliation as worthy of subsidy and incentive. It made no sense that it is the most tenuous, least permanent, of our intimate relationships that is afforded the most significant and privileged position in both public and private institutions— subsidized on both ideological and economic levels. Certainly the law both reflects and facilitates this.

With these experiences in mind, I began teaching family law in the mid-1980s. The third situation that confirmed for me the hold of sexual affiliation on our thinking were the responses to an exercise I developed in 1990 to focus my students' attention on questions of the social construction of the core family connection and the creation of deviancy.

During the semester, I ask my students to define for me and themselves what they believe to be the "core family unit." I use the concept of "core" to describe the configuration below which one no longer imagines there is a "family," attempting to get the notion of a primal or basic unit. I suggest there may be alternatives to the traditional nuclear image of husband/father, wife/mother, and child, bound by a conglomeration of blood and legal bonds. What about two adults? Is it necessary that there be children in order to call something a family? Is it even necessary to have more than one person for the label to apply?

A few students venture that marriage, formal and celebrated the way it has been for generations, is the basic building block of family formation and that it should remain so. Others are quick to point out that formality should be irrelevant and that couples not legally tied together can, nonetheless, constitute a family. They often feel this is particularly true when there are children.

What seems to occupy my students' attention (and, I might add, passion) is the issue of whether informal, nonlegal relationships should be considered the equivalent of marriage for the purpose of defining a family. Sometimes there is a debate about how "far" to go in equating informal relationships with marriage. Heterosexual unions are the easiest analogy, but some students have difficulty with same-sex relationships.

About this point in the class debate, I suggest that, instead of trying to fit more and more relationships into the legal space that marriage occupies by asserting that they are entitled to the same set of privileges and protection as marriage, we abolish marriage as a legal category. In other words, I suggest that all relationships between adults be nonlegal and, therefore, nonprivileged—unsubsidized by the state. In this way, "equality" is achieved in regard to all choices of sexual relational affiliations. I suggest we destroy the marital model altogether and collapse all sexual relationships into the same category—private—not sanctioned, privileged, or preferred by law.

My "reform" is, of course, far more radical than just the removal of formality attending the formation of family. It addresses the nature of the way individual intimacy is understood in our society and legal culture. To illustrate this, I return to the initial question, identifying the core, primal, basic family affiliation. I tell my students at this point that I define my core unit as mother and child. Typically there is silence, perhaps some laughter (in disbelief?), and, eventually, the inevitable response, "But that's sexist— it excludes men."

"Why," I respond, "do you think that men's major, definitive role in the family is only expressed in terms of their sexual affiliation with women? Don't men also find their places within the unit as sons, or as a mother's brother, as uncles to her children? What about grandfathers? Why are you disturbed by a paradigm that challenges the way we typically think about intimacy between men and women—a vertical rather than a horizontal tie; a biological rather than a sexual affiliation, an intergenerational organization of intimacy?"

I continue by pointing out that in defining a core family unit, what has happened is the creation of a norm, a baseline. It does not mean that other adult family characters are excluded: fathers, or nonprimary caretakers who have sexual affiliation to the primary caretaker, are certainly free, under my model, to develop and maintain significant connections with their sexual partner and her children if she agrees to such affiliation. The mother may also wish to forge ties and relationships with nonsexual affiliates.

Under my intimacy scheme, however, single mothers and their children, indeed all "extended" families transcending generations, would not be the "deviant" and forgotten or chastised forms that they are considered to be today because they do not include a male head of household. Family and sexuality would not be confluent; rather, the mother-child formation would be the "natural" or core family unit—it would be the base entity around which social policy and legal rules are fashioned. The intergenerational, nonsexual organization of intimacy is what would be protected and privileged in law and policy.

The purpose of this exercise is to help my students understand that our definition of a core, primal family unit is also a definition of deviancy. Those configurations that cannot be analogized—that fall below our ideological (and emotional) minimum—will not be considered "normal" families entitled to privacy and respect. They will be cast as deficient and therefore will be at risk of more direct and intrusive state regulation and control—even sanction and prohibition. I hope that this exercise makes my students think about their firmly entrenched beliefs about what is "natural," "desirable," and, hence, defensible in regard to the institution of the family.

This book is a further attempt to grapple with these issues. It reflects my conviction that legal regulation is grounded on societal beliefs and expectations that continue to reflect unexamined gendered politics, policies, and practices. There have been massive structural changes during the past several decades in the ways many of us live our family lives. We have created, then valorized, new patterns of family formation, holding them out as the equivalent (moral and/or functional) of traditional marriage. But the tenacity and vitality of our inherited beliefs or ideologies about the family has meant that the changes are in some ways superficial—merely altering form, while leaving aspiration and expectation undisturbed. Our ideological understanding of the functioning and societal role of the family (whatever its form) has not undergone much transformation.

This book is also an exploration of the extent and tenacity of the ideological components of patriarchy and their role in the construction of gender as reflected in law and policy. The exploration results in a pessimistic assessment of the possibility for more than superficial changes in the social construction of the family and the functions it is designated to perform in its relationship to the state. We seem destined to perpetuate the old mistakes even if they are cast as "reforms."

II. Family As Usual

On a general level, the public and political rhetoric about families retains predictable orthodoxy. We all shun the characterization of "deviance" and seek to align ourselves and our behavior with the safety of normalcy. Some may accept, even embrace, altered norms of family formation and functioning but still resist the application of ideological labels to their personal experiences. Thus, women who support equal rights at work and are unhappy with the unequal burdens they bear at home are careful to indicate that they are not "feminists." At the same time, many of those brave enough to live "alternative lifestyles" still struggle to analogize their situations with the traditional norm—as "marriage-like." This strategy of attempting to expand the categories of the "normal" has limits. Categories can only be stretched so far and retain credibility. Moreover, as the 1992 presidential campaign rhetoric illustrates, the backlash of the traditionalists has been mounted and is vicious, as the family is openly designated as a site of cultural embattlement.

The attacks on "family as usual" have been vigorous as social movements such as feminism and groups organized around issues such as children's "rights" have addressed the exploitative potential of traditional roles and patterns of dominance. Proponents of a different type of family functioning, largely professional and educational elites, have successfully recast the modern family as nonhierarchical—expressing an egalitarian ideal. But, even when newly crafted societal aspirations have been reflected in reforms to traditional laws, they have not heralded changes in practice. In spite of the significant rhetorical reorientation of family law, the functioning family remains the most gendered of our social institutions. The new family formations merely replicate old concepts and beliefs and there is little fundamental challenge to the ways we think about the institution of the family and its relationship to society. Shared societal presumptions about the naturalness and inevitability of existing gendered role definitions and divisions continue to be pervasive.

There is a great deal of attention in this book to the creation and perpetuation of this ideology. Definitions and discussions of patriarchy as ideology are central to the theoretical positions developed about motherhood and the primacy of sexual affiliation. The basic message is that, from the perspective of law reform, the role of ideology is conservative. Our individual experiences are structured and reinforced by discursive structures (including law) that surround us, defining the contours of our everyday lives. These unexamined constructs reflect ideological concepts that act as limitations on our imaginations.

The articulation of the issues, as well as the re-visioning of the societal purpose of the family and the role of family law that concludes this volume, grew out of my frustration with the ways in which our laws organize and regulate intimacy. However, this book—although ostensibly focused on the regulation of family relationships—is concerned with more than mere legal rules and legalistic reasoning. Consequently, the next two chapters include some historical material on the development of contemporary debates about intimacy and families in feminist legal theory. I consider the many ways in which our lives are "gendered" in American society and argue for some accommodation of relevant differences. I also reflect on the limitations of law as a major tool for societal transformation. Subsequent chapters specifically address the title concepts of "neutered mother" and "sexual family" as well as develop the myriad "tragedies" inherent in the way our society casts and contains intimate connections.

In the final chapter of this book, I propose the end of family law as we know it with the suggestion that marriage be abolished as a legal category. I offer a utopian re-visioning of the family—a reconceptualization of family intimacy that redefines the legal core unit away from our current focus on sexual or horizontal intimacy. My vision of the appropriate core family unit for purposes of law and policy may anger and alarm many readers. Troubling to some feminists in particular will be the fact that in redefining familial intimacy and the role of law I develop two different archetypes of dependency that have gendered as well as policy implications.

"Inevitable dependency" is the term used to describe the status of need for caretaking embodied in the young, many of the elderly and disabled, as well as the ill. "Derivative dependency" results because the caretaker is dependent on external resources to fulfill the caretaking role. The relationship between these two types of dependencies is exemplified in this book by the metaphor of Mother/Child—the intimate connection to be protected and subsidized by state policy and law in my scheme. This caretaking dyad would replace the historic dyad of the heterosexual married couple as the core intimate family unit upon which family policy and law are constructed.[1]

Although I know it is destined to be misunderstood, I will point out initially (and will reiterate in chapter 9) that in this context I am using the

Mother/Child pairing as a metaphor. This metaphor was deliberately chosen because as a cultural symbol in its positive aspects it exemplifies caretaking. I want to build on those positive aspects and confront the negative and oppressive manifestations of the stereotypes about mothering. In doing both of these things, I hope to extend the image of mothering to contexts well beyond the nuclear family.

My argument is that, as a society, we do not value caretaking or caretakers and this is true outside as well as inside the family. In fact, we burden those who would caretake with ideological and actual impediments that make their tasks more difficult. I purposefully use the term "caretaker" rather than the more common "caregiver" in this book to describe the nurturing work mothers typically do. Caretaking, in common usage, involves more "commercial" forms of "taking care of" something (or someone). Caretaking, often undertaken on a "temporary" basis and/or for an absent "owner," implies that the caring activity will be compensated. Nurturing work should not be assumed to be "given" as a gift, to either the dependent or the society that benefits from the "caregivers' " sacrifices. Taking care of someone such as a child while they are young, until they "become their own person," is work, represents a major contribution to the society, and should be explicitly recognized as such.

Note

1. Some people would describe the nuclear family as a triad, with the components being father, mother, and child. As I argue in chapter 6, the child is not a full focal point for policy and politics. The child is an abstraction, significant for assessing the status of the adults—for measuring the dimensions of power and control lost or accumulated in the symbolic struggle between men and women, in which the family is a primary contemporary battleground.

PART I

Concepts and Constructs

IN THE TWO CHAPTERS IN THIS SECTION, I set forth some of the basic theoretical and historical concepts I am using in approaching the topic of motherhood, family formation, and the regulation of intimacy. This section constitutes an "abbreviated primer" on feminist jurisprudence, with a few "new" theoretical directions developed. This material will be generally familiar to some readers, but the specific application of legal feminist themes to the institution of the family is relatively unexamined territory and should be of interest to even the most sophisticated reader. This section is the most abstract in the book, but the concepts are foundational to the arguments developed in later chapters.

In chapter 2, I address some of the obstacles to any project of social transformation. First, there are the limitations that adhere in the use of law as an instrument for societal reform. Law has its own set of interpretive and conceptual rules that must be addressed when it is the subject of critical inquiry and rhetorical analysis. Law is a conservative discipline, not easily used for ends that undermine the status quo.

In the second part of chapter 2, I describe what I mean when I use the concept of "ideology." I argue that ideology operates as an independent limitation on the use of law because dominant ideology is the conceptual or intellectual mechanism whereby "radical" ideas are tamed and made consistent with dominant power alignments in society. Of course, patriarchy is the most relevant ideological concept to explore in the context of a consideration of the family and motherhood and is specifically discussed in its role of dictating even reformist discourses.

There has been some recent rethinking of the relationship between feminist theory and traditional legal paradigms such as equality. This rethinking has contributed to and been assisted by the evolution of complementary critical legal thought, loosely defined as "perspective scholarship," which is discussed in chapter 2. Perspective scholarship is the term applied to a body of scholarship that is built explicitly upon the assertion of relevant differences among people, whether they be found in race, class, sexual orientation, social situation, or gender.

Chapter 2 concludes with an assessment of the failure of much of feminist legal theory to confront the family in general, and the institution of motherhood in particular, as serious and central to its overall project of considering law as implicated in women's oppression. I assert that the family is typically considered as an afterthought (if at all) by feminist legal theorists whose attention remains focused on equality in the workplace and on issues surrounding sexuality and violence against women. When it is addressed, the family is considered more of an anomaly to be corrected than an institution so pivotal to the maintenance of societal structure and operation that it seems impervious to reform.

In chapter 3, building on what I see as the failure of feminist legal theory to take the family seriously, I explore the uneasy confrontation of legal feminists with notions of difference. This chapter traces the evolution of the feminist debates about differences and ultimately concludes that feminist theory that focuses on law must take the unequal position of women as a present given and must incorporate gendered differences as an explicit part of its analysis.

It has proven difficult for feminist legal theorists to offer remedies for unequal circumstances within an equality paradigm that emphasizes sameness of treatment and is suspicious of accommodating differences. Our institutions, particularly the family, are gendered. And, women are disadvantaged not only by the fact of gender differences but also by rules that ignore the different cultural and social mandates and restrictions built on gender differences.

In the last part of chapter 3, I describe my concept of a "gendered life," a descriptive term that references the actual or potential situations and circumstances women as a group may encounter in our society. This is my proposed "corrective" device for the direction of feminist legal theory. I argue that actual or potential gendered experiences distinguish women's "reality" from men's in our society. Men (and therefore, men's experiences) cannot continue to be considered the universal norm, the omnipotent rule makers and law givers. Women's experiences must also be incorporated into the law, made central to the rules that govern our lives.

I argue that the gendered life concept, while establishing a way to think about differences between women and men, can also be useful in forging (temporary) alliances among women across our differences. All women are, at least to some extent, judged as "Woman" (according to gendered expectations) in our society. Therefore, we have an interest in working together on issues such as motherhood, domestic violence, sexual harassment, and rape that affect us all.

The material set forth in this section is largely conceptual and helps to put the rest of the book in perspective. Throughout the subsequent chapters, I rely on some of these initial ideas in developing the concepts of the neutered mother and the sexual family and in exploring our impoverished and punitive social policies that constitute twentieth-century tragedies. Of particular importance is the concept of patriarchal ideology and the notion of a gendered life. My arguments about the limitations of law and the interaction between law and larger societal precepts is also relevant to the later discussions of the family as a social institution.

2

Law, Ideology, and the Perspective of Feminist Legal Theory— Limitations on Imaginations

MANY OF THE SUBSEQUENT CHAPTERS in this book consider the process of change or, more accurately, the difficulty of initiating and/or implementing societal change through law. They concentrate on families and motherhood and the ways in which language, professional assumptions and assertions, historic biases, and just plain old stereotypes confine and limit our ability as a society to address the problems that families—particularly families composed of single mothers and children—face at the end of the twentieth century in the United States. There is little disagreement that we face a crisis. There is also surprisingly little disagreement about the range of possible solutions—solutions that tend to merely replicate old family models and ignore emerging patterns of nonnuclear family formation.

In all arenas for reform there are practical and ideological restrictions upon change. Possibilities are contained by the contexts in which they arise and to which they often remain ideologically tied. In this chapter I set forth some of the larger themes and theoretical suppositions about law, ideology, and the traditional perspective of feminist legal theory that inform my consideration of the neutered mother, the sexual family, and the contemporary regulation of intimacy that constitute part of what I designate as twentieth-century tragedies.

It is important to remember in considering the possibility for reform that our history and our dominant cultural ideologies embody symbolically powerful notions of such elementary things as what is the appropriate family formation, what behavior constitutes "good" motherhood, the desirability and attainability of autonomy and independence for individuals, and the nature of responsible sexuality. On an empirical level, however, more people are living lives that call into question the continued viability of many of our historic paradigms for individual behavior and family intimacy. In several areas of the law, the initial responses have seemed to accommodate change, establishing some legitimacy for diverse family forms, even if in confined and marginal ways.[1]

Increasingly, however, the official responses to behavioral trends that diverge from the traditional nuclear family model have seemed punitive and panicked. Policy on the national and state levels, for the most part, attempts to revitalize and replicate idealized traditional modes of intimate connection symbolized by the nuclear family. This failure of creative imagination on the part of law and legal institutions has resulted in an impoverished approach to the dilemmas of poverty for mothers and children in our society. I do not mean to imply that these failures are the products of law alone, however. Law as a discipline has historically been more explicitly evident (and considered more legitimate) in regulating "public" behavior rather than "private" relationships. The private sphere has been, more often than not, an area where proxies for state power have been issued to designated actors whose status and role within the family privileges them as the enforcers or conduits for social norms and values. Men, in their roles as heads of household—husbands and fathers—have historically employed and enjoyed reflected state power in this regard.[2]

This does not mean legal definition and regulation have not existed in intimate areas, as laws governing marriage and divorce most obviously reveal. But it is the larger society—the cultural and ideological context in which law is fashioned and employed—that defines (and confines) our legal future.[3]

I. The Limits of Law

Why do we struggle about law? Why does resorting to law seem so appealing to would-be social reformers of all political persuasions? Some reformers consider law as "unique" in that it is viewed as the formal repository of state power. As such, law has the potential for coercive imposition of ideological norms by sanctioning certain behaviors. The law is a site of struggle within the more encompassing terrain of the state upon which many groups contest over institutions such as the family. Law can be experienced as the codification of a (temporary) public truce in an ongoing struggle, but winning at law seldom ends the larger struggle.

Law is part of a dynamic process; therefore, the processes whereby legal norms are generated, selected, interpreted, and implemented are relevant for critical investigation. Also of interest is the relationship between established legal norms and the more generalized, often more diverse, and, therefore, contested and competing societal norms. What role does law play in the process of manufacturing and perpetuating these norms in the first place? What role does it have in mediating between conflicting norms when viable alternatives to dominant social paradigms present themselves?

A. Law and Imagining Society

Viewing law as an ideological system confined within the context of the larger society calls into question the assumption that law has a particular, inherently superior, or special advantage in terms of shaping beliefs. In spite of its coercive potential, law does not seem to have a unique or particularly compelling role in proscribing behavior. Religion, group identification, even fads and the media, seem equally or more compelling than formal legal rules in shaping behaviors in many instances. Perhaps the postmodern message is that, on this more generalized level, law is nothing special, merely one normative construct competing with other, equally valid, options. Merely one of multiple discursive systems, each of which expresses a variety of images that together convey or express the "imagination" of our society,[4] law should be realistically understood as both enmeshed within and contained by the overarching normative systems that reflect dominant cultural and social ideologies.[5]

The imagination of society seems more contained than creative in regard to undertaking innovative or radical reform. This social imagination, diffuse, shifting, and amorphous, defines both the possibilities available to individuals and the limits of larger social and cultural aspirations. It seems evident that legal change will be elusive because law is largely reflective of dominant societal values.

In certain contemporary reformist political discourses, however, the law continues to be considered as ideologically or normatively powerful. Law is spoken of as though it were something to be captured, tamed, and utilized—a tool to manipulate in refashioning and reforming an inequitable society. Law, in this frame of reference, certainly is envisioned as existing outside of culture and society—independent of the societal forces it would be employed to confront. The aspiration is that "good people" can generate "good laws," which will then be evenhandedly imposed on society as corrective, coercive, normative measures. Even those who realize that law is the product of political struggles (and therefore the product of power) often discuss law's potential as though it were essentially separate and distinct from the society in which it is to operate. Many feminists trained in law approach their new discipline with the inspired but misguided visions of the avid legal reformer.[6]

In stating that law is not a major catalyst for social change or a powerful tool for cultural transformation, I do not mean to suggest that law reform has no role in social change or that law is not worth struggling over. When societal changes are under way, changes in law must accompany them, providing support and concrete embodiment of the changes. Law has a symbolic role that alone would make it worthy of struggle. Furthermore, law can often be usefully manipulated in specific cases to do good for individuals—an extremely important and necessary endeavor.

The instrumental characterization of law as a tool for the potential transformation of society is far too simplistic. Law is a crude and limited device and is circumscribed by the dominant ideologies of the society in which it is produced. Existing beliefs and assumptions shape knowledge and understandings, including those about law and law reform. Therefore law reform cannot, in and of itself, be effective as a catalyst for more generalized reforms. The significance of dominant ideologies in this process on the shape and content of law and legal process makes the idea of "progress" problematic.

Furthermore, even when reforms are forthcoming, implementation presents a separate set of problems. Even when changes are successfully made on a doctrinal level, they can and will fail if judges or others charged with the application of new laws revert to interpretations that merely replicate old results. Some reformers forget the extent to which "context" controls the ultimate practical content of the purist ideal and distorts worthy goals beyond recognition. As a result, quite often reforms not only fail to have the desired impact but even make things worse for those they were designed to help.

B. Classification and Residue

In addition to the premises stated above, it is important to emphasize that when law is the object of analysis, certain unique methodological and conceptual constraints operate upon any theoretical endeavor. Every intellectual project in law, of course, is defined in the first instance by the characteristics of law and legal institutions. Our responses to law are shaped by our perceptions about law and its role and function in society. Law is a system that reflects existing allocations of state coercive power, and legal discourse both reiterates and reconstitutes the consequences of that power in our society—the processes whereby explicitly coercive rules are generated and implemented.

If law is understood to be enmeshed in society, also problematic are some of the prevalent notions about the neutrality and objectivity of law with which policy makers and politicians, judges, and attorneys drape their processes. Once the ideas of neutrality and objectivity are exposed as myths rather than as attainable and maintainable goals, the law is put into perpetual contest. If law is merely one of multiple, interactive normative systems, how can society justify the coercive nature of law—the costs exacted from transgressive individuals? Societal norms shift, new "truths" appear. If law is not based on extrasocietal realities, it must constantly relegitimate itself.

Another significant limitation for a theorist is the explicit reliance in legal doctrine on classification. Classification is the process whereby facts are given legal meaning.[7] The law is a system of rules and/or norms, many of which are designed to have universal application. Similar situations are to be treated the same. All rules, therefore, have potential application beyond any specific set of factual circumstances. Thus, the process of lawmaking relies on broad generalizations about groups or classes of things and people at the legislative level. On the individual case level, law is also a process of classification—courts make decisions using analogies and distinctions within the context of "precedent" and "*stare decisis,*" tying "like things" together in a web of consistent and coherent doctrine.

Classification, inevitable though it might be, is nonetheless a process that is susceptible to criticism because it invariably both includes inappropriate cases and excludes appropriate ones.[8] Since classification involves line drawing and assessments of similarity and difference, it is mired in stereotypes. It seems clear that both as a process and in terms of fashioning responses, classification should be understood to be a political act. It generates controversy. Murray Edelman has noted:

> The character, causes, and consequences of any phenomenon become radically different as changes are made in what is prominently displayed, what is repressed, and especially in how observations are classified. Far from being stable, the social world is therefore a chameleon, or, to suggest a better metaphor, a kaleidoscope of potential realities, any of which can be readily evoked by altering the ways by which observations are framed and categorized. Because alternative categorizations win support for specific political beliefs and policies, classification schemes are central to political maneuvering and political persuasion.[9]

In addition to the problems inherent in classification, whatever its institutional manifestations, other problems exist because law must operate in a "practical" or pragmatic manner. Decisions must be made even if the processes are imperfect and the results unpopular. What happens in this regard to the unrepresented, the residue not encompassed within the classification?

The formation and implementation of legal rules quite often proceed in haste, without deep reflection. Rules are typically formulated in response to political and social pressures—adopted for their symbolic rather than for their pragmatic characteristics and contents. Even the best-intentioned legal actors find themselves with imperfect and incomplete information yet are required to make decisions that have significant, immediate impacts on people's lives.

C. Those Who Would Reform

Related to and exacerbated by the failure to fully understand the deterministic nature of the social and ideological contexts of law reform is the tendency of legal theorists to believe grand principles can be bent to their idiosyncratic intellectual will. Too many would-be reformers proceed as though the specific doctrine or principle they advocate as an analytical ideal has no historic limitations that impede its use for transformative purposes.[10] Concepts such as "equality" and "justice," for example, are treated as clean slates upon which can be written the reformers' specific (often idiosyncratic) aspirations. The fact that these abstract concepts have documentable legal histories that function as implicit or explicit boundaries on the nature of reform is often ignored.

There is a parallel and more personal kind of limitation on the effort of legal transformation. Many of us who are attracted to law as a potential means of societal change are as limited by our own contexts and histories as legal principles are by theirs. Trained as lawyers, beginning as people who "chose" to study law, we are steeped in certain discursive structures that shape and reflect our own professional and personal "realities."

To fail to recognize this is to underestimate the extent to which *all* individual assessments about value—what everyone considers basic, inevitable premises about social ordering and hierarchies, including our conclusions about law—reflect widely shared and even traditional norms. In other words, working within a legal context is committing to "law reform" and is probably more indicative of the acceptance of significant societal norms than it is of the adoption of a truly oppositional stance.

Because law is enmeshed in the overarching normative ordering of society, there is no "uncontaminated" alternative to reference for those who seek to reform law. Of course, there is some potential for change, particularly on an individual case-by-case basis, where doctrine can be manipulated without systemic implications. But when large-scale transformations threaten the system, it (and usually we) inevitably references the dominant social and cultural constructs that are powerfully evident across multiple sites of ideological production. Social imaginings, ideologies that are the products of diverse entrenched and complementary systems, are extremely hard to change.[11]

II. The Role of Ideology

One way to understand the concept of ideology is to consider it as an information-processing system. An ideology is constituted by a complementary collection of symbols, beliefs, and assumptions that, in combination, rationalize and give meaning to discourses. One further aspect of an ideological system is that it performs its meaning-giving role in the context of social and political power.[12] Ideology in this regard can be considered functional—a selection and sorting mechanism that provides coherence, structure, and form to social and political discourses.

A. Ideology and Discourse

The study of discourse reveals something about the existence and content of the underlying ideology. If ideology is a rationalizing set of principles and concepts that link discourses to power, it follows that a close examination of discourse reveals implicit aspects of an underlying ideology. Discourses are linguistic framings or stylized appeals to parts of ideologies; the broad parameters of ideology are what define and structure the contours of discourse. In order to be influential, to be dominant, discourse must reference the concerns of power. This inquiry—exploring the relationship between ideology and discourse—in turn exposes something about the location of power within society.

In defining these interrelationships, I pursue the suggestion made by Terry Eagleton that "discourses . . . produce effects, shape forms of consciousness and unconsciousness, which are closely related to the maintenance or transformation of our existing systems of power."[13] Eagleton went so far as to assert that ideology can be taken to indicate no more than the connective link between discourse and power.[14] This understanding of ideology—as having systemic implications—has theoretical as well as practical implications.[15] On a practical level, it means that dominant ideology is more likely to operate as a conservative force, serving to tame or domesticate discourses by exerting a confining pressure on their initial development, ultimately channeling even the most radical ideas into categories approved by the existing conceptual system.

Within this perception of ideology, meaningful conflict and competition are confined to the level of discourse. To be labeled "dominant"—i.e., providing the recognized links between power and discourse—an ideology may not be too sharply contested. A dominant ideology, therefore, is relatively stable, although it may be altered over time, adapting in response to the tensions generated by violent or prolonged demands from discourses.

If we posit ideology as a system of symbols and beliefs, it must be experienced as both complex and dynamic, meaning that it will seldom be totally revealed in the context of a specific political debate or contest of discourses. It will also not easily be expressed in abstract terms outside the context of a specific set of assumptions. As a dynamic system, ideology represents a process that is not easily reduced to a finite set of clearly stated principles that are operational outside of any specific application.

The definitive shape and content of an ideology is only partially revealed in its symbols: fragmented and shadowed traces discernible within discourses from their initial formulation to their ultimate translation and transformation within institutions of power. As part of a cluster of social and cultural symbols and beliefs, the threads of an ideology may appear in seemingly dissociated discourses. The ideology provides a path for information; it can be imagined as a series of synapses that contain the possible permutations. It directs the nature and content of the various appeals (discourses) to the institutions of formal power in our society.

My preoccupation with ideology leads me to be more pessimistic about the possibility for social transformation than are social critics who focus solely on structure. Dominant ideologies are subtly and conclusively expressed and repressed in the very creation and recreation of social norms and conventions. They define the contours of culture and of society and its institutions. A dominant ideology is transmitted through everyday discourse—through language, symbols, and images as well as through the operations of formal institutions and structures of power.

Conflicts that are developed and located in these discourses concern the political implications or meanings of the symbols and beliefs that comprise the ideology, but do not dispute the existence or potency of the symbol. Oppositional discourses—including feminism—often reference the shared aspects of the ideology in what are attempts to compel and convince.

B. Patriarchal Ideology

Understanding of patriarchy as an ideology is of particular relevance to this book. Patriarchy as a system is constituted by a set of concepts and symbols that are more complex and convoluted than the simplistic notion that men are the formal holders of power within the family and society (what one might call "a parody of patriarchy"). More accurate and descriptive is Gerda

Lerner's definition of patriarchy as the "manifestation and institutionalization of male dominance over women and children in the family and the extension of male dominance over women in society in general."[16]

I resist the emphasis, however, that this definition places on "manifestation" and "institutionalization" of dominance. This focus presupposes (even mandates) that societal structures (such as the nuclear family) become the focal point for critical assessment. Such an approach may foster the belief that structural changes alone can transform society. But to me it seems clear and essential that we must go beyond structural critique in considering the power of an ideology so dominant and pervasive as patriarchy.

The ideological aspect of patriarchy presents a more elusive and resistant social and cultural product than any structure. That ideology affects us even before birth with a gendering process that shapes our future lives. It is impressed upon us in myriad ways and we adopt it, internalize it, and impose it on others. It is the ideological power of patriarchy that explains why an individual can resist or reject its structures by, for example, refusing to participate in a nuclear family but still find herself defined and ultimately controlled by the ideology underlying and supporting the structure.

The ideological construction and maintenance of the family is pervasive and persistent. Paradoxically, while the family may be hailed as fundamental, its very significance in the maintenance and perpetuation of patriarchy has meant that it must ultimately be rendered invisible. The patriarchal family is an "assumed institution" with a well-defined, socially constructed form complete with complementary roles—husband/head of household, wife/ helpmate, child. The significant family tie is the sexual affiliation that, when legally sanctified, creates marriage. The assumed inevitability and primacy of this form of intimate connection reinforces patriarchy in that it defines male presence as essential and dominant within the family.

The family, as assumed, is the institution upon which the "public" (and therefore designated "important") aspects of society are built. As an assumed institution (and considered to be what I refer to in subsequent chapters as "natural"), the family has been only marginally evident in legal theory or jurisprudence, including feminist legal theory.

In feminist legal theory, patriarchal ideology has also had significant constraining influence. For example, much legal feminist theory seems to rank social institutions and concerns in the same way that patriarchal culture in general does.[17] It adopts the hierarchies even as it criticizes the system for perpetuating divides such as the separate spheres of "public" and "private"—those relationships conceptually contained in the private sphere, receiving little sustained critical attention except as they relate to the public domain. Even when feminist legal theorists do focus their energies on "domestic" issues, the concern seems to be with sexuality and violence. If they occur at all, considerations of nonsexual family relationships, such as the institution of motherhood, are likely to be based on a rejection of the status and the social implications it bears.

These assertions have implications for the methodology that I have adopted in examining discourses about motherhood and other matters in this book. The task is to uncover and understand the appeal to ideological components—the link to power. But if patriarchy is a *shared* cultural construct, it affects us all. Its core images of intimacy and sexuality define the discourses produced by both the proponent of the status quo and its critic. As chapter 5 will demonstrate, I have found in examining different discourses about motherhood that the underlying symbols and values are more uniformly shared than the apparent differences in discourses would superficially indicate. This tendency toward replication operates even though critiques of law and legal institutions have been blossoming during the past few decades.

III. Feminist Legal Theory

Feminist legal theory is "perspective scholarship,"[18] a term that encompasses an ever-growing body of work connected by the fact that it challenges the traditional notion that law is a neutral, objective, rational set of rules, unaffected in content and form by the passions and perspectives of those who possess and wield the power inherent in law and legal institutions. In some regards, perspective scholarship is merely the most recent expression of a critical scholarly movement known as "legal realism," which during the 1920s and 1930s called into question the prevailing idea of law as an autonomous system of rules and principles. The early legal realists stressed the factual context of cases, not abstracted legal principles.[19] They urged the use of extralegal material—such as that produced by social scientists— to aid in resolving the social and political issues that found their way into courtrooms and legislatures.[20]

Perspective scholars begin with the same initial skepticism about the objectivity and neutrality of law and legal institutions as do the legal realists. They also look to the social, cultural, and political, in addition to the legal, to provide a context for understanding the operation and impact of law in our society.

The perspective scholar's definition of "law" is broad, and law is to be discovered in actions as well as in words—in the interpretation and implementation of rules as well as in their formal doctrinal expression. Law is not only something "out there"—an independent body of principles—but a product of society, acted upon and responsive to political and cultural forces. For this reason, it is as essential to understand societal and cultural forces as it is to decipher doctrine in order to understand "the law."

Perspective scholarship adds the explicit consideration of diverse perspectives to the realist, law-in-society tradition. Perspective scholarship is based on the premise that certain groups historically have been unrepresented (or underrepresented) in law and that their exclusion has led to biases—an incompleteness or deficit in contemporary legal analysis and legal institutions.

Furthermore, perspective scholars argue the corresponding contention that historically excluded groups have different, perhaps unique, views and experiences that are relevant to the issues and circumstances regulated and controlled by law. Perspective scholarship adds nuance to the traditionally rather monotone canvas of law. It adds the possibility of color and texture to the legal palette by introducing diverse and often divergent viewpoints based on the social and cultural experiences of race, gender, class, religion, and sexual orientation, for example. It makes more complete and more complex our consideration of the questions "What is law?" and "What are the roles and functions of law in our society?"

A. Women in Families in Feminist Legal Theory

Of particular relevance to this book are the perspectives of women within the family context—women who, as members of the gendered categories of "wives," "mothers," and "daughters" have borne the burdens of intimacy in our society. The presence of children creates dependency not only because the children are themselves dependent, but also because the person who assumes primary care for them becomes dependent on social and other institutions for accommodations so that such care can be delivered. However, institutions in our society do not facilitate the care of children, and sacrifices are expected in career plans and other goals if one is to have children. The same is true in regard to caring for the elderly or any dependent adult with whom one is intimate and, therefore, for whom one is likely to feel some responsibility.

Typically, it is women who bear the costs of the expectations associated with such intimate relations in our society. Women are not compensated for bearing these costs, and in the make-believe world of abstract legal equality they are, in fact, penalized. Women have been defined in feminist legal discourse mainly as "wives," not as mothers. As wives, it is argued that women are equal and in need of neutral rules. Neutral treatment in a gendered world or within a gendered institution does not operate in a neutral manner, however. Women are not only (and not always) wives, but often also mothers. There are more and more empirical studies that indicate that mothers' relative positions have worsened in our new ungendered doctrinal world.[21] Ignoring differences in favor of assimilation has not made the differences in gender expectations and behavior disappear. These differences operate to women's disadvantage as the material implications of motherhood, for example, have negative consequences in the context of career development and opportunity.[22]

In spite of the gendered nature of dependency and its location within the family, much of feminist legal theory fails to place the family and the role of mother as central institutions for the development of theory. Rather, the focus has been on prematernal or extramaternal concerns such as employment discrimination or gathering political power. When maternity has come into play, typically the "dilemmas" raised have related to the presence of children and have been resolved on a theoretical level by resort to the need for shared parenting, the inevitable panacea being involving fathers with children. Theoretical work on the family is typically segregated and marginalized—when mentioned at all—in feminist legal theory collections or casebooks, and motherhood is hardly mentioned at all.[23]

In pointing out that feminist legal theorists have "neglected" the family, I do not mean to minimize the very important contributions of feminist thought in law or the important advances in thinking about law that feminist scholars have made. I am concerned, however, by recent attempts to establish a canon of so-called basic feminist jurisprudential works, most of which either ignore the family as a significant structure or consider it only tangentially in exploring the "main" issues of work, sexuality, and violence.

As soon as such steps are taken, as soon as boundaries are drawn (no matter how strenuously their significance is denied in prefaces and introductions), it becomes crucial to look to what is left out, the silences, those things still not spoken about. Notably, what is left out tends to be a discussion of the family as a foundational patriarchal structure. The tendency has been instead to consider a critique of the family as only one facet in the study of other areas of concern. The institution is seldom a central focus and rarely presented as an essential aspect of the core of feminist jurisprudence.[24] The family may be presented as a site of inequality or an institution to be reformed, but it is neglected as an independent focus for feminist legal theory, clearly not considered as important an institution as the market and only peripheral in considering the issues surrounding sexuality and violence.

For example, some feminists accept traditional configurations of family but criticize historic role divisions. They couple their acceptance with appeals for egalitarian reform so that women can participate as equals in the nonfamily world of market work. In the subsequent chapters, I argue we should not assume the primacy of the nuclear family form nor the inevitability of our social family adhering to the biological (or heterosexual) configuration necessary for reproduction.[25] In fact, it seems to me that reliance on reform of the traditional family for the liberation of women has been clearly demonstrated to be misguided. On a doctrinal level we now have an egalitarian model for the family, but it operates in a social context that remains very gendered. This is extremely detrimental to many women and children, and I therefore argue that we leave our aspirations for the traditional family form behind and reimagine what should be our core family connection.

An inability to move beyond dominant heterosexual constructs in defining family intimacy has been a serious limitation in feminist legal theory.[26] This book's attempt to open up this area of discussion will inevitably be mired in its (my) own cultural context, but it is a self-conscious attempt to look beyond the dominant ideological imagery of sexual affiliation and the nuclear family. I consider motherhood to be a unique but legally invisible social experience. The potential for the experience of motherhood is what has historically differentiated female from male public existence in our society. Motherhood has been the basis for discrimination and devaluation. This has not changed with legal feminism's inattention to that status or with pretenses (or beliefs) that mother is no different than father.

What has changed, partly as a result of feminist legal theorists' refusals to address questions of differences within family roles and reproductive positions, is that motherhood as a legal construct is significantly different today than it was at the beginning of the century. In (and outside) of law, mothers are systematically separated and alienated from their children as fathers gain rights based on assertions of sameness and rejection of ideas of difference between the social roles of mother and father. This has been accomplished in the name of legal equality, which renders differences invisible or irrelevant. The next chapter explores the evolution of feminist legal theory in relation to the question of differences between men and women.

Notes

1. *See Griswold v. Connecticut,* 381 U.S. 479 (1965) (holding that the state could not prohibit use of contraception by married couples); *Eisenstadt v. Baird,* 205 U.S. 438 (1972) (providing that the state could not infringe on the right of single people to use contraception); *Roe v. Wade,* 400 U.S. 113 (1973) (holding that a woman had a privacy right in determining whether or not to have an abortion); *Moore v. City of East Cleveland,* 431 U.S. 494 (1977) (holding that zoning restrictions could not bar a grandmother, her son, his son, and another grandchild, from living together as a single family); *Wisconsin v. Yoder,* 406 U.S. 205 (1972) (providing that Amish parents had the right not to send their children to secular high schools).

2. Even if, as Frances Olsen argues, it is theoretically true that there is no place in society where state power does not reign, it seems that there are some circumstances in which it is more diffuse and abstracted. *See* Frances E. Olsen, "The Myth of State Intervention in the Family," 18 *Univ. of Michigan Journal of Law Reform* 835 (1985). For example, power directly wielded by the police or social service caseworkers who take a child from an "unfit" parent would in most instances be experienced and understood as more coercively interventionist than the requirements that parents have children vaccinated or see that they attend school. It is also true that private or family exercise of authority, even if state supported and condoned, is increasingly susceptible to direct supervision by the state. Domestic violence, including child abuse, is not only criminalized

and subject to other sanctions, but recent cases have allowed actions to be brought against police departments that do not enforce the laws. When the state is the abuser, however, accountability is harder to attain. The direct rather than proxied social control over private lives by the state often comes within the confines of immunities or other protective doctrines. *See Deshaney v. Winnebago County Dept. of Social Services,* 489 U.S. 189 (1989).

3. I often tell groups of students or would-be students of law that if they are interested in changing society they should not go to law school. I suggest that they pursue a career writing for television. Their impact (and creative license) would be much greater. Of course, I realize that all arenas of production of cultural and societal images, including television, are limited. Some arenas, like law, seem more limited than others, however.

4. This phrase has been used to define the way authors of all texts through the language of writing represent or imagine a variety of social worlds, acting in that regard as the imaginations of actual societies. Steven Marcus, *Representations: Essays on Literature* xiii (Morningside Edition 1990). The imaginations and representations are as diverse as the authors and each, alone or in combination, provides at best only a glimpse of the "actual" world.

5. This idea is expanded and illustrated in the context of patriarchal ideology and families as well as the stereotypical fashioning of motherhood in sections 2 and 3 of this book.

6. *See* Chapter 3.

7. Claims under the Equal Protection Clause of the Fourteenth Amendment provide a familiar example of this classification process. State action, which itself distinguishes between groups of actors, is analyzed at a level of scrutiny dependent upon the classification of the right or status of the group in question. Where a law classifies people according to their race, "such classifications are subject to the most exacting scrutiny." *Palmore v. Sidoti,* 466 U.S. 429, 432 (1984). Where the distinction is based on gender, however, the law is given an intermediate level of scrutiny. *See, e.g., Mississippi Univ. for Women v. Hogan,* 458 U.S. 718 (1982). Race and gender are separate bases for classification.

   The extent to which the process of classification pervades all legal analysis is evident in the very research tools that are used by lawyers, judges, and other legal scholars. Classification is the process whereby the diverse and broad range of factual circumstances that might become the subject of legal scrutiny are channeled into discrete categories, ultimately susceptible to the application of rules and norms operating on such categories of facts—rules and norms that can be referenced in key-word indices and treatises on specific subject matter.

8. However, the creation of fixed categories with concrete legal implications has often been a feminist (and other) objective in law reform. Classification in this

regard is seen as an alternative to more amorphous processes such as "balancing," "weighing," or other devices to implement judicial discretion; fixed rules are seen as preferable to unrestrained judicial bias. *See* Martha Albertson Fineman, *The Illusion of Equality: The Rhetoric and Reality of Divorce Reform* (Chicago: Univ. of Chicago Press, 1991), ch. 3, for a discussion of this phenomenon in the context of rules governing the distribution of property at divorce.

9. Murray Edelman, *Category Mistakes and Public Opinion,* 1 (1992) (unpublished manuscript, on file with author).

10. The concept of "equality" was employed in the divorce context with disastrous results because the history of the abstract concept is one of formal equality with sameness-of-treatment as the appropriate goal; *see* Fineman, *Illusion* [chapter 2, note 8].

11. In an earlier work, I pointed out Carol Smart's concern with the "totalizing tendency" evident in the work of many of the best-known North American legal feminists, which she calls "the construction of a 'scientific feminism,' " and her explicit criticism of such grand theorizing. *At the Boundaries of Law: Feminism and Legal Theory* Martha A. Fineman and Nancy Sweet Thomadsen, eds. (New York: Routledge, 1991), p. xii. I further noted that the grander the feminist theory, the more it resembles mainstream scholarly format and content, and concluded that some feminist theory "represents the creation of a new form of positivism in a search for universal truth discoverable . . . within the methodology of critical legal analysis. Middle-range theory, by contrast, mediates between the grand realizations that law is gendered, that law is a manifestation of power, that law is detrimental to women" *Id.* Middle-range theory connects the empirical with the abstract so that both are enriched. I realize that for many, choices are confined and directed by traditional indices of success, by the need to get tenure, or by the desire to gain positions within elite social and legal institutions that value grand theoretical constructs. *Id.* at xii-xiii.

12. The power is not equalized in society, and ideologies are dominant or marginalized depending on their relationship to the maintenance and reflection of power.

13. Terry Eagleton, *Literary Theory: An Introduction* (Oxford: Basil Blackwell, 1983), p. 210.

14. *Ibid.,* p. 73

15. I am also influenced by the work of Christine Harrington and Sally Merry, who cast legal ideology in terms of the mobilization of "symbolic resources by groups promoting different projects." Christine B. Harrington and Sally Engle Merry, "The Making of Community Mediation," 22 *Law & Society Review* 709, 714 (1988).

16. Gerda Lerner, *The Creation of Patriarchy* (New York: Oxford Univ. Press, 1986), p. 239.

17. In the Introduction to *Boundaries* [chapter 2, note 11], I explored the limitations of a focus on legal concepts and grand theoretical assertions such as "equality" and "justice". The transformative potential of feminist thought is blunted, because in order "to be incorporated into and considered compatible with legal theory, feminist thought must adapt, even if it does not totally conform, to the words and concepts of legal discourse. Feminism may enter as the challenger, but the tools inevitably employed are those of the androphile master. And the character of the tools largely determines the shape and design of the resulting construction" at xii–xiii.

18. Kimberlé Crenshaw traces the ideal and (unreal) concept of "perspectivelessness" (an analytic stance that law has no specific cultural, political, or class characteristics) and the growing challenges to the ideal in the context of arguments for a race-conscious approach to specific legal issues. Kimberlé Williams Crenshaw, "Foreword: Toward a Race-Conscious Pedagogy in Legal Education," 11 *National Black Law Journal* 1 (1989).

19. *See, e.g.,* Laura Kalman, *Legal Realism at Yale* (Chapel Hill: Univ. of North Carolina Press, 1986), pp. 9–10.

20. *Ibid.,* pp. 17–18.

21. This is true economically, as demonstrated by recent statistics. *See e.g.,* Victor R. Fuchs, *Women's Quest for Economic Equality* (Cambridge: Harvard Univ. Press, 1988). For more recent statistics regarding divorce and the poverty of children, *see* Jason DeParle, "Child Poverty Twice as Likely After Family Split, Study Says," *New York Times,* (March 2, 1991), p. A8.

22. Furthermore, even for women choosing to forgo gendered roles and to accept the male-worker standard as the norm, entry into previously male-dominated institutions does not guarantee equality. Many such women encounter incremental obstacles to their advancement as glass ceilings and other impediments appear.

23. Feminist legal theorists have generally not focused on the family as basic to patriarchy. *See, e.g.,* Stephanie Wildman, "The Power of Women," 2 *Yale Journal of Law and Feminism* 435, 446–452 (1990); reviewing Catharine A. MacKinnon, *Toward a Feminist Theory of the State* (Cambridge: Harvard Univ. Press, 1989), in which she critiques MacKinnon's failure to address the caretaking role so central in many women's lives. Other feminist theory has been amaternal, not only minimizing the practical implications and material consequences of motherhood but ignoring it altogether along with differences in circumstances it may represent. *See also* Carol Sanger, "M is for the Many Things," 1 *Southern California Review of Law and Women's Studies* 15 (1992).

24. One recent publication that explicitly neglects the family in this regard is D. Kelly Weisberg, ed., *Feminist Legal Theory: Foundations* (Philadelphia: Temple Univ. Press, 1993). Weisberg states in the Preface that the book is the first of two volumes planned: "The first volume, *Feminist Legal Theory: Foundations,* exploring theoretical issues in feminist legal theory; the second volume, *Feminist Legal Theory: Applications,* exploring applications of feminist legal theory to specific substantive areas of law (e.g., criminal law, family law, employment law, and the legal profession)." *Ibid.,* p. xi. Although the family is listed in the index to the *Foundations* volume, when it is discussed it is only in the context of separate spheres ideology. The one place in this volume where the family is listed as a specific heading is within an article by Richard Posner called "Conservative Feminism." Posner spends some time in this article extolling the market virtues of womb rental in surrogacy cases. The family is considered, therefore, to be not a "foundation" but an instance of "application."

Patricia Smith's recent anthology *Feminist Jurisprudence* (New York: Oxford Univ. Press, 1993) contains several articles exploring reproductive inequality, sexual violence against women, and the gendered nature of judicial reasoning. However, these articles do not examine the family as a central institution. Only one article therein specifically addresses the structural significance of the family to market society generally—Frances Olsen's "The Family and the Market: A Study of Ideology and Legal Reform." I am glad to see this article here. However, what I am suggesting cannot be contained within a single article, and I believe the Olsen piece supports this contention. A critique of the family as an ideological and foundational structure must be infused within all feminist jurisprudence. It is not insignificant that this same article is the only article dealing with family in this way in yet two other volumes dealing with feminism and the law. The first of these is Katherine T. Bartlett and Rosanne Kennedy, eds., *Feminist Legal Theory: Readings in Law and Gender* (Boulder, CO: Westview Press, 1993).

The second is a new casebook by Mary Becker, Cynthia G. Bowman and Morrison Torrey, titled *Cases and Materials: Feminist Jurisprudence—Taking Women Seriously* (St. Paul, MN: West, 1994). While this book deals with the particularities of inequities resulting from traditional family ideology, those feminists that are left out are again those that move from a critique of traditional family ideology as a fundamental base structure for patriarchy. There are chapters on "Women and Reproduction," "Women and Marriage," and "Women and Children," but the Olsen article is the only piece in the section designed to give an overview of feminist theory. The general theoretical significance of sexuality is evident, but the ideology of the family and its significance to feminist jurisprudence is dealt with only superficially. The efforts of these editors to establish a resource from which further feminist theory can be developed is certainly worthwhile, even if incomplete. However, I want to emphasize that this book is different in that it attempts to enlarge the theoretical frame offered feminist legal theorists by providing a critique of the ideological and structural power of "The Family" and by showing how such a critique is crucial for any analysis of patriarchy.

25. This distinguishes this book from work by people like Susan Moller Okin. *See, e.g.,* Sara Rapport, "Justice at Home," 16 *Law and Social Inquiry* 835 (1991) (reviewing Susan Moller Okin, *Justice, Gender, and the Family* [New York: Basic Books, 1989]).

26. In addition, and quite ironically, for members of a group that explicitly distinguishes itself from other schools of thought by questioning and rejecting the traditional and rigid categories of knowledge and thought, a whole industry seems to have been generated by those legal feminists who seek to place others into rather tritely contrived categories and thereby implicitly or explicitly to value them. This practice of boxing other feminists seems to me to shed little light and typically is performed in a rather sloppy and idiosyncratic manner, resulting in groupings that are over or underinclusive.

   In the first place, the level of engagement should be with the arguments, not the individuals. Arguments can appropriately be classified as "postmodern" or "radical." Condemning specific women to such categories seems designed to marginalize them and their ideas. The categories sometimes seem designated according to the specific classifiers' preference for or against abstraction as contrasted with empiricism. Other categories seem to relate to nothing more than the subject matter the "other" feminist discusses and to completely ignore differences in methodology, analysis, or emphasis in the classified work.

   Furthermore (and specifically related to the devaluation of family and motherhood work) is the fact that feminists who write about the family tend to be cast as "cultural" feminists even when they are concerned with issues of power and dominance and specifically reject any notion of an inherent "woman's nature." It seems that addressing the subject of the family or motherhood inevitably will result in the author being classified as one who believes in inherent, biologically based differences, as though the selection of family topics invokes a corollary concession to the dominance of nature.

   This reactionary response to any demonstrated interest in such topics is not only exclusionary and condemning of feminists interested in such topics, but also represents an intellectual phenomenon that would seem to implicate the vast majority of women who are members of families and mothers.

3

Differences in Context— Feminist Legal Theory and Gendered Lives

THE LAW AS A DISCIPLINE relies heavily on the process of classification. This fact has meant that some part of the feminist project in law has historically been focused on the question of "differences." The assessment of differences is central to the process of legitimating distinctions in legal treatment among categories of persons. The centrality of the classification processes to law and legal reasoning probably means that a move away from consideration and debates about the theoretical significance of gender difference is not likely to occur as quickly or completely in legal feminism as seems to have happened in other academic disciplines.[1]

In the broader academic feminist world, the whole question of differences between men and women earlier generated a lot of debate. In general, unanswerable questions have arisen concerning causation and the respective roles of "nature" and "nurture." In some disciplines, feminists are concerned with definitively establishing that it is society and culture that construct gender roles and that there are no fundamental biological distinctions that produce differences between women and men.[2]

While some feminist legal scholars seek to transplant aspects of this debate into a legal context, an argument can be made (and defended) that the concern with origin is not of central importance to the feminist legal project. Even if differences are considered to be socially rather than biologically constituted, nothing is resolved. Feminists who dawdle over this debate seem to assume that social construction is easier to handle or alter than biological differences. I disagree. In fact, if differences were merely found in biology, then technology and medical innovations might be enlisted in the construction of an androgenous future.[3]

Society is not easily manipulated. To state that something is socially constructed, in my opinion, is to concede that it is powerful and resistant to change. All of us—even those who are critically inclined—must operate within our cultures. None of us may totally escape that culture: to some extent it defines us all. The point is that differences, however constructed, have real material effects on women. For me this means that the task of feminist legal theorists is to consider in what ways the law can remedy inequities that have occurred and that continue to operate to disadvantage women.

In fact, engaging in debates about origin and differences will only siphon energy needed for tasks of more immediate or practical concern for law and legal theory. A fundamental role of theoretical approaches in law should be to generate critical discussions of current policy regarding specific societal choices and to reveal the inequitable aspects of legal regulation. My position is that law has a concrete, immediate impact on women's lives and that legal feminists do not have the luxury of indulging in esoteric debates about the origin of differences. Regardless of how fashioned, or whence derived, differences matter.

Upon the respective reproductive roles of the sexes are built social and cultural assumptions and expectations; these have significant material consequences that are enshrined in policy and, therefore, are susceptible to some legal redress and remedy. Differences in this regard are "real." They are manifest and are harmful to women.[4] Differences are also obscured by legal rhetoric in which law and legal concepts are deemed neutral and objective. Differences, therefore, must be brought to light so their relevance can be debated and discussed.

The assertion that differences exist does not resolve much for a legal audience. In fact, the acceptance of the basic premise generates further questions. For example, what legal significance should any specific differences between women and men have? Should, or must, any or all differences be accommodated? In law this is partly a question of remedies, although there are important theoretical implications to the question as well: If ultimate legal accommodations are not sought, why should a theorist even explore the question of differences?

A second set of legal questions associated with differences revolves around the possibility of using law as a tool of reconstruction: Can the law be used to eliminate some of the socially constructed (and destructive) differences? Can law assist in the project of fashioning an egalitarian, genderless world? If law is to be useful in either regard, can we as a society (or even as feminists) agree on the goals to be achieved? Many legal feminists find themselves occupied with answering these questions.

I. The Evolution of Difference in Feminist Legal Thought

A. The Initial Feminist Project—Women Into Law

The century's earliest feminist project in law[5] was fairly clearly defined by the explicit nature of doctrinal assumptions about differences. Because of their perceived biological or "natural" attributes, women were considered appropriately excluded from the practice of law and other positions of public power. They were relegated to the "private" or family sphere.[6] In his much quoted concurring opinion in *Bradwell v. Illinois*—the Supreme Court case that upheld an Illinois prohibition on women practicing law—Justice Bradley explained that the civil law

> as well as nature herself, has always recognized a wide difference in the respective spheres and destinies of man and woman. . . . The natural and proper timidity and delicacy which belongs to the female sex evidently unfits it for many of the occupations of civil life. The constitution of the family organization, which is founded in the divine ordinance, as well as in the nature of things, indicates the domestic sphere as that which properly belongs to the domain and functions of womanhood.[7]

In Bradley's rhetoric in *Bradwell,* as well as that of Justices in other cases setting forth "protective" doctrines, women's perceived differences from men operated to exclude women from the "public" or market sphere, to set them apart, outside of the main avenues to power and economic independence.

Since the *Bradwell* era, the consideration of differences in legal feminism has been a contentious task. In fact, much of the rather antagonistic early interaction among legal feminists arose from disagreement about the fundamental question of whether there are cognizable differences between women and men.[8] The early "founding mothers" who began the broadly defined legal feminist project when they entered law school during the 1960s and 1970s rejected an exploration of the differences between women and men. Because these differences had serious exclusionary consequences, many feminist legal scholars and practitioners who finally did make it into the profession during the 1960s argued for equality in terms of sameness of treatment as a matter of moral and legal right.[9] The push for equal treatment required those feminists to ignore the existence of differences or to assert that differences were of no significance.[10] Legal feminism, or feminism with a legal focus, was thus fashioned.

This brand of legal feminism, dominant until recently, was primarily an equality-based strategy that assumed no legally relevant differences between men and women, an emphasis determined by the many ways in which the law historically both facilitated and condoned women's exclusion from the public (i.e., overtly powerful) aspects of society. Difference had provided the rationale and the justification of such exclusion—women's unique biological role in reproduction demanded their protection from the rigors of public life. It was no surprise, therefore, that when significant numbers of women began to make inroads into public institutions such as the law, they sought to dismantle the ideology that had excluded them. Assimilation became the goal and equality the articulated standard.

Arguments for a positive or remedial consideration of differences designed to help women were often assailed as harboring the inevitable potential for exclusion and differentiation that harmed women. These early feminist legal reformers attacked existing classifications and categories based on gender and favored a "gender-neutral" paradigm of equality that linguistically assumed and asserted sameness between men and women.

The most ambitious of such symbolic reforms was the movement for the Equal Rights Amendment[11] to the Federal Constitution that, although it ultimately failed on a national level, mothered changes in some state constitutions forbidding distinctions based on sex.[12] The momentum for gender neutrality also generated significant statutory and case law alterations in family law and other doctrinal areas.[13] In general, it was clear to legal feminists in the 1960s and 1970s that the best way to ensure that perceived differences between men and women were not used to put women at a disadvantage was to refuse to recognize any differences as legally relevant. However, it is time to reconsider the question of difference and the role of feminist legal theory in responding to societal changes.

Relevant to this contemporary reconsideration are the limitations of assimilation as a feminist goal. Of particular significance is the fact that law is a conservative discipline, resistant to change. As discussed in chapter 2, law operates by establishing categories that then become entrenched because of the adherence within the discipline to values such as consistency and continuity. Precedents are followed and rules change by increments, if at all. This characteristic of law is crucial given that the exclusion of women from voting, jury service, even the practice of law, was the societal norm until fairly recently in our country.[14]

This historic exclusion should signal that there may be significant problems for women's adherence to an equality or neutrality model. Law as an institution—its procedures, structures, dominant concepts, and norms—was constructed at a time when women were systematically excluded from participation. Insofar as women's lives and experiences were (are) the subjects of law, they were (are) of necessity translated into law by men. Even social or cultural institutions such as "motherhood," that women occupy exclusively as legally significant categories, were what I call "colonized categories"—initially defined, controlled, and given legal content by men. Male norms and male understandings fashioned legal definitions of what constituted a family, of what was good mothering, who had claims and access to children as well as to jobs and education, and, ultimately, how legal institutions functioned to give or deny redress for alleged (and defined) harms.

Of course, women had been politically active and legally conscious during the *Bradwell* era. Some had even sought to implement their views about women's unique position into law. But the lessons from that era seemed clear about the dangers of a policy of difference. Florence Kelley and others from the National Consumer's League, for example, attempted to introduce a "female standard" into employment law—a standard that, although initially proposed to help women, ultimately worked against many women's interests.[15] Early women reformers such as Kelley, who believed that the only way to achieve equality was through the legal recognition and accommodation of women's differences, were handicapped. Unfortunately, they had to rely on men as litigators and legislators to be the translators and transmitters of their views. This was a process fraught with peril; male legal actors such as Felix Frankfurter, comfortable with and in control of "Law," shaped and reshaped ideas with feminist orgins until they were no longer recognizable as such.[16] Difference was ultimately translated in law and policy as inferiority, resulting in stigma and exclusion.

In regard to assessing the prospects for contemporary legal accommodation of differences, an important distinction between our own era and that of *Bradwell* is, of course, that feminists are no longer dependent upon the Frankfurters of the world for the translation of our ideas. Women now occupy professorships, are members of the bar, and make up almost half of law classes. A few of us are even legislators and judges.[17] While the full integration of the profession is far from complete (especially at the most powerful levels), feminist women can at least give our own legal voices to our ideas.

The current field of rich and diverse feminist legal theory is an example of what can happen when such voices are raised. A variety of feminist theorists articulate a spectrum of strategies for change. From continued adherence to the equality model to ideas of accommodation and acceptance of "special" needs, legal proposals are fashioned by feminists seeking to use law to better the position of women. In some specific areas, such as in developing the "battered woman's syndrome," concepts of difference have been successfully introduced and generally accepted by the larger legal community.[18] In most areas of legal regulation, however, existing concepts that fail to account for differences are not easily dismantled, and the law is assumed to be appropriately gender neutral, at least in its aspiration.

B. The Shape of the Contemporary Debate

A theory of difference is necessary in order to do more than merely open the doors to institutions designed with men's experiences in mind. A theory of difference calls into question the presumed neutrality of institutions, questioning their legitimacy because they are reflective of primarily male concerns. In this way, a theory of difference has the potential to politically empower women by making their participation central to the legitimation project.[19]

Interestingly, the attachment of some of the early legal feminists to the equality standard first seemed to falter around the issue of pregnancy. Staunch equal-treatment feminists found themselves divided along the parameters of a sameness/difference debate focused specifically on reproductive biology. In the articulation of similar earlier debates during the 1960s and 1970s, the dominant position of equality feminists was that a recognition of differences, even in the context of pregnancy, would lead to writing the separate spheres ideology back into law.[20]

For example, Wendy Williams' classic argument, published in 1982, was that the "problem" of pregnancy be dealt with using an equality strategy that analogized pregnancy in the workplace with illness. She asked the question, "On what basis can we fairly assert, for example, that the pregnant woman fired . . . deserved to keep her job when any other worker who got sick for any other reason did not?"[21] Her argument was for gender-neutral but improved sick leave policies that offered both men and women protection in the event of a "disability."

Deviations from a strict equality/sameness-of-treatment theme began to emerge in the early 1980s. These were the first signs of what would become a significant attempt to acknowledge differences in some contemporary feminist legal theory. Arguments fashioning distinctions between types of equality sought to draw meaningful lines between concepts such as "equality of treatment" (mandating same treatment) as contrasted with "equality of result" (which allowed for some different treatment). My own early work attempted to draw such lines in a broad family context. As early as 1981, I was arguing for distinction between "rule" and "result" equality and developed a critique of the trend toward gender neutrality in law reform as prohibiting any assessment of differences. The critique of gender neutrality, as well as the distinctions between equalities, was subsequently applied in other areas by other legal feminists.[22]

Even some of the most hard-line, sameness-of-treatment feminists have altered their positions in recent years, conceding that equality needs to be supplemented by an appreciation of difference in at least some narrowly defined class of situations. For example, Herma Hill Kay, one of the prominent early legal feminists, recently partially recanted her commitment to sameness-of-treatment by fashioning an "episodic" approach to equality.[23]

Kay notes that, although she adheres to the idea that women and men are basically the same, the law needs to acknowledge some biological difference. That legal acknowledgment should come in the form of validating some sex-specific rules in regard to pregnant, nursing, or menstruating women.[24] Biological sex differences would thus be "legally significant," but only when they were being utilized for specific, episodic, reproductive purposes. In assessing whether pregnancy discrimination had occurred, for example, the comparison would not be among broad categories of persons such as "women" and "men" (or to use the Supreme Court's peculiar categories, between "pregnant" and "non-pregnant" individuals).[25] Instead, the law would focus more narrowly to compare women and men who have engaged in the same reproductive behavior (sexual intercourse resulting in pregnancy) and ask if discriminatory treatment had occurred.[26] The episodic analysis leaves in place the basic equality framework, merely distorting it for some specific events that have increasingly come to be seen by many legal feminists as not fitting comfortably within the equality/sameness-of-treatment paradigm.

Other legal feminists are more disillusioned with sameness models and seem willing to move beyond equality rhetoric altogether. These feminists call attention to the fact that subtleties are often lost in legal formulation and application and that quite often calls for "equality" are translated as a mandate for sameness of treatment across crude categories that look like the application of "equality with a vengeance." The unique doctrinal position of equality as sameness in American legal culture actually operates as a conceptual obstacle to the formulation and implementation of solutions to the unique economic and societal problems women encounter within the confines of the status quo.[27]

The "postegalitarian feminists" (among whose ranks I count myself) move well beyond biological differences. We urge a theoretical focus on the role of law in maintaining the existing unequal allocations of societal and economic power between women and men. The argument is that legal theory must recognize the reality of existing systemic and persistent inequality and move beyond the simplistic equality paradigm, establishing an affirmative feminist theory of difference.

While initial adherence to an equality concept might have been necessary in taking the first steps toward trying to change the law and legal institutions, equality has proven insufficient as a concept with which to both assess and address the position of women under law. Equality may still have some use in circumscribed circumstances, such as in the context of arguing about measures when women and men stand in relatively equal positions (e.g., equal pay for equal work or equal voting rights), but there are many situations where positions are too unequal for equality to be of use. The argument is not that the concept is useless, but rather that equality should no longer be the overarching goal of feminist legal theory—the meta-objective that drives all other considerations.[28]

With a move away from equality as one of the paramount organizing principles of feminist legal thought, the emerging feminist legal theory becomes more oppositional. It explicitly challenges the status quo by disputing the presumed neutrality of law and calling into question the universality of the overarching abstract principles that have buttressed business as usual at most levels of society.

But, even if united in this basic first step of moving beyond equality, there are still differences among postegalitarian feminist theories. For example, legal feminists who argue for "accommodation" as well as those who urge "acceptance" believe that differences should be explicitly addressed, but they may differ on defining what differences are legally relevant and what form the legal arguments should take.

Those who argue for accommodation often approve "special" treatment for women only when "real" (biologically based) differences are at issue. The deviations from the equality model may be thus narrowly defined as fundamental reproductive differences.[29] By contrast, acceptance arguments, as advanced early on by Christine Littleton, encompass both biological and cultural sexual differences and seek to ensure "symmetry" in the ultimate positions of women and men by taking account of those differences. In this way, acceptance arguments are similar to the earlier attempts to fashion different types of equality to gain equality of results.[30] The acceptance approach, therefore, seems to many legal feminists to be the most promising way to address the questions of difference in societal position and economic strength. To date, however, the acceptance concept has not been used to discuss much beyond the "easy" case of pregnancy.

Other feminists, although clearly disillusioned with equality and sameness of treatment (and, therefore, postegalitarian), resist incorporation of discussions of difference into feminist legal theory. They argue that any attention to difference is a concession to male power in that it accepts that power as the relevant defining force—men are the beginning and the end of discussions about differences. Catharine MacKinnon, a leading proponent of this critique, urges that concepts of "dominance" and "subordination" be used to rectify legal inequality.[31] Sometimes this model productively leads to grounded considerations of gendered circumstances, but it has a tendency toward abstract presentation[32] and has been attacked as essentialistic and insensitive to differences in experiences.[33]

Another problem with concepts such as dominance and subordination is that they are inherently negative characterizations of women's subjective realities. As such, they may not be considered by many women to be appropriate descriptive labels to attach to the experience of sexuality, motherhood, or other forms of intimate connection. The danger is that the theoretical language of dominance and subordination is too distanced from the way many women view their own lives.

One additional type of postegalitarian legal feminist argument that is more often tied to insights of disciplines other than law and typically labeled as "postmodern" should be noted. Some of these arguments are simplified and reductionist renditions of French feminist and literary theories, but the important thrust of the best of these arguments is to be wary of essentialism.[34] Such insights have been challenging and provoked a lot of creative introspection on the part of feminist legal theorists seeking to preserve the overarching category of "Woman" as a political tool. As a result of the postmodern challenge, feminist legal theory typically now refers to subcategories within the larger construct of "Woman" and emphasizes that there are other defining characteristics such as race or sexual orientation that complicate the category.[35] This is necessary lest one be dismissed as an essentialist, believing in inherent, inimitable characteristics, but it has also unmasked an inherent problem with feminist use of any categories, even the basic one of "Woman" itself. The danger is that the postmodern sensitivity to essentialism results in a kind of hyperindividualism, with the potential to have very conservative consequences. This is particularly true when the additional defining characteristics become more than just necessary components for feminist theory, but rather requirements for defining who may speak for or about women.

C. Questions of Representation in Feminist Legal Theory

The thorny theoretical questions of what are the relevant differences among women and how should they be accommodated within feminism have been among the most hotly debated recent issues in the difference debates.[36] While I think feminists in general are to be commended for their concern with these differences and for their desire not to indulge in essentialism, I am concerned that recent developments seem to have paralyzed many—silencing or restricting voices as women determine that they cannot speak for anyone other than those women with whom they share major nongender characteristics such as class, sexual preference, or race.

1. Differences Among Women

Some writers have gone so far in accommodating differences among women that they suggest it is problematic to even use an unqualified category of "Woman" upon which to build theory and/or assign social, cultural, or political considerations or consequences.[37] There are additional questions as to whether we can speak even for ourselves—challenging the concept of "self" and asserting there are no unitary beings that exist over time, in space, to whom one can pretend to give coherent voice.[38] Under this view, we are thus reduced—either in a group, a cluster, or as an individual—to multiple categories and divided from each other.[39] The implications of these arguments are problematic.

In response to concerns about the essentializing of women, I think it is important to remember that, as the questioning of categories (in fact, the questioning of the whole process of categorization) goes on, society has generated—and continues to re-create and act upon—universalized, totalizing cultural representations of women and women's experiences. Cultural images of women, portrayed in the media, literature, movies and advertising range from victim to vamp, whore to madonna. Women are portrayed as mothers, selflessly devoting themselves to their children; as career women, selfishly denying their children adequate mothering; as wives, ecstatic over the newly waxed floor or anxiously awaiting their husband's return from work; as sex objects in pornography, from the soft-core versions found in advertising and fashion magazines to the more hard-core images in male-fantasy magazines; as dumb blondes; and as little girls in the current fashion craze. These images of women are pervasive and, "true" or not, they are presented as essentialistic. We are all of them even if we are none of them: they matter. Even those critical of essentialist images of women must recognize the force these culturally constructed images hold.[40]

None of us completely escapes the dominant images of the society within which we operate. Interpretation of life events, the processes whereby events are given meaning, is not an atomistic, individualistic procedure. Social action and interaction, as well as dominant cultural images, significantly contribute to individual interpretation of, and reaction to, events. Furthermore, the law utilizes and facilitates the construction of these totalizing social and cultural images.

2. Representation and Tokenism

As a theoretical issue, the direction of the debate about differences among women also raises some important conceptual problems. Insofar as it is understood to be an assertion that only women who occupy a category—i.e., have a qualifying characteristic—can speak with any legitimacy or authority about the significance of that category, the antiessentialist position is inherently divisive and the implications for feminist politics are troubling. In contemporary political discourse, there is a disturbing trend toward excessive attention to and reliance on the individual characteristics of the speaker. It seems indefensible, however, to assert that merely by "having" or embodying a characteristic or set of characteristics, an individual presumptively also has the authority and legitimacy to represent the position of women sharing such characteristics. It is equally indefensible to assert that someone who lacks the characteristics cannot speak with any authority. In using such arguments to legitimate (or delegitimate) some discourses, we also erroneously further the idea that the individual is the agent of social change and mask the manifold ways in which oppression takes place and is fostered within the structures and dominant ideologies of our society.

Some discourses are placed beyond criticism; they are accepted as authentic, not because of the nature of the rhetoric but because of the nature of the individual speaker. It should not be the characteristics of the speaker that are considered most relevant, however, but the quality and nature of that which is spoken. We must focus on the discourse, the ideology, the message—not the messenger. While certain differentiating characteristics may indicate experiences that should be added to the general theoretical construct, merely occupying a category should not, in and of itself, be considered sufficient or even necessary in a political context. No group or individual should be immune from a critical and political assessment of what they advocate. No group or individual should be freed from the responsibility to try to understand and speak out against injustice even if it is not directly experienced by them or the group to which they belong.

An individualistic version of representation was evident in the earlier, token moves to incorporate women into law. In the not-too-distant past, feminists observed how the legal profession integrated itself with the presence of a woman (or even several women) while social institutions and legal ideology remained unchanged. Experience should have taught feminist theorists that, from the most rudimentary political perspective, adhering to a notion that authority or authenticity can be located in specific individuals is dangerous and leads to the mere token inclusions of such individuals. The included representative is then seen as the "solution" to the problems suffered by the larger group. This tokenism fails to accommodate feminist concerns and criticisms and is profoundly reductive. Individualistic manifestation of "representation" equates one woman with another, making us fungible objectifications of the essential Woman.

This type of representation eradicates the perception of differences between women and men because it is a strategy focused on characteristics rather than experiences or ideology. Not surprisingly, a woman chosen to "represent" her gender often is one whose interests and values coincide with those of the normalized male institutions that have deigned to include her. Parity is achieved by the inclusion of a representative of a category, not by accommodation of different experiences and ideas. Since ideology and structure are not relevant in the selection of a representative, the representative woman also often finds herself accommodating the behavioral norms and the professional standards of the institution. Her token position makes challenge difficult, even if she initially had oppositional ideals. She, as token, is isolated.

The focus on the characteristics of the individual reveals the circular assumption of tokenism: an individual having the designated characteristic can and does represent members of a community now defined by that characteristic. The process of legitimation is accomplished within unchanged institutions that hold up the representative woman against the radical potential and challenge of a discourse of gendered experience and ideology. The gendered experience, however, is not capable of location within any individual woman.

It is important to remember (so we see its attractiveness) that while the notion of individual representation facilitates tokenism, it can also operate to empower an individual woman. Her gain in position and status is seductive even though it may simultaneously render her the most effective weapon to silence the interests and voices of the women she is supposed to represent. The ambition of individuals quite often means that the individualized mode of representation operates to exclude discordant voices by cooptation.

Thus, a notion of representation that is dependent on the characteristics of the individual poses serious difficulties. It carries with it not only the potential for divisiveness but also the certainty of exclusion within the hypothetically available community of feminists. Moreover, individual-based representation allows tokenism to flourish and nurtures continued resistance to the radical potential for change through the ideological and structural implications of feminism within institutions.

II. Shared Position—The Concept of A Gendered Life

The lessons learned from postmodern arguments, in particular, have enriched the development of theoretical approaches to the question of differences. In general, it seems that an increasing number of legal feminists are concluding that a so-called neutral equality model for law reform will serve as an artificial limit on the feminist project in law. While there are multiple feminisms, there is some agreement about the overall nature of the feminist project in law—consensus on the significance of defining affirmative uses of law to attempt to understand and address the social inequities women experience in our society as the result of their gender, including those resulting from their gendered roles as wives and mothers. Referencing ideals such as "justice" and "fairness" rather than focusing on equality, some feminists seek to make poor and working-class, nonprofessional women's circumstances more visible. They may not have menus of solutions, but their goal is to present the pain that the status quo has wrought in the hope that it will make some in positions of power rethink the tired and trite images and ideological impositions that have crippled public policy to date.

A. Making Gender Central

I have been developing the concept of a "gendered life" in order to give content to, and legitimate, a legal concern for differences. The idea of a gendered life is based on the premise that as a socially and legally defined group, women share the potential for experiencing a variety of situations, statuses, and ideological and political impositions in which their gender is culturally relevant. These experiences, be they actual or potential, provide the occasion for women to develop an identifiable perspective that is rooted in their appreciation of, and reaction to, the gendered nature of our social world. This concept does *not* assume that women respond identically to an appreciation of gendered existence. It does presume that with gender revealed as a central social and cultural consideration, women's attention in many areas can be directed productively toward confronting and challenging the gendered implications of our lives.[41]

This concept of gendered life begins with the observation that women's existences are constituted by a variety of experiences—material, psychological, physical, social, and cultural—some of which may be described as biologically based while others seem more rooted in culture and custom. The actual or potential experiences of rape, sexual harassment, pornography, and other sexualized violence that women may suffer shape individual experiences. So, too, does the potential for reproductive events such as pregnancy, breast-feeding, and abortion guide women's constructions of their gendered lives.

On the question of superficial similarities, I concede that while some gendered experiences are events that are shared with men, there is, nevertheless, often a unique way in which these events are generally or typically lived or experienced by women in our culture. Aging as a life event falls into this category. While both women and men age, the implications of aging from both social and economic perspectives are different for the genders.[42]

This concept of gendered life is my attempt to create a way to argue that a consideration of differences is necessary to remedy socially and culturally imposed harms to women. Notice that the formulation of the differences question is distinguishable from that of Justice Bradley's opinion in the *Bradwell* decision. In Bradley's opinion, differences were based on biology, nature, and, ultimately, God, and they operated as an exclusionary device to limit women's participation. My difference argument by contrast is grounded in empirical realizations, in gendered experiences, and, therefore, in women's lives as constructed in society and culture. It is an affirmative position, poised for the demand for remedies, for differentiated treatment to rectify existing pervasive social and legal inequality.

B. Gendered Life in Application

An example of this type of sensitivity to differences is found in *Ellison v. Brady,* a recent employment discrimination case.[43] In that case, Judge Beezer (a Reagan appointee on the Ninth Circuit) adopted a "reasonable woman" standard for the assessment of allegations of sexual harassment:

> We believe that in evaluating the severity and pervasiveness of sexual harassment, we should focus on the perspective of the victim. If we only examined whether a reasonable person would engage in allegedly harassing conduct, we would run the risk of reinforcing the prevailing level of discrimination. Harassers could continue to harass merely because a particular discriminatory practice was common. . . .

> Because women are disproportionately victims of rape and sexual assault, women have a stronger incentive to be concerned with sexual behavior. . . . Men, who are rarely victims of sexual assault, may view sexual conduct in a vacuum without a full appreciation of the social setting or the underlying threat of violence that a woman may perceive.[44]

The majority opinion adopted a reasonable woman standard in recognition of the fact that women experience at least some aspects of the world differently than men.

Judge Beezer was opposed to a purely subjective test and indicated that the "objective" reasonable woman standard was fashioned "in order to shield employers from having to accommodate the idiosyncratic concerns of the rare hyper-sensitive employee."[45] He noted that the court found it necessary to "adopt the perspective of a reasonable woman primarily because we believe that a sex-blind reasonable person standard tends to be male-biased and tends to systematically ignore the experiences of women."[46] The court reversed the trial judge's finding that the woman, who had received "love letters" that she found frightening from a male colleague, had failed to state a *prima facie* case of hostile environment sexual harassment.

On a very significant level, the opinion in this case was a victory for feminist legal theorists who emphasize the different ways in which men and women in our culture experience events. Feminist legal writers' works are found in the text of the opinion.[47] Even more important, certain relevant aspects of women's gendered lives were not systematically ignored and male experiences were not adopted as the norm. In referencing the "real" world context of sexual violence toward women, Judge Beezer recognized that such reality can shape an individual woman's reception of insistent and unwanted declarations of affection.

Before feminists do too much celebrating, however, it is important to remember that winning one battle is not the same as winning the war. Just articulating that women's experiences are the relevant ones does not mean that male judges will "get it right." Compare *Ellison* with *Scott v. Sears, Roebuck & Company*,[48] in which a different appellate court found that allegations of repeated propositions by a supervisor, along with experiences such as slapped buttocks and sexual comments from coworkers, did *not* poison a woman's work environment. Also ominous for those who want to hold onto hope for a rosy future for the reasonable woman standard is *Rabidue v. Osceola Refining Company*.[49] In that case, a majority of the Sixth Circuit Court of Appeals held that sexually explicit and derogatory remarks about women and the presence of pinups in the office did not seriously affect the female plaintiff's psychological well-being.[50] Other courts have shown similar tendencies to coopt the concept of reasonable (applied to women explicitly or generically), making it coterminous with the "common sense" of (mostly) male judges.[51]

We must also be aware that opinions such as Judge Beezer's in *Ellison* reflect an aspect of the difference-among-women portion of the differences debate. At the same time that Judge Beezer affirmed that there are relevant legal differences between the social and cultural experiences of men and women, he assumed that a reasonable woman standard could be applied in the context of the fact-finding process. The opinion does note the possibility of relevant differences among women, but banishes any doubt that realization might have generated in the interests of protecting the employers from the "idiosyncratic concerns of the rare hyper-sensitive employee."[52] Any potential differences among female perspectives are not the occasion for withholding a gender-specific new standard given the need that exists, the court concludes, for "[a] gender-conscious examination of sexual harassment

[that] enables women to participate in the workplace on an equal footing with men."[53]

C. Differences Among Women

While the distinction between women's and men's experiences with sexual harassment is welcome, the question arises in *Ellison* what about the "dilemma" presented by the recognition that there are relevant differences among women?[54] I think that the concept of a gendered life may be helpful in this inquiry also. To explore this claim, I want to return to the issue of motherhood.

I earlier referred to the institution of motherhood as a "colonized category"[55] in law. I argued that regardless of the differences among us, all women must care about social and legal constructions of motherhood. Although we may make individual choices not to become mothers, social construction and its legal ramifications operate independent of individual choice. As is demonstrated in everyday existence, as well as in legal doctrines and political language, women *will* be treated as mothers (or potential mothers) because "Woman" as a cultural and legal category inevitably encompasses and incorporates socially constructed notions of motherhood in its definition.[56] In addition, it is important to note that, although the social and legal construction of motherhood occurs in a variety of different social and legal contexts, there seems to be a common image of the ideal "mother" that emerges and against which women in different circumstances will inevitably be judged.[57]

A comparison of images of single motherhood that emerge in both poverty and in divorce discourses, for example, demonstrates that concepts and totalizing ideals tend to "cross over."[58] The ideas (and ideals) forged in one context constrain and direct the debates in another. It is not necessary that the transference be a complete one. There is significantly shared imagery, and connections are made between discourses about mothers in different circumstances so that they (we) should be able to see the reflections of each other shaping the total cultural construct. Motherhood is a totalizing, culturally defined institution that applies across race and class lines. The mother is objectified—heterosexual, married, chaste, self-sacrificing—a rather statistically improbable and oppressive construct.

This process of objectification is inevitable. Murray Edelman theorizes:

> It is the expression of ideas that makes it possible to hold them, think about them, react to them, and spread them to others. There must be an image, as articulated in art, in words, or in other symbols. The notion that an idea can somehow exist without objectification in an expression of any kind is an illusion, though the expression may take the form of a term or image in one's own mind: i.e., as a contemplated exchange with others.[59]

However, inevitable though it may be, the process of objectification does not mean that the form of the image is not up for contest and ultimate reconstruction.

The assertion that there is a totalizing tendency represented in the social and legal construction of women as "Woman" (and "Mother") suggests a basis for women working together across their differences. This rather hopeful twist on the oppressive extent of gender stereotyping is premised on its utility for unifying different groups of women. Using the concept of gendered lives that I earlier developed to distinguish women's from men's lived experiences in our culture, it is possible to see some unifying potential in the very extensiveness of the cultural stereotype. The existence of the social construction suggests that, while few could legitimately dispute that characteristics such as race, class, and sexuality are significant to one's experiences, it is an error for women to proceed as though these differences were always relevant. For example, I believe that age, physical characteristics (including "handicaps" and "beauty" or the lack thereof), religion, marital status, the level of male identification (which is independent of both marital status and sexual orientation—what Gerda Lerner has referred to as "the man in our head"[60]), birth order, motherhood, grandmotherhood, intelligence, rural or urban existence, responsiveness to change or ability to accept ambivalence in one's personal life or in society, sources of income (self, spouse, or state), degree of poverty or wealth, and substance dependency, among others, shape existence in both how individual women experience the world and how others, particularly those in power, relate to them.

The postegalitarian feminist concept of a gendered experience, offered initially in an attempt to open a space for women's perspective in law as distinct from men's, can also provide the occasion for unity among women over some specifics of their lives. Women have characteristics or clusters of characteristics related to the gendered aspects of their lives that have social and legal significance and, therefore, give women a basis for cooperation and empathy.

In fact, in some instances gender may not be relevant and women's lives can be viewed as analogous to men's.[61] In other contexts, sets of interests may more appropriately be articulated in ungendered terms such as race or class.

By using the terminology of "gendered lives," I mean to problematize the so-called "feminine," recognizing it as developed in specific historical, social, and political contexts.[62] Because the concept of gendered experiences focuses us on specific experiences that are confined to such contexts, hopefully it can avoid perpetuating an idealized, universal notion of "Woman."

Furthermore, as I have already argued, many of the terms applied in feminist legal theory attempting to describe the uniqueness of women's position in society are problematic. A benefit of the gendered life concept is that it does *not* contain any inherently negative connotations as does a domination model, which brings with it notions of victimization. Many women may not be comfortable with a theory that rhetorically places their life experiences in a hegemonic web of oppression and domination. To return to the experience of motherhood as an example, while it may be a burdensome status in many regards, most mothers do not experience motherhood as "oppressive." There is a need for the development of theoretical language to express women's experiences so as not to alienate women who live some aspects of traditional lives. Feminists should not trivialize women's voluntarily shouldering of material or social disadvantages as caretakers, labeling their doing so the product of false consciousness or resulting in individual or group pathology.[63]

I think the gendered lives concept has advantages over other ways of discussing differences simply because it anticipates that women's lives are always composites of concerns, characteristics, and components that constantly shift as situations and circumstances change. Gendered life assumes the relational nature of experience, presumes that we are all affected by social patterns and material circumstances. It is an abstracted term with built-in complexity, just like the idea of women's lives.

III. Conclusion

The force that an imposed (and in that sense, therefore, "common") socially constructed concept of gender exercises upon aspects of all women's lives presents an opportunity for diverse women to participate in resisting that imposition. Women can coalesce across differences to work together on the project of defining for ourselves the implications and ramifications of the gendered aspects of our lives.

I'm interested in exploring whether it is possible to have an affirmative politics of difference that defines groups and classifications tenuously, whereby group identification is recognized as politically necessary but is also seen, in the words of Iris Marion Young, as "ambiguous, relational, shifting," without "clear borders" that bind people in all circumstances for all time.[64] Women need not be considered to be inevitably either in opposition to or having little in common with other women because of nongender group differences. Women can and should converge to organize around overlapping experiences.[65]

My hopes for a development of the concept of gendered lives as a creative way to simultaneously address both distinct aspects of the differences debate may be too optimistic. I am convinced, however, that the renewed interest in difference in feminist legal theory that has occurred during the last decade is positive because it reaffirms that our struggle over content and meaning in law is inherently political and that perspectives count.

I recognize that the focus on difference at the core of the gendered life concept is fraught with potential pitfalls. Difference can be used to divide women, diluting our collective potential as a group to challenge male-defined and controlled notions of law that systematically disadvantage women in a variety of contexts. I defend my attempt here by stating only that this is a search for pragmatic ways for legal feminists to work with law, recognizing its gendered nature and the need for the contexts supplied by considerations of differences.

Notes

1. Lise Vogel questions why feminist legal theorists are still so caught up in the equality versus special treatment debate; she considers other feminists in different disciplines to have moved beyond such issues. Lise Vogel, *Mothers on the Job:*

Maternity Policy in the U.S. Workplace (New Brunswick, NJ: Rutgers Univ. Press, 1993). Since differences are generated by and essential to legal process, it is not surprising that they concern feminist legal thinkers.

2. For a discussion of the feminist debate over social construction of gender versus female essentialism, *see* Linda Alcoff, "Cultural Feminism Versus Poststructuralism: The Identity Crisis in Feminist Theory," 13 *Signs* 405 (1988).

3. Altering the biological capacities of men so that they could carry a fetus might be the only way to evoke significant change in other areas. Many people reflect on the fact that American men are assuming more responsibilities for children. How male interest in children is expressed, however, may reinforce rather than dismantle existing power relationships. I believe this is illustrated by three clippings I occasionally distribute to my family law classes. The clippings represent to me three competing models of the "new father."

The first clipping is a letter to Ann Landers, in which an expectant mother confessed that while she considered herself "lucky" in comparison to the women who complained about their husbands not paying much attention to their newborns, she was "concerned." The soon-to-be Mom wrote: "Larry doesn't want me to breast-feed our child because he wants to play a significant part in the care of our newborn. He recently read that if the father isn't involved in the feeding of the infant, bonding won't take place. I've always believed that breast is best, but I certainly don't want to deny my husband the opportunity to bond with our baby." Ann responded: "It's wonderful that your husband is so eager to be part of the baby's early life. But a breast-fed child has a decided advantage. . . . Your husband can hold the child after he feeds. He can burp, cradle, coo and establish bonding in this way." Ann Landers, *Wisconsin State Journal* (February 18, 1988): p. 6.

The second clipping announces the development of something called "Dr. Goldson's Baby Bonder." The device is described by Barbara Roessner thus: "[A man's] chest is cloaked in a biblike garment with breast-shaped protuberances into which ordinary baby bottles have been inserted." She quotes from the advertisement: "Something new for the mouths of babes. . . . Now, nursing can be done by anyone for just $19.95. . . . Breast-feeding isn't just women's work anymore." Barbara Roessner, "Device to Let Fathers 'Breast-feed' May Be the Latest Sign of the Times," *The Capital Times* (March 15, 1988): p. 8.

The most radical (and technology-dependent) vision of the new father, however, was offered by the British Magazine *New Society* 76 (1219) (9 May 1986): p. 7, which reported scientists as saying that "the technology exists to enable men to give birth." The Associated Press followed up on this story with interviews and reported:

Male pregnancy would involve fertilizing a donated egg with sperm outside the body. The embryo would be implanted into the bowel area

where it could attach itself to a major organ. The baby would be
delivered by Caesarean section. . . .

The embryo creates the placenta, so theoretically the baby would
receive nourishment.

Mr. Mom: Scientists Say Men Could Give Birth, Wisconsin State Journal, May
9, 1986, p. 2. The question of whether or not there would be a market for this
technology is an interesting one. It was dismissed by one fertility researcher
with the comment, "Nobody has tried it—and why would they? It's bizarre
and fanciful." Others, however, saw the potential for a limited market: "[C]andi-
dates for male pregnancy might be homosexuals, transsexuals or men whose
wives are infertile." *Ibid.*

These three stories represent three possible male adaptations to the existence
of a biologically based difference between men and women that actually favors
women in regard to the establishment of a claim to children. In the first story,
the male response is to force the woman to deny the implications of difference,
even at the possible cost of harm to the child. She is coerced into conforming
her conduct to the male's physical limitations so that she does not garner any
advantage.

The second story, however, in my opinion represents an even more insidious
response. The male merely makes a superficial adjustment, donning an obviously
artificial imitation (almost a caricature) of maternity while not altering the
reality of his physical situation. Such subversion disguises the fact that a move
from breast to bottle has occurred at the same time that it asserts on an ideological
level the erroneous notion that breast-feeding is nothing special, an activity that
can be duplicated by some wire, material, strings, and a great deal of smoke
and mirrors. This example of resorting to gimmicks in order to assume away
any significant biological difference may be tempting to advocates of equality.
It has the potential to backfire, however. What may occur is the devaluation
and minimization of an important biological, social, and cultural event (breast-
feeding) in order for us to pretend that fathers can "breast-feed." See Sherry F.
Colb, "Words that Deny, Devalue, and Punish: Judicial Responses to Fetus-
Envy?" 72 *Boston Univ. Law Review* 101, 119 (1992) (noting the effect of the
trial court's naming the award of the embryo to Mrs. Davis "temporary custody," in the Tennessee frozen embryo case, *Davis v. Davis,* 1989 Tennessee
Appeal, Lexis 641. This gender-neutral term allowed the pretense that men can
be pregnant, thereby denying that pregnancy is special, since men as well as
women may have temporary custody, but only women can become pregnant.)

The third story illustrates my point that technology can in some circumstances
eliminate differences. While it is true that this story involves gestation, not
breast-feeding, the hope is that once this step is accomplished the subsequent
nurturing may be expedited. Surely for the advocate of equality, the direction,

which is toward the elimination of differences, is the right one. The goal is assimilation, although this time it is the conformity of the male to the female that is sought. As the comments quoted above indicate, however, even if the technology exists, the cultural and societal arrangements make it unlikely that anyone other than those who have no woman ready to do their bearing for them will ever use it.

4. For a collection of essays organized around the difference theme, *see* "Papers from the 1986 Feminism and Legal Theory Conference." 3 *Wis. Women's Law Journal* (1987).

5. The answer to the question, "What is the feminist project in law?" changes over time as either the law or circumstances change or as perceptions of the problems alter. At any one time there are many feminist projects in law. The designation of what are the most pressing feminist projects varies with the feminists consulted; some are concerned primarily with issues of legal knowledge and the production of doctrine, others with women's opportunities within the profession. Many are concerned with the impact of law for the perpetuation of an historically inequitable and gendered social existence.

6. Feminism has been one significant source for contributions to the contemporary conclusion that the separate spheres of public and private or market and domestic are a myth. For some of the early significant attacks on the separate spheres metaphor *see* Nancy F. Cott, *The Bonds of Womanhood: "Woman's Sphere" in New England 1780–1835* (New Haven, CT: Yale Univ. Press, 1977):p. 197–206. Nadine Taub and Elizabeth M. Schnieder, "Perspectives on Women's Subordination and the Role of Law," in *The Politics of Law: A Progressive Critique* David Kairys, ed. (Boston: Pantheon, 1982); Sylvia A. Law, "Rethinking Sex and the Constitution," 132 *Univ. of Pennsylvania Law Review* 955, 1020 (1984).

7. *Bradwell v. Illinois,* 83 U.S. (16 Wall.) (1872) pp. 130, 141 (Bradley, J., concurring).

8. *See* Wendy W. Williams, *The Equality Crisis: Some Reflections on Culture, Courts, and Feminism,* 7 *Women's Rights Law Reporter* 175 (1982).

9. In a classic article on the subject, Wendy Williams expressed the concerns of those advocating for an equality model. While noting the "instinct to treat pregnancy as a special case" (*Ibid.,* p. 195) Williams warned:

> The same doctrinal approach that permits pregnancy to be treated *worse* than other disabilities is the same one that will allow the state constitutional freedom to create special *benefits* for pregnant women. The equality approach to pregnancy . . . necessarily creates not only the desired floor under the pregnant woman's rights but also the

> ceiling. . . . If we can't have it both ways, we need to think carefully about which way we want to have it.
>
> My own feeling is that, for all its problems, the equality approach is the better one. The special treatment model has great costs. . . . (195–96)
>
> At this point we need to think as deeply as we can about what we want the future of women and men to be. Do we want equality of the sexes—or do we want justice for two kinds of human beings who are fundamentally different? (200)

10. *See* Wendy McElroy, "The Roots of Individualist Feminism in 19th Century America," in *Freedom, Feminism, and the State* Wendy McElroy ed. (Washington, DC: Cato Institute, 1982).

11. House Joint Resolution 208, passed House 117 Congressional Resolution H35815; passed Senate 118 Congressional Record S9598

12. Eighteen states and territories have constitutional amendments that specifically mandate sexual equality under the law. *See,* for example Alaska Const. art. I, §3; Colorado Const. art. II, §29; Connecticut Const. art. I, §20; Maryland Const. Decl. of Rts. art. 46; Massachusetts Const. Pt. 1, art. I; Montana Const. art. II, §4; New Hampshire Const. Pt. 1, art. II; New Mexico Const. art. II, §18; Pennsylvania Const. art. I, §28; Rhode Island Const. art. I, §2; Texas Const. art. I, §3a; Utah Const. art. IV, §1; Virginia Const. art. I, §11; Washington Const. art. XXXI, §1; Wyoming Const. art. I, §3.

13. *See, e.g.,* Fineman, Illusion [chapter 2, note 8]; Isabel Marcus, "Reflections on the Significance of the Sex/Gender System: Divorce Law Reform in New York," 42 *Univ. of Miami Law Review* 55 (1987).

14. The nineteenth amendment to the U.S. Constitution giving women the right to vote was proposed in June 1919 and ratified in August 1920. It is of note that it was not ratified in Florida and South Carolina until 1969, Georgia and Louisiana in 1970, North Carolina in 1971, and Mississippi in 1984. As late as 1961, women were not treated equally with regard to jury service, *see Hoyt v. Florida,* 368 U.S. 57 (1961) (Court upheld Florida statute requiring that women register to vote before being eligible for jury duty). *And see Bradwell,* Chapter 3, note 7, in which the U.S. Supreme Court upheld an Illinois prohibition on women practicing law. It wasn't until the early 1970s that women were admitted to law schools in significant numbers. *See* Chapter 3, note 17.

15. For a documentation of this process in regard to the litigation involving industrial equality, *see* Sybil Lipschultz, "Socialism, Feminism and Legal Discourse, 1908–1923," in *Boundaries* [chapter 2, note 11] p. 209.

16. *Id.*

17. As of 1988, approximately 42 percent of those enrolled in law school were women. *Review of Legal Education in the United States,* Fall 1988, 1988 ABA Sec. Legal Educ. & Admission to B. 65. The Census Bureau reports that as of 1989, 22.3 percent of all lawyers and judges were women. U.S. Department of Commerce, Bureau of the Census, *Statistical Abstract of the United States* (Washington, DC: U.S. GPO 1991) 395.

18. There has been recent controversy over these changes. The battered woman's defense has been criticized as stigmatizing and failing to give acknowledgement to women's agency. *See* Holly Maguigan, "Battered Women and Self Defense: Myths and Misconceptions in Current Reform Proposals" 140 *Univ. of Pennsylvania Law Review* 379 (1991). There is a great deal of concern over women being cast as "victims" and thus as passive receptors of definition and action by powerful men in society. *See* Elizabeth M. Schneider, "Describing and Changing: Women's Self-defense Work and the Problem of Expert Testimony on Battering," 9 *Women's Rights Law Reporter* 195 (1986); Elizabeth M. Schneider, "Particularity and Generality: Challenges of Feminist Theory and Practice in Work on Woman-abuse," 67 *New York Univ. Law Review* 520 (1992); Christine A. Littleton, "Women's Experience and the Problems of Transition: Perspectives on Male Battering of Women," 1989 *Univ. of Chicago Legal Forum* 23, and Martha R. Mahoney, "Legal Images of Battered Women: Redefining the Issue of Separation," 90 *Michigan Law Review* 1 (1991).

19. Differences can be empowering, providing opportunity not stigma. This assertion is made without the intent to obscure the fact that a focus on differences holds potential dangers for women. However, the problems women face in law and in the larger society are not the same as they were even ten years ago.

20. *See* Williams [chapter 3, note 8]. There are many explicit criticisms of Williams position. For example, it seems clear that Williams fails to recognize her own inherent commitment to a disadvantageous system in that she does not question the designation of work as the preeminent social goal. In criticizing gender-neutrality, Sherry Colb observes that Williams herself implicitly concedes the weakness of the equality approach in confronting the argument that pregnancy is voluntary, unlike disability, and that pregnancy therefore need not be accommodated. Williams argues that pregnancy is no more voluntary than eating or sleeping and that a gender-integrated work place must provide for pregnancy-related absence just as it provides time for employees to eat and sleep. This is, of course, a departure from gender-neutrality and the gender-neutral antidiscrimination enterprise of finding male analogues for female experiences that arguably deserve accommodation. *See* Colb [chapter 3, note 3] p. 126 (discussing Wendy Williams, "Equality's Riddle: Pregnancy and the Equal Treatment/Special Treatment Debate," 13 *New York University Review of Law and Social Change* 324, 354 n. 114 (1984—85).

21. *Ibid.* p. 196.

22. *See* Martha L. Fineman, "Implementing Equality: The Rhetoric and Reality of Divorce Reform," 1983 *Univ. of Wisconsin Law Review* 789. Other scholars have continued along the lines first suggested in that 1983 article and have sought to draw distinctions among modes of equalities. *See, e.g.,* Mary Becker, "Prince Charming: Abstract Equality," *Supreme Court Review* 1987: p. 201. *And see* Herma Hill Kay, "Models of Equality," 1985 *Univ. of Illinois Law Review* 39; Lucinda M. Finley, "Transcending Equality Theory: A Way Out of The Maternity and the Workplace Debate," 86 *Columbia Law Review* 1118 (1986); Christine A. Littleton, "Reconstructing Sexual Equality," 75 *California Law Review* 1279 (1987). However, I soon realized that equality is a legal concept, considered foundational and thus carrying with it a significant and vital history of interpretation. It is not a term so easily captured and manipulated as to be readily available for feminist reforms. I subsequently argued for the "abdication" of equality and a resort to middle-range ideals. *See* Fineman, *Illusions* [chapter 2, note 8].

23. Herma Hill Kay, "Equality and Difference: The Case of Pregnancy," 1 *Berkeley Women's Law Journal* 1 (1985).

24. *Ibid.*

25. *Geduldig v. Aiello,* 417 U.S. 484 (1974) (upholding California's disability insurance program against an equal protection challenge because the distinction it made was between pregnant and nonpregnant persons, not males and females). "There is no risk from which men are protected and women are not. Likewise, there is no risk from which women are protected and men are not. . . . The California insurance program does not exclude anyone from benefit eligibility because of gender but merely removes one physical condition—pregnancy—from the list of compensable disabilities." *Id.* at 496–97. Perhaps the Court was prescient, *see* chapter 3, note 3 regarding new technology that may allow men to give birth.

26. Herma Hill Kay, "Equality and Difference: A Perspective on No-Fault Divorce and its Aftermath," 56 *Cinncinati Law Review* 1 (1987). The author also sees a limited role for male-specific rules, as in the case of rape. This an "accommodationist" model that validates "special" treatment when it is used to accommodate "real" (that is, physiologically based) difference. *See* the description and critique in Vogel [chapter 3, note 1] pp. 83–84, 142–43.

27. *See, e.g.,* Fineman, *Illusion* [chapter 2, note 8]; Diana Majury, "Strategizing in Equality," in *Boundaries* [chapter 2, note 11] p. 320; Marcus [chapter 3, note 13].

28. A simplistic notion of equality has created a particularly harmful set of problems in the family context. For example, the rhetoric surrounding the equality debate

has raised questions in the context of adoptions. Unmarried fathers are employing equality models to attack the rules that treat them differently from the child's mother in terms of due process and substantive rights when a child is to be placed for adoption. *See Caban v. Mohammed,* 441 U.S. 380 (1979) (single father who had lived with his children for five years may block adoption of children by withholding consent); *but see Quilloin v. Walcott,* 434 U.S. 246 (1978) (natural father who had never exercised custody over or legitimated the child could not object to adoption). *See also Lehr v. Robertson,* 463 U.S. 248 (1983) (refusing to strike as unconstitutional a law that provided different procedures and rights to fathers of nonmarital children up for adoption than to mothers). In *Lehr* the court found it significant that the father had not maintained a relationship with the child since her birth, quoting with approval Justice Stewart's dissent in *Caban:* "The mother carries and bears the child, and in this sense her parental relationship is clear. The validity of the father's parental claims must be gauged by other measures. By tradition, the primary measure has been the legitimate familial relationship he creates with the child by marriage with the mother. . . . In some circumstances the actual relationship between father and child may suffice to create in the unwed father parental interests comparable to those of the married father." *Id.* at 260, n. 16 (quoting *Caban,* 441 U.S. at 397 [Stewart, J., dissenting]). *See* discussion below pp. 111–114.

29. *See* Kay [chapter 3, note 26].

30. *See* Littleton [chapter 3, note 22].

31. Catharine MacKinnon, "Difference and Dominance in Sex Discrimination." In *Feminism Unmodified: Discourses on Life and Law* (Cambridge: Harvard Univ. Press, 1987).

32. *See Boundaries* [chapter 2, note 11]. p. xi–xii (discussing Carol Smart's concerns with Grand Theory).

33. *See,* generally, Martha R. Mahoney, "Whiteness and Women, in Practice and Theory: A Reply to Catharine MacKinnon," 5 *Yale Journal of Law and Feminism* 217 (1993); Sanger [chapter 2, note 23] (discussing why motherhood has been ignored as a relevant topic for serious research.)

34. *See, e.g.,* Martha Minow, "Feminist Reason, Getting it and Losing It," 38 *Journal of Legal Education* 47 (1988); Angela P. Harris, "Race and Essentialism in Feminist Legal Theory," 42 *Stanford Law Review* 581 (1990); and Mary Joe Frug, "Progressive Feminist Legal Scholarship: Can We Claim "A Different Voice?" 15 *Harvard Women's Law Journal* 32 (1992).

35. Harris [chapter 3, note 34]; Patricia Cain, "Grounding the Theories," 4 *Berkeley Women's Law Journal* 191 (1989–90).

36. Harris [chapter 3, note 34]; Deborah L. Rhode, "Feminist Critical Theories," 42 *Stanford Law Review* 617 (1990); Joan C. Williams, "Deconstructing Gender," 87 *Michigan Law Review* 797 (1989); Sanger [chapter 2, note 23] (discussing "maternal essentialism").

37. For a further exposition of this view, *see* Patricia Cain, "Feminism and the Limits of Equality," 24 *Georgia Law Review* 803, 838–41 (1990). Cain argues that the category "Woman" is multifarious and cannot be made into a unitary whole. She says that a postmodern feminism would focus not on "woman" but "women." This is her answer to the criticism that there is not an appropriate category around which feminism can operate in postmodern theory.

38. *See Ibid.*, pp. 806–810. Cain describes the social constructionist position of "Woman" as a category whose content is filled out by the creators of the category. "Self-definition," she claims, is "never something I can do independently." *Ibid.* at 808. She does suggest that one brand of radical feminism hopes to reconstruct the category in feminist terms. *Ibid.*, pp. 832–35.

39. Robin West has voiced a powerful critique of this tendency. *See* Robin West, "Feminism, Critical Social Theory and Law," 59 *Univ. of Chicago Legal Forum* 84–89 (1989). For attempts to provide a postmodern connection, *see* Drucilla Cornell, "The Doubly-Prized World: Myth Allegory and the Feminine," 75 *Cornell Law Review* 644 (1990).

40. For a fuller treatment of this phenomenon, *see* Helen Benedict, *Virgin or Vamp* (New York: Oxford Univ. Press, 1993).

41. In a world in which gender is more than semantics, feminist legal theory cannot be gender neutral nor can it have as its goal equality in the traditional, formal legal sense of that word. Feminist theory must be woman centered, gendered by its very nature because it uses women's experiences as its raw building material. Since women live gendered lives in our culture, any analysis that begins with their experiences must of necessity be gendered. Addressing the real material consequences of women's gendered life experiences cannot be accomplished by a system that refuses to recognize gender as a relevant perspective, imposing "neutral" conclusions on women's circumstances.

42. *See* Paul E. Zopf, *American Women in Poverty* (Greenwich, CT: Greenwood, 1989): pp. 109–111.

43. 924 F.2d 872 (9th Cir. 1991). However, the particular aspect of protectiveness evidenced in *Bradwell* may still be detected in court cases. *See, e.g., International Union, UAW v. Johnson Controls, Inc.*, 886 F.2d 871 (7th Cir. 1989), where the court sitting *en banc* upheld a company policy that banned women of childbearing years from occupying particular positions of employment because of evidence that exposure to lead in those positions would cause severe birth defects if a woman were to become pregnant. While this was later overruled

by the Supreme Court—*International Union, UAW v. Johnson Controls, Inc.,*
111 S.Ct. 1196 (1991)—the Court did not reject the basic premise of the lower
court—that is, that all women should be viewed as potential mothers—but
instead emphasized the woman's right to make choices regarding childbearing
and pregnancy.

44. *Ellison,* 924 F.2d at 878–79.

45. *Id.* at 879.

46. *Id.*

47. Judge Beezer cites the following feminist writing in the area of sexual harassment:

> Ehrenreich, "Pluralist Myths and Powerless Men: The Ideology of
> Reasonableness in Sexual Harassment Law," 99 *Yale Law Journal*
> 1177, 1207–1208 (1990) (men tend to view some form of sexual
> harassment as "harmless social interaction to which only over-sensitive
> women would object"); Abrams, "Gender Discrimination and the
> Transformation of Workplace Norms," 42 *Vanderbuilt Law Review*
> 1183, 1203 (the characteristically male view depicts sexual harassment
> as comparatively harmless amusement). (*Ibid.,* pp. 878–879)

48. 798 F.2d 210 (7th Cir. 1986)

49. 805 F.2d 611 (6th Cir. 1986), *cert. denied,* 481 U.S. 1041 (1987).

50. Another ominous episode in regard to the progress being made in the sexual
harassment area was the treatment Professor Anita Hill received in her appear-
ances before the Senate Judiciary Committee in conjunction with her allegations
against Supreme Court nominee Clarence Thomas. Whether one believes that
Hill was sexually harassed or not, it is clear that the manner in which her
credibility was assessed reflected male bias and ignorance of women's experiences
even though the experience of sexual harassment is essentially a gendered event.

 Throughout the Hill/Thomas hearings, the nation watched as a woman was
judged by an all-male panel and a predominantly male media who repeatedly
raised questions as to why she would continue her employment with Thomas
in the first instance and maintain contact with him after she had left the Justice
Department if she had in fact been sexually harassed. Senator Orrin Hatch, in
particular, seemed to feel it was unbelievable that Hill did not do something
drastic if things were as she reported.

 I find it incredible that these men could think Hill's inaction was of any
significance. Even if they chose to ignore the argument that many women in
this position fail to act, their own experiences with (nonsexual) harassment
from superiors who had power over them should have provided some insight
into the dilemma someone in Hill's position would face. No doubt in their
professional lives—as law students, as young associates in law firms, or as junior
governmental officials—they suffered humiliation, indignities, or insults at the

hands of powerful supervisors, yet continued their employment and actively fostered continued contact for the future references and opportunities the person in the explicit position of power would supply.

The senators and the male media did not place Hill's experience of sexual harassment in the context of "normal" hierarchical power relationships with which they might have had some basis for identification and empathy. Instead, and perhaps because the indignities and humiliation she suffered were sexual in nature, what transpired was the application of the tired, old, traditional, patriarchal male vision of female virtue and how it should be expressed—"death before dishonor."

51. *See, e.g., Lipsett v. University of Puerto Rico,* 740 F. Supp 921, 925 (1990), in which the court refused, as unnecessary, expert testimony regarding sexual harassment because it would be within the "common sense" of jury to determine whether the evidence indicated a hostile environment.

52. *Ellison,* 924 F.2d at 879.

53. *Id.*

54. Martha Minow develops the various aspects of the "dilemma," which she describes as "the risk of recreating difference by either noticing it or ignoring it," in her book, *Making All the Difference: Inclusion, Exclusion, and American Law* (Ithaca, NY: Cornell Univ. Press, 1990).

55. For a more extensive discussion of this concept, *see Mothers in Law: Feminism and the Legal Regulation of Motherhood,* Martha Fineman and Isabel Karpin, eds., (N.Y.: Columbia University Press), forthcoming 1995.

56. The trial court opinion in *International Union, UAW v. Johnson Controls, Inc.,* 886 F.2d (7th Cir. 1989), rev'd 111 S.Ct. 1196 (1991), graphically illustrated this assertion. The company policy excluded "all women who are pregnant or who are capable of bearing children" from working in areas of the plant where lead levels were above a certain concentration. 886 F.2d at 876. Only women who had medical confirmation that they were infertile were excluded from the policy. *Ibid.* at 877–78. The trial court accepted the company's argument that the exclusion was justified as a bona fide occupational qualification and that men were not similarly affected by the lead levels. Even though eventually overturned on appeal, the sets of assumptions engaged in by the trial court were by no means outside of dominant societal constructs. In reversing the decision, the Supreme Court quoted from the earlier company policy which recognized that " 'Since not all women who can become mothers wish to become mothers (or will become mothers), it would appear to be illegal discrimination to treat all who are capable of pregnancy as though they will become pregnant.' " 111 S. Ct. at 1199. The Court went on to state: "The bias . . . is obvious. Fertile

men, but not fertile women, are given a choice as to whether they wish to risk their reproductive health for a particular job." *Ibid.* at 1202.

57. *See, e.g.,* Julia Kristeva's discussion of the "imaginary construct" of motherhood as exemplified by the Virgin Mary popularized in Christianity. Julie Kristeva, "Stabat Mater," *The Kristeva Reader* (Toril Moi ed. 1986). *Kristeva* thinks feminists need to create a new discourse on motherhood, redefining the image in "postvirginal" terms. *Ibid.,* p. 161. In attempting to define a new image of mother, feminists have confused the "idealized archaic mother [with] the idealization of the *relationship* that binds us to her," resulting in their rejecting motherhood or accepting the traditional view. *Id.* Christianity embeds the feminine within the maternal—the Virgin Mary. Religious tradition holds that Mary/Mother, like Christ was without sin, did not die—she was transported into heaven and represents both "courtly" and "child love." *Ibid.,* pp. 164–65. The Virgin is, at one and the same time, the "*mother* of her son and his *daughter* as well, Mary is also, and besides, his *wife* . . . the threefold metamorphosis of a woman in the tightest parenthood structure." *Ibid.,* p. 169. The Virgin has the "attributes of the desired woman and of the holy mother." *Ibid.,* p. 171 She is the source for the "humanization of the West in general and of love in particular." *Ibid.* She is "modest and humble" and a "devoted, fond mother." *Ibid.* Kristeva's view of the purpose of maternal love as conceived by man is instructive. She notes that he "overcomes the unthinkable of death by postulating maternal love in its place—in the place and stead of death and thought. This love . . . is perhaps a recall . . . of the primal shelter that ensured the survival of the newborn." *Ibid.,* p. 176.

58. The idea of cross-over discourses in regard to single mothers is explored in chapter 5.

59. Edelman [chapter 2, note 9] p. 11.

60. From conversations between Gerda Lerner and the author. By the term "man in our head," reference is made to the masculinist culture and society that defines for us what is right and wrong, good and evil, male and female—a male voice of authority that is internalized and operates as a social control. For a general discussion of a male hegemony over that which is defined socially as "universal truth," *see* Lerner [chapter 2, note 16] pp. 219–29.

61. Of course, a correlative project under the gendered lives analysis will be for men to explore the nature and content of *their* gendered lives.

62. *See* Cain [chapter 3, note 37]; Mary Joe Frug, "A Postmodern Legal Manifesto (An Unfinished Draft)," 105 *Harvard Law Review* 1045 (1992).

63. The battered woman's syndrome can be criticized for this tendency. *See* Maguigan [chapter 3, note 18]; Mahoney [chapter 3, note 33].

64. Iris Marion Young, *Justice and the Politics of Difference* (Princeton, NJ: Princeton Univ. Press, 1990): p. 171. Young argues that in this way women of different races, classes, and sexual preferences can seize the power of naming their differences as women without being frozen into essentialist categories. Differences can be understood and accommodated in the context of specificity, variation, and heterogeneity. She defines this as "relational understanding" of difference. The relevance of differences depends on context and shifts in the contexts.

65. A gendered experience approach is also consistent with the philosophy underlying feminist methodology since it focuses on the concrete and not the abstractions of women's lives. In feminist theory, methodology is step-by-step a part of theory. For the most part, feminist methodology is about making theory more concrete, about bringing in stories and other ways of identifying and describing women's experiences as they exist and as they have been left out of the legal system. Angela Harris refers to shifting methodology as a way to get around dangerous gender essentialism. *See* Harris [chapter 3, note 34]. Deborah Rhode turns to it as a way to assure that critical theory does not become so abstract so as to remove itself from women's experiences. *See* Rhode [chapter 3, note 36]. Methodology, not always explicitly as such, includes literature (Adrienne Rich is as quoted as any legal scholar) and psychology (note the role of Carol Gilligan's, *In a Different Voice: Psychological Theory and Women's Development* [Cambridge, MA: Harvard Univ Press, 1982]) as a way of bringing in women's experiences seemingly excluded from traditional legal rhetoric.

Katharine Bartlett argues that feminist method is feminist theory. Her recommended method of "positionality" suggests that truth shifts according to position, but that feminists must try to posit this contingent truth—yet be willing to change. Bartlett says that asking the "woman question" is what starts feminist method; she then discusses the importance of "practical reasoning" and consciousness raising. She criticizes both Robin West and Catharine MacKinnon for what she calls "standpoint epistemology" because it cannot adequately describe or follow feminist knowing. These epistemologies rely too heavily on essentialism to take account of real knowledge. She also criticizes postmodern deconstruction because it cannot move past its own sense of contingency to recommend reform. Bartlett says her argument for "positionality" recognizes the contingency of a "truth" but allows the feminist reformer to embrace a truth long enough to advance reform and explore experience. Katharine T. Bartlett, "Feminist Legal Methods," 103 *Harvard Law Review* 829 (1990).

PART 2

The Neutered Mother

THIS SECTION DEVELOPS the notion that motherhood has been divested of many of its traditional, positive aspects in legal discourse. This process has been undertaken within the context of a commitment to equality, in which sameness of treatment is symbolically essential. The institution of "Mother" has been transformed in law, collapsed and merged with "Father" in the generic concept of "Parent." In this process, any distinctive or unique aspects of mothering are erased and the symbolically significant rhetoric is that of gender neutrality (hence, the "neutering" of Mother).

Mother has been neutered in several senses. She is taken out of contexts. In policy discussions, just as she is de-gendered, Mother is also de-raced and de-classed. Mother is treated as though she has no ethnic or cultural community that helps to define her. Equality makes Mother an empty legal category, robbing real-life mothers of the protection of their specificity. This neutering happens in the context of a racist and misogynist culture that paradoxically fills the neutered Mother with idealized and demonized contents.

Legal definitions of equality have taken a toll on Mother. She is conceptually separated from her child as a matter of policy and law. She is forced into competition with state and father over her child. As chapter 4 argues, fathers have gained significant rights that allow them to exert continuing control over single-mother families, whether these have been created by divorce or by decisions to mother without marrying. But the neutered Mother has been deprived of her power—law and rhetoric devalues and undermines the traditional tasks that form part of "her" socially constructed identity. The treatment of mothering in modern American society casts caretaking as inconsequential and unworthy of subsidy (in welfare policy) or ultimate reward (in the context of custody rules at divorce).

As an explicitly positive symbol, with unique connotations and significance in regard to her relationship with her child, Mother has been moved out of the text and into the margins of family law discourse. Neutered into Parent, Mother is at the same time transformed or reconstructed into "Wife"—a role considered to be more appropriate as it connotes an equal or full partner in the family and in extrafamily contexts.

One result of this transformation is that a primary focus now is on women as economic actors, a role that requires a degree of independence that is difficult, if not impossible, to reconcile with the demands of "traditional" motherhood. Changes in family law are justified by the need to refashion Mother—manipulating her so as to permit the construction of an appropriate egalitarian parental role that will position women for participation in the market and public spheres.

One consequence of this emphasis has been the alteration of women's relationship to the market. Women and wives as equal partners are expected to work, to be self-sufficient and to assume equal financial responsibility for their children. This is now true at divorce. However, the implications of neutering Mother are not confined to "private," middle-class families when they encounter the divorce system. Liberal legal arguments for gender neutrality and family structuring to facilitate market participation have had an impact on "public" families (i.e., those receiving state assistance) as well.

As developed in chapter 5, an important component of the neutering process has been the designation of untraditional forms of motherhood as "pathological" or deviant. This stigmatizing process makes mothering outside of the context of a two-parent, traditional family susceptible to extensive legal regulation and supervision. Mother and child alone are incomplete and insufficient—the cause and perpetuators of social decay and decline.

A second consequence of the neutering of Mother and her transformation into Wife is that Mother is disembodied—representations of women's bodies are un-Mothered. The body of Mother is neutered by advertisements and cultural representations in which women are portrayed without hips or breasts (no physical manifestations of mothering). The Motherly body is rejected by current standards of beauty and reconstructed. The neutered Mother becomes the sexualized Woman. The sexual, ultrathin, very young female body, unmarked by gestation and nursing, is the idealized image of women. And even if this woman is portrayed as Mother, her relationship with her child is sexualized. Mother's Day advertisements in newspapers drape a seductive young mother's body in lacy peignoirs and position her with an adoring son, giving vision to Oedipus's challenge.

The neutering of Mother is a tragedy. It has implications far beyond the law and legal institutions. It presents a vision of society in which children and the values of nurturing and care are suspect, a vision that abandons us all to a restricted notion of intimacy and connection.

4

The Neutered Mother

THE "NEUTERED MOTHER"—words in contraposition to each other, incompatible when placed together, a gendered noun de-gendered by its modifier, an opposition of meaning that mirrors the conflicts in culture and in law over the significance and potency of the symbol of Mother.[1] "Neutered Mother" is a term that represents the conflict and contradiction generated in the context of many women's lives by negative images of motherhood and mothering.[2]

In this chapter I assess the evolution of the practical as well as the symbolic content of Mother in modern law reform. I ultimately condemn the legal rules and rhetoric that are consistent with the gender-neutral fetish of liberal legalism. The evolution of de-gendered legal rules regulating families is more than a mere change in language reflecting the aspiration that all parents, male as well as female, will nurture and care for their children. Gender neutrality has substantive implications and signals a change in orientation in which caretaking is devalued and biological and economic connection are deemed of paramount importance.

There are no longer formally different expectations for, or responses to, mothers and fathers in much of family law.[3] However, it is my contention that in practice the egalitarian rhetoric of modern reforms results in unrealistic, punitive responses that are harmful to mothers and children. The harm is particularly evident in two groups of mothers who are central to my consideration of the neutering or de-gendering of motherhood—those mothers who encounter custody challenges in the context of divorce and those mothers who have not married the fathers of their children.

To a great extent, the law and legal language incorporate the feminist notion that Mother is an institution that must be reformed—that is, contained and neutralized.[4] In middle-class family law (the law of marriage and divorce), this has been accomplished by transfiguring the symbolically positive cultural and social components of parenting typically associated with the institution of motherhood into the de-gendered components of the neutered institution of "parenthood." Custody policy at divorce reflects the determination that parents are assumed equally entitled to custody regardless of the "mothering" they did (or did not do) during the marriage.[5]

The implementation of the contemporary fetish with gender neutrality and equality has been retarded in the context of never-married mothers. In such situations, there is no male legally attached to the mother (and, hence, to the child) upon whom to confer equal rights and responsibility; thus the first task is to make that connection. The equality rhetoric is more muted as a result, although it has been implicit and is becoming more central in the increasingly heightened significance given to unwed fathers in a variety of contexts.

Furthermore, as more fully developed in chapter 5, poor mothers who deviate from the marriage norm bring forth proposals from policy makers who seem even more vigorous and intent on obliterating the positive cultural connotations of motherhood, at least for single women.[6] The discourses of politicians as well as social workers and others in the "disciplines" reflect their belief that this group of mothers is clearly dangerous and their behavior pathological. On a concrete level, plans for Norplant incentives and punitive measures denying additional benefits for additional babies conceived and delivered while on welfare can be said to be literally state plans designed to neuter these mothers.

I. Mother As Symbol

"Mother" is a universally possessed symbol (although its meaning may vary across and within cultures). We all have a mother—some of us are mothers. These are experiences that help to define for us on an individual level the content of the symbolic Mother. As a lived experience, Mother is shared virtually universally in our culture and, is therefore, more intimately and intensely personalized than many other symbols. There are additional social and cultural dimensions to the construction of Mother that help to shape and, therefore, are at least as significant as personal experiences. In many instances these generalized constructs are the most symbolically salient because they form the contours against which experiences and events are measured and valued.

In its various configurations, Mother is a pivotal factor in defining our understanding of our own familial, sexual, and social circumstances. In this way, Mother is also significant in our construction of universal meanings, defining the general qualities of life for us. Mother is an ambiguous symbol— one about which there is social and cultural contest. For that reason, focusing on Mother may be considered too dangerous: Mother is neither fixed nor containable.

Nevertheless, the unique potential of Mother as a symbol with which to assess the social and cultural meanings of intimacy and the regulation of families by law is too powerful to forego due to unfocused fears of dangerousness. Any concept potent enough to be useful in attempting social and cultural change is bound to have the capacity to be dangerous—change is an inherently dangerous undertaking. The symbolic potential of Mother is greatly enhanced on both individual and societal levels by the very ambiguity that lends to it this aura of danger.

Concern with the danger of Mother arises in and references ideological interpretations of the practice of mothering. In contemporary society, Mother has accumulated negative as well as positive symbolic content. Two major twentieth-century contributors to the construction and perpetuation of negative images of motherhood have been neo-Freudians (very loosely defined) and contemporary liberal feminists. The discourses of these two groups, often encapsulated within the same text, have been significant due to the coherency and comprehension of their articulations of the negative aspects of Mother.[7]

These rhetorical constructs, for different purposes and in different contexts, have typically cast Mother as a problem-laden social and cultural institution. Mother embodies dependency at the same time she is trapped by the dependency of others. In both discourses, the symbol of Mother is negatively implicated by the specter of her dependence on husband and child. At the same time, in both discourses, she is marred by her burdens of obligation and intimacy in an era where personal liberation and individual autonomy are viewed as both mature and essential.

The focuses of the two Mother-negative discourses are different. Neo-Freudian rhetoric seems more concerned with the ability of the child to extricate himself (and I do mean himself) from the clutches of Mother so as to attain independence and accede to the law of the Father.[8] Much of feminist discourse, by contrast, is concerned with the ability of women (potential mothers) to avoid the psychological and material burdens of the symbolic Mother that society has placed on them through the generations.[9] I am concerned with the feminist discourse in this chapter, specifically the framing of Mother issues in liberal legal feminism.[10]

The concerns with the burdens of motherhood appeared most vividly in the feminist literature of the 1970s.[11] However, the concern is of earlier origins. Simone de Beauvoir extolled the view that too much self-sacrifice made for inferior mothering and an impoverished life for a woman:

> The woman who works . . . is the one who undergoes pregnancy most easily . . . ; the woman who enjoys the richest individual life will have the most to give her children and will demand the least from them; she who acquires in effort and struggle a sense of true human values will be best able to bring them up properly.[12]

To Beauvoir, a "rich individual life" for women did not consist entirely, even primarily, of mothering. Demanding the least from one's child was the ideal. Children, at best, were a burden.

De Beauvoir's biographer reports that, in response to a question about whether she felt deprived that she didn't have children, the "mother of modern feminism" replied, "I wrote in my memoirs about how children never held any attraction for me. Babies filled me with horror. The sight of a mother with child sucking the life from her breast, or women changing soiled diapers—it all filled me with disgust. I had no desire to be drained, to be a slave to such a creature."[13]

More recent feminist writing does not totally disavow the role of the Mother, but rather simultaneously praises and rejects her. Mother is seen as a desirable status at the same time that it is viewed as a threat to one's personal autonomy. Nancy Rubin provides an illustration of this ambivalence:

> Mother isn't forever. It's a limited altruistic and narcissistic endeavor, albeit one of the most important experiences a woman can have. . . . Somehow we have to maintain a balance between our feelings of empathy, devotion, love, and identification with our children without losing the whole of ourselves to it.[14]

The idea of mother as a specifically gendered concept is cast by some feminists as particularly threatening to women's sense of individuality. Barbara Rothman exemplifies this reaction with the statement, "I would like us to get rid of our 'mommy' and 'daddy' language. We are individuals, in individual relationships with our children, and not the embodiment of gender-based parental roles."[15]

Some feminists feel that Mother has gotten too much contemporary attention. In an article entitled "Motherhood—Reclaiming the Demon Texts," Ann Snitow schematically presents the evolution of liberal feminist thinking about motherhood.[16] The "demon texts" Snitow refers to are those early second-wave books that first called into question the idea of reproductive determinism. She defends them and notes they were "demonized, apologized for, endlessly quoted out of context, to prove that the feminism of the early seventies was strangely blind [about motherhood]."[17] Snitow labels the disillusionment with equality and concern with the material disadvantages women face as mothers "backlash" and dismisses authors who argue that Mother has been harmed by feminism. Quite ironically, Snitow demonizes a whole new set of texts in this article, those texts that address the material and social implications of the status of motherhood.[18]

Snitow's text seems defensive, even anti-Mother, although she explicitly states, "It's no part of my argument to say women shouldn't want children. This would be to trivialize the complexity of wishes, to call mothering a sort of false consciousness—a belittling suggestion."[19] Yet one wonders if this is not what she believes when she ends her article with the rather cryptic comments about the "idée fixe" for "our wave" of feminism, which she identifies as access to abortion: "There will be much resistance to letting the right to abortion expand to its larger potential meaning. We seem—this time around—to really want abortion. And this right carries within it the seed of new identities for women."[20]

In their increasingly important role of effecting changes in law and legal institutions, liberal legal feminists have picked up on some of the themes in general feminist literature. Legal feminist arguments have tended to present women's issues and represent women's concerns as partly related to or caused by the distortion of the traditional institution of motherhood. The result is that much of the reformist rhetoric directed at family law constantly reaffirms the notion that the disabilities and disadvantages of Mother must be overcome—the family refashioned so that the individual woman is left unencumbered.

The societal ideal for accomplishing the task of freeing Mother is "shared parenting." This concept has been fashioned into complementary legal principles, such as joint custody, with their own set of symbolic components where men as fathers are envisioned as (and empowered in) assuming their "appropriate" parental role within the egalitarian family.[21]

II. The Construction of Mother in Law

There are two types of mothering practices in which traditional rules have been transformed by symbolic measures designed to "free" Mother. The first context involves the rules governing custody at divorce. Mothers who are cast as the central images of this type of reform activity in mainstream family law are typically the (sometime) housewife mothers who are now encouraged (or expected) to be also interested in pursuing a career (or compelled to take a job). These mothers have been caught in the rhetoric of equality that casts their situations in aspirational terms. They have become "partners" in an egalitarian marriage, no more or no less capable of raising children (or mothering) or of earning a family wage than their husbands. Their gender-neutral statuses as "spouses" and "parents" are consistent with the stated expectations of a true partnership marriage.

The second context is that of women who attained their status as mother outside of the institution of marriage. Never-married motherhood has generated many proposals for reforms by conservative politicians and pundits in recent years. Motherhood outside of marriage has historically been susceptible to punitive regulation and the object of policies designed to curtail the practice. While the theme of punishment has not been abandoned, single motherhood has also been transformed—increasingly caught within the symbolically potent egalitarian imagery. As a result, the never-married mother has also lost ground to the biological father.

The symbolically driven changes in laws concerning motherhood have been generated by different political actors. In earlier policy discussions, housewives experiencing divorce and never-married mothers received very different legal treatment as well as social support in regard to their mothering. It is significant, however, that both groups of mothers, designated (and demonized) as "single mothers," together now share the spotlight of increased societal concern with the "breakdown of the family"—a societal concern that often results in state intervention and supervision of these mothers' behavior in attempts to control Mother. As is developed more fully in chapter 5, the threat to society is often articulated as the fact that these mothers are single. This threat, defined by marital status, reveals the extent to which law and policy reinforce the heterosexual family as the exclusive core social institution.

Single mothering is threatening and dangerous because it is out in the open, not hidden in the confines of the private, nuclear family. This makes it (and single others) vulnerable politically. It is in the context of considering these designated deviant mothers that public and political discourses explicitly reveal core notions about the way society views the institution of Mother in general. We turn now to a consideration of the transformations in law.

A. The Law of the Mother

It is important to position the discussion of the neutering or de-gendering of Mother within the confines of traditional family law discourse. Family law is that area of law whereby the state regulates certain intimate relationships by defining a legal family relationship and assigning formal legal consequences and obligations within the context of that definition. Family law has important symbolic significance and both reflects and contributes to our cultural understandings of the traditional family roles of wife-mother, husband-father, and child.

1. Early Law—Motherhood at Divorce

Well-defined references to Mother are found in the early nineteenth-century Anglo-American rules regulating custody decisions at divorce. During marriage Mother was clearly designated the legally "inferior" parent, and it was a battle getting her established in law as a potential contender for custody of her children at divorce. Under English common law, fathers had an absolute right to ownership and control over their children—as if they held title—and a corresponding duty to support them. Mothers, according to Blackstone, were entitled to "no power, but only reverence and respect."[22]

Early American custody law operated in a relatively simple and straightforward manner. Judicial decision making was limited to determining if a particular set of circumstances constituted an exceptional case requiring deviation from the stated standard of father custody and control. It was not until the latter part of the nineteenth century that the notion of paternal possession was successfully challenged.

Invoking the powerful cultural Mother imagery of the day, domestically oriented feminists stressed the importance of the mother's special nurturing and caregiving roles to the welfare of her children.[23] This feminist agitation, coupled with the efforts of turn-of-the-century, welfare-state do-gooders, was instrumental in shifting the focus of custody law toward concern for the child's right to the best custodial situation and away from the property interest of the father.[24]

The move away from automatic paternal right came with the adoption of the "best interest of the child" standard as the governing substantive principle in custody adjudications. Instead of merely implementing a father's right to custody, the courts were directed to select the best custodial placement for the child.[25] The indeterminacy of this test created problems for the legal system, however, as it required judges to assess a multitude of factors in making substantive comparisons and judgments on a case-by-case basis.

Many jurisdictions developed subsidiary rules to give coherence (from their perspective) and content to the best-interest standard. One such rule was the presumption in favor of maternal custody based on the belief that, in most instances, it would be in a child's best interest to continue to be nurtured by its mother. This rule, which became known as the "tender years" doctrine, incorporated the positive symbolic aspects of Mother, favoring and fostering mother custody, in implementing the best-interest rule.[26]

The movement away from the father's absolute right incorporated contemporary notions of domestic ideology that recognized a mother's socially productive labor in raising future citizens. Although these early pro-mother custody rules were predicated on positive perceptions about Mother, they were not problem free when viewed from a modern feminist perspective.[27] The revised custody rules were premised on the middle-class gendered assumptions and assertions of the late nineteenth and early twentieth centuries. Prevalent domestic norms reinforced women's exclusion from the public or market aspects of life under the guise of protecting or sheltering women so they could fulfill their true roles as bearers and nurturers of the species.

In addition, even the gains in the family arena for women were ambiguous. Both social and legal systems conditioned women's enjoyment of their newly found custodial rights on their submission to patriarchal norms such as fidelity, temperance, and so on. For that reason, these apparent gains may be better understood as being consistent with the dominant paternalistic rhetoric of the time.[28] While the wave of domestic feminist ideology that raised Mother as a powerful symbol initially challenged patriarchy, its more radical implications were absorbed and deflected, illustrating the elastic nature of patriarchal ideology.[29] Individual men had to relinquish some control over the private or domestic sphere, in that they did not retain an absolute right to their children's custody, but the basic structures as well as the ideological underpinnings of the system remained patriarchial.[30]

Women's role within the private sphere did not alter, and codes of wifely conduct could be enforced through a custody doctrine that denied deviant mothers custody of their children. Mothers received custody of young children unless they were "unfit" to provide care for them. Sexual indiscretions in particular provided grounds upon which to base a finding of unfitness and to deny mothers custody under the tender-years doctrine. Common bases upon which to establish unfitness included promiscuity, adultery, cohabitation, and sexual orientation.

In spite of these limitations, however, this early law of Mother had unrealized radical potential to empower mothers within the context of divorce. Women no longer had to fear losing their children as a result of divorce. Once this significant advance was complemented by the economic gains women made during the last half of the twentieth century, it became apparent to many women that they could practice motherhood independently of men. The potential for independent motherhood was strengthened by increased (if modest) employment opportunities, child support, and public assistance. The phenomenal increase in independent single mothers created by divorce therefore set the stage for demands that the advantages to mothers of the tender-years preference in custody decision making be eliminated.

Mother had to be explicitly controlled and reconfined. Hence, the direction of modern reforms in family law that focus on ensuring that fathers maintain their positions as patriarchs. Altered custody rules, revolving around notions of equal rights for fathers and ideals of shared parenting—most vividly exemplified by joint custody—have been imposed. Other reforms significantly restrict custodial mothers' abilities to care for themselves and their children in order to ensure noncustodial fathers have liberal visitation rights. Statutes prohibit custodial parents from leaving the state with the children unless they are able to convince a judge that they have good reasons and that the move will not interfere with the noncustodian's relationship with the child.[31] Mothers who resist visitation (or cannot compel their children to visit) risk punishment, even punitive modifications of custody to the father, by courts intent on securing the father-child bond.[32]

2. Early Law—Never-Married Mothers

The rules governing nonmarital children have also been significantly transformed. During the past several decades, the rights of unmarried fathers in regard to their children have evolved and greatly expanded. Historically, our laws regarding nonmarital children derived from English common law. Transplanted into the colonies, it eventually developed some contrasts between the legal articulation of obligations and rights of unmarried Mothers when compared with Fathers. Traces of these differences remain today and underscore the continued vitality and centrality of the marriage tie in defining the relationship between father and child.

In early common law, however, the treatment of unwed parents was similar, and their child was severely disadvantaged socially and economically. The child was labeled "filius nullius" or the son (sic) of no one.[33] Another, less elegant, term used to refer to such a child was "bastard." Unlike the situation in Europe, even a subsequent marriage between her or his parents was not sufficient to change the status of the child.[34] Furthermore, and equally harsh, the children of annulled or void marriages were also declared bastards with the pronouncement of the invalidity of the parental tie.

Nonmarital children were not entitled to inherit from their fathers (or, initially, from their mothers). Furthermore, while the ecclesiastical courts enforced some duties of support on some fathers, the common law contained no obligation for maintenance of bastards until the enactment of the Elizabethan Poor Laws in the sixteenth century.[35] These laws, which imposed a duty of maintenance on mothers as well as fathers, were explicitly designed to relieve the parish of economic responsibility for children.[36] As to parental rights, in early English law neither mother nor father had a "right" to custody of the children born to an unsanctified union, although mothers typically had *de facto* custody.[37]

The English law, with its legally imposed disadvantages to children, was adopted in the colonies, but after the Revolution it was increasingly questioned.[38] For example, in common law a child considered *filius nullius* did not have a domicile, since she or he was not tied to the father and, under English law, was not considered part of the mother's family either. The child was assigned the town of birth as her or his place of settlement, a location that might have been different from the mother's. That town, since it was responsible for the child's support, could also legally assume custody of the child.[39] In a legal innovation, laws passed in the colonies required fathers to support their illegitimate children, and there is some evidence that the inchoate right to custody was thus also transferred to the father.[40]

Unwed mothers quickly made inroads on any initial recognition of paternal rights, however, and clearly overtook any earlier concessions concerning custody to fathers by the end of the colonial period. In most states, by the end of the nineteenth century nonmarital children were considered legally to be members of their mothers' families and had inheritance rights within those families as though they were legitimate.[41]

This American development was significant. A "new" legally recognized family unit thus came into being: the unwed mother and her child formed a unit not officially recognized at common law. Unwed mother and child were bound together legally with inheritance implications and the imposition of reciprocal rights and duties enforceable in law, including the right of the mother to custody of the child.[42] Fathers for all practical purposes were not legally or formally a component of the newly recognized unwed family.[43]

Michael Grossberg locates the development of the unwed mother-child family at a formative stage in American law, characterizing the changes as resting on new notions concerning the welfare of the child and the rights of its mother. Grossberg identifies these mothers and children as the main family beneficiaries of the "rights consciousness" embedded in post-Revolutionary legal ideology.[44] The positive rights that were being developed in the nonmarital situation derived from the biological connection of Mother and child—a perceived "natural" connection that came to be mirrored in legal doctrine. The law recognized no such "natural" tie governing rights of unwed fathers to their biological children. Grossberg locates the developing maternal right within the cult of domesticity that "pervaded nineteenth-century American culture." He notes that this ideological development generated immense pressure on legal authorities to place children with their mothers. In this regard, the distinction between married and unmarried mothers coalesced—the unmarried mother's claims were strengthened along with those of her more traditional sisters.[45]

In contrast to the establishment of a biologically based legal connection directly between mother and child, fathers' custodial rights increasingly came to be viewed as derivative. A father's rights to his biological children arose from and were based upon the marital tie with the child's mother.[46] The significant affectional and familial legal tie for men was thus construed as marriage. Under this scheme, unwed fathers were out of luck. They might have legally imposed support obligations for their biological children, but these financial obligations were viewed as independent of the relational rights of parenthood. The rights to custody and control continued to be based on a father's marital relationship to the child's mother.

This disjunction between paternal economic responsibility and unwed fathers' affectional or relational rights reflected the primarily punitive orientation of the legal system toward nonmarital reproduction. The law singled out that parent socially assigned as responsible for nonmarital births. The unwed mother was positioned as the "victim" of male sexual excess rather than as an equal participant in inappropriate sexual conduct and socially deviant reproduction.[47]

This tendency toward punitive legal regulation of nonmarital reproduction continues to shape policy in contemporary legal reasoning and rationales when addressing the social and legal "problems" of nonmarital births. Today, however, the position of the father has changed. In legal rhetoric and policy proposals he is viewed as the "solution" for child poverty. The law's objective is to secure his ties with the mother-child unit. The punitive focus, therefore, is no longer primarily on fathers. Rather, the weight of societal wrath has shifted and seems more directed at unwed mothers, rhetorically cast as the progenitors of a new and great social harm.[48]

B. Modern Trends

1. Motherhood Descending—Transformations at Divorce

The maternal preference embodied in the tender years doctrine applicable at divorce stood relatively unchallenged for decades. However, as the incidence of divorce increased in the early 1970s, so did conflicts over the law governing child-custody determinations. The conflicts were generated in part by the formation of gendered interest groups with family law as their focus. For example, stringent state and federal provisions for the collection of past-due child support fostered the formation of fathers'-rights groups, which expressed resentment that men were not equal parents in regard to child custody. To a great extent, these groups represented a backlash to some of the successes of the feminist movement, such as the impetus to take child support awards seriously.[49]

Fathers' groups advocated reforms in the family law area that had as their subtext the perceived inequality in the family law process.[50] In efforts to exonerate "deadbeat dads," for example, the widespread nonpayment of child support was justified by images of beleaguered fathers victimized by a court system that consistently awarded mothers custody and treated fathers as nothing more than "walking wallets."[51]

Predating the fathers' groups assertion of their interest in achieving equality within the family, mainstream liberal feminists were attacking gender-specific legal tests in the public sphere as inherently discriminatory. They also articulated the ideal of an egalitarian, genderless family where child care and household responsibilities were shared equally by husband and wife.[52]

The fathers'-rights movement picked up the banner of gender neutrality and turned it to their rhetorical advantage in the custody area. They effectively criticized child-custody rules and decision making for manifesting what they perceived to be a "pro-mother" bias.[53] Their attacks seemed all the more forceful because of the equality reforms that were being implemented in response to the economic consequences of divorce. Male backlash to family law economic reforms, and the liberal feminist gender-neutral rhetoric it appropriated, helped to set the stage for challenges to custody rules and processes of decision making that relied on the positive aspects of Mother.[54]

Most state statutes now specifically provide that both parents are "equal," thus forbidding consideration of gender in custody cases.

Both the liberal feminists and the fathers'-rights groups undermined the earlier acceptance of Mother as being something distinct from, separate, and, perhaps, superior to the generic term "parent." In place of the maternal presumption, custody arrangements that formally equated parents, such as joint custody, were proposed and defended on the grounds of furthering equality between the sexes. "Shared parenting" was the objective, and custody and visitation rules were manipulated to facilitate this ideal. Some commentators even went so far as to assert that gender neutrality required that considerations of "typically Motherly" characteristics be eliminated from judicial consideration.[55] Others extended the equality goal to its most extreme limits in the suggestions that custody disputes be resolved by a toss of the dice.[56]

In a world in which custody is characterized as "competition" and in which symbolism is more significant than substance, nurturing has become suspect as gendered behavior giving Mother an advantage over fathers. Fathers' rights and role, characterized as unfairly suppressed, had to be paramount. One men's-rights group, The Association Hommes Separés ou Divorcés de Montréal phrased the struggle thus: "Children need to break out of the 'very primitive, simplest' relationship they have had with their mother since their birth and move into a relationship in which they must fight to earn the esteem of their father, who is recognized as more socially competent."[57]

What has resulted is a legal system that empowers fathers. Anne Marie Delorey places the movement toward joint custody in a critical light: "Joint legal custody gives rights and responsibilities to mothers, but it gives rights without responsibilities to fathers. Mere legal control of children is simply an assignment of power, and when this type of power is given to fathers, judges are merely reinforcing patriarchal power."[58]

2. Motherhood Descending—Nonmarital Motherhood

The unique (or at least "privileged") status of the never-married mother in regard to custody that evolved during the nineteenth century has come under attack in an interesting and effective way. In the early enthusiasm of liberal reform, social workers and "progressives" argued for eliminating the distinctions between "illegitimate" and "legitimate" children. These arguments were couched in terms of the child's "rights" or need for "protection" and the unfairness of discrimination based on the marital status of one's parents.[59]

The legal system has responded to these arguments as well. The negative economic consequences of nonmarital status for children have been lessened or removed in many states.[60] Although allowing some difference in treatment between marital and nonmarital children, the Supreme Court has given nonmarital children some protection in regard to governmental benefits and would-be discriminatory state rules governing inheritance. In doing so, the Supreme Court has given some legal teeth to the principle that the state may not punish children by "attempt[ing] to influence the actions of men and women by imposing sanctions on the children born of their illegitimate relationships."[61]

The statutory schemes that disadvantage and discriminate against nonmarital children are obviously more vulnerable to attack than those that draw distinctions between classes of parents. Children are not responsible for their parents' behavior. As one leading family law case book indicates, "the trend is clearly to reduce the disparity between marital and non-marital children, and it will probably continue, particularly as paternity becomes easier to establish."[62]

But the advances made in nonmarital children's interests have greatly expanded the legal rights of unwed fathers as well. Reversing the nineteenth-century accommodation of the mother-child nonmarital family are the transformations in law that occurred during the latter part of the twentieth century. We have seen the articulation and rapid expansion of a program of legal rights for unwed fathers.

In contrast to the divorce context where the state judges and legislators have played such a prominent role in defining the rights to children, the Supreme Court of the United States was initially the major author of the rights of unwed fathers. The initial movement away from nineteenth-century law, which granted unwed fathers few rights, came in *Stanley v. Illinois*,[63] in which a father lost custody of his children to the state because he was deemed, by virtue of his lack of a marital tie to the children's mother, to have no interest that required protection. In Illinois, unwed fathers were not within the statutory definition of "parent" and were considered to have no more rights than a stranger when the state considered what was in a child's best interest.[64] In *Stanley,* the Court set aside the state's presumption that unwed fathers were unfit to have custody and held that an unwed father who had always resided with his children was entitled to a hearing before the children were taken away from him after their mother's death. Couching its decision in constitutional language, the Court concluded that the Illinois system infringed on unwed fathers' "liberty" interest in their children and noted that the parental bonds "were often as warm, enduring, and important as those arising within a more formally organized family unit."[65]

In cases that followed, unwed fathers' rights were further defined. Of particular interest is the extent to which these cases followed the lead of *Stanley,* conditioning the developing rights on the presence of long-standing familial relationships between unwed father and child. In fact, the more the unwed family looked and functioned like a traditional family, the more secure the father's claims seemed to be. Unwed fathers did not have equal rights with unwed mothers, but, if they participated in nuclear-family-like behavior, they were gaining parity with married fathers. The requirement of the formal tie was disappearing, to be replaced by the experience of a "natural"[66] family—a family that functioned and operated as an analogue to its formally constituted marital cousin.

Biology in this regard was central to the fathers' claims; it at least opened the door to something more. But, in the evolving articulation of "rights," biology had to be coupled with some familial relationship or demonstrated commitment on the part of unwed fathers. For example, while Justice Stevens wrote in one case that a mere biological relationship cannot *alone* establish legal paternal rights, he noted that "the significance of the biological connection is that it offers the natural [unwed] father an opportunity that no other male possesses to develop a relationship with his offspring."[67] Thus, biology "plus" commitment was sufficient to convince a majority of the Court that paternal rights should be recognized.

There have been further changes that put unwed fathers closer to divorced fathers in regard to visitation, and a lot of debate and arguments urge that these fathers have parallel claims to custody against mothers. Cases have begun to redefine the comparative positions of unwed father and mother. In *Caban v. Mohammed*,[68] a majority of the Court rejected the argument that "a natural mother . . . bears a closer relationship with her child . . . than a father does."[69] However, other Justices have expressed reservations about this aspect of unwed fathers' equality. Justice Stewart and Justice Stevens have both voiced concerns that the parents are not similarly situated when no formal nuclear family exists. Justice Stewart summarized by stating that "the absence of a legal tie with the mother . . . may . . . appropriately place a limit on whatever substantive constitutional claims might otherwise exist by virtue of the father's actual relationship with the children."[70]

Furthermore, just as in the colonial era, paternal economic obligations for the nonmarital child have facilitated the extension of fathers' rights to other aspects of parenthood. In our contemporary era of equality rhetoric, the connections between financial responsibility and eventual equal rights for unwed fathers appears to be both destiny and progress.

While judicial resolutions thus far seem to be tempered by the continued primacy of maternal interest in regard to nonmarital children, the preference for mothers is eroding rapidly. Assumed maternal custody in nonmarital cases is not likely to survive contemporary assaults by those arguing for equal fathers' rights and equating children's best interest with equal legal ties to two biological parents.[71]

The evolution of unwed fathers' rights continues and courts are increasingly receptive to their claims. Some commentators urge increasing their rights. For example, law professor John Hamilton argues for an unwed father's "right to know" of the existence of a pregnancy and a corollary right to resist adoption plans by the mother.

> The decision to surrender a child for adoption without informing the father is undoubtedly one of the most difficult decisions the mother will be forced to make in her life . . . [but] the unilateral decision by one individual to deprive a person of the opportunity to know his child—without any showing of fault on the part of the person so deprived—would not . . . be accepted—or tolerated—in any other context. It is difficult to see why the legal status of an "unmarried male" serves to alter our perceptions. The real question seems not to be whether the right to know should be protected, but rather why it has taken us so long to ensure that it is.[72]

In several recent and difficult adoption cases—cases where children have been living in adoptive homes after being legally relinquished by biological mothers—the fact that fathers were not notified has been successfully used to set aside the adoption.[73] These cases, and arguments of many fathers'-rights advocates who agree with them, raise paternal biological connection to the same level as that associated with motherhood. Some popular sentiment has condemned these adoption cases as sacrificing the present and future interests of the individual child to the father's demands based on his past (and often fleeting) biological connection.[74] In these cases the child is removed from a traditional and stable home, often the only one it has ever known, and given over to untried "strangers." The perceived harshness of this result for many underscores the social and emotional costs of equality for unwed fathers. These costs seem clearly to be most cruelly borne by the child (at least in the short term).

Proponents of unwed and other fathers' rights argue, however, that there are no relevant differences between mothers and fathers that should have legal significance and dismiss, out of hand, arguments based on statistically demonstrated disparities in investment in and commitment to children. Nor do these advocates find persuasive the vast differences in the nature of women's physical and psychological reproductive functions during pregnancy. The father's biological connection is considered equally primal and, as in the divorce context, biology is destiny when it comes to fathers' rights. The direction seems set as the rights of fathers, wed or unwed, ascend.

III. Conclusion

Although women as Mothers are not well represented in the legal or the political process, it is essential that their perspectives be articulated in the context of law and policy proposals. Yet feminists have been reluctant to make Mother a legislative agenda. There may be attention to the child, or references to the family, but discussions about motherhood are likely to be labeled "pronatalism" and condemned as harboring the subtext that all women must mother.

Liberal legal feminists, the most obvious source for an articulation of the alternative, nonpatriarchal legal discourse about Mother, seem disinterested in the undertaking, perhaps even in the subject. Legal feminists have for the most part centered their attention on nonfamily circumstances and have expressed ambivalence about challenging concepts of family relationships except insofar as they are viewed as hindering or assisting market and economic equality for women.[75]

Even if a reexamination of the legal implications of motherhood from a feminist perspective were undertaken, it is not clear how successful it would be. As developed in chapter 1, the nature of law is conservative. It tends to reformulate, not render obsolete, the core tenets of our society, and any challenges that are too radical or extreme are typically deflected. In the family context, the basic ideological construct is patriarchy—a decidedly anti-Mother perspective reflecting power relationships in which pater consistently trumps mater and the law assists in this endeavor. Furthermore, even in this social context, the liberal legal feminist position on family reforms, exemplified in the paradigm of gender neutrality, makes it likely that equality will remain the ideological medium for the construction of legal images. Equality in the context of patriarchy is a medium that threatens further destruction of Mother.[76] Consistent with the feminist commitment to gender neutrality, parenthood—like personhood—has become the preferred designation because it encompasses both father and Mother without the idealized (and real life) distinctions associated with those terms.

The desire for gender-neutral rules represented an important symbolic component of the legal feminists' battle to demonstrate that there were no relevant differences between the sexes and thus no basis for unequal treatment in law. Certain feminists even anticipated that the rise of these egalitarian expectations in language would have concrete effects on behavior patterns in marriage and divorce situations.[77]

But commitment to gender neutrality meant the legal system had to eliminate any preferences based on a gendered concept of Motherhood. This had to be accomplished for important symbolic reasons, regardless of whether a gendered rule accurately conformed to either intuitive or empirical evidence as to which parent actually was most likely to systematically and continuously invest time and effort into raising children.

The law's reluctance to recognize and accommodate the uniqueness of Mother's role in child rearing conforms to the popular gender-neutral fetish at the expense of considerations for Mother's material and psychological circumstances. Even if the ultimate goal is gender neutrality, the immediate imposition of rules embodying such neutrality within the family law context is disingenuous. The effect is detrimental to those who have constructed their lives around gendered roles.

In this regard, reformed divorce laws impose the risk of significant emotional as well as economic costs for Mother. For example, shifting custody policy creates an increased threat that mothers will potentially lose their children at divorce. To Mother, this risk is too great to contemplate. As a result, mothers may exchange a bargained-down property settlement to avoid a custody contest because they tend, in contrast to fathers, to consider custody a nonnegotiable issue.

Needless to say, the shifts in policy based on such ideology have operated to harm the most disadvantaged and defenseless mothers. The unanticipated by-product of earlier liberal feminist attempts to achieve economic equality has been that the new images of Mother operate to disadvantage many women encountering the law in the context of nonmarket circumstances. Such women are caretakers, nurturers who live lives of dependency—their child's and their own—generated by their roles as Mother.

However, the boundary between gender-neutral legal discourse and the gendered operation of society cannot be maintained. The significance of Mother as an institution and cultural symbol continues to have a shadowy impact on law; it cannot be erased. Mother has disappeared only rhetorically. In social and extralegal institutions that embody both idealized and practical cultural expectations, Mother continues to exist and to function.

It is only the legal discourse, not society, that is now formally Mother purged. The very gendered and Mothered lives most women live continue. Equality rhetoric successfully neutered Mother as a unique legal construct, but has failed to erase Mother on the societal level, nor has it removed the material manifestations of the institution of Motherhood. Furthermore, the disparity between the experience of Mother and her neutered legal presentation is potentially threatening to the legal system's commitment to gender neutrality. If Mother continues to be experienced as "different," "special" accommodations will be demanded (and delivered) even within a formally neutral family law system.

Notes

1. In this chapter I capitalize the "m" in mother in order to signal that I am using the term in its symbolic sense. When real-life mothers are under discussion, the lower case is used.

2. The following definitions are based on Funk and Wagnall, *New Practice Standard Dictionary,* (New York: Funk & Wagnall, 1954)

   mother: a female who has borne offspring
   female: of or pertaining to the sex that brings forth young
   neutered: neither masculine nor feminine in gender
   gender: the quality of being male or female

3. For further information on the specifics of family law reforms, *see* Fineman, *Illusion* [chapter 2, note 8].

4. Liberal legal feminists constantly reaffirm their commitment to gender neutrality in the family context. Gender neutrality is the paradigmatic expression of the values and norms of the dominant legal concept of equality that, even if—perhaps, especially if—rephrased in feminist terms, precludes the consideration of Mother as something different or distinct from father. In legal texts, statutes, and cases, Mother is collapsed into the legal generic category of "Parent" and is suppressed.

5. Martha L. Fineman, "Dominant Discourse, Professional Language, and Legal Change in Child Custody Decisionmaking," 101 *Harvard Law Review* 727 (1988) (discussing this phenomenon and recommending that courts give more weight to the primary caretaker). *See also* David Chambers, "Rethinking the Substantive Rules for Custody Disputes in Divorce," 83 *Michigan Law Review* 477 (1984) (urging the adoption of the primary-caregiver standard).

6. *See New Jersey Stat. Ann.* §§44:10, *et seq.,* especially §10–3.5 (West 1993) (eliminating incremental increase in benefits for birth of additional child); *see also Ga. Stat.* §49-4-115 (1993). *See* Madeline Henley, "The Creation and Perpetuation of the Mother/Body Myth: Judicial and Legislative Enlistment of Norplant," 41 *Buffalo Law Review* 703 (1993) (discussing such reforms in New Jersey, Wisconsin, California, and other states). Virginia plans to require Aid to Families With Dependent Children (AFDC) recipients to work and to eliminate increases in benefits for additional births. Note that "a mother with two children [receives] $285 per month, not including food stamps . . . [and] $61 more for each additional child up to five." *See* Peter Baker, "Virginia Jumps at Chance to Shake up Welfare," *Washington Post,* Feb. 22, 1994, p. B1.

   See also Tenn. Stat. §71-5-133 (1993) (requiring that the department of human services provide to all AFDC recipients written information regarding the availability of Norplant when they apply or are recertified for benefits.) *See also* a bill filed in the 1994 session of the Florida legislature establishing a pilot program that will provide financial incentives for designated female AFDC recipients or males or females whose income is below 125 percent of the federal poverty level. Females who voluntarily use an approved contraceptive method can receive $100 per quarter for ten years or an annual dental voucher of $400 for ten years or postsecondary educational vouchers for $400 per year for ten years. Payments would be made only for as long as the woman continued to use the contraceptive. Males who voluntarily consent to vasectomies will receive a one-time payment of $500. PSC/HB 1451.

7. *See e.g.,* neo-Freudians: Nancy Chodorow, *The Reproduction of Mothering* (Berkeley: Univ. of Calif. Press, 1978); Dorothy Dinnerstein, *The Mermaid and the Minotaur: Sexual Arrangements and Human Malaise* (New York: Harper & Row, 1977); Carole Klein, *Mothers and Sons,* (Boston: Houghton Mifflin, 1984); David M. Levy, *Maternal Overprotection* (New York: Norton, 1966): pp. 121–40. *See, e.g.,* Feminists: Shulamith Firestone, *The Dialectic of Sex: The Case for Feminist Revolution* (New York: Morrow, 1970); Jennifer Allen, "Motherhood: The Annihilation of Women," in *Mothering: Essays in Feminist Theory* (Joyce Trebilcot, ed.) (Totowa, NJ: Rowand Allanheld, 1983); Simone De Beauvoir, "The Mother," in *The Second Sex* (New York: Alfred Knopf, 1974). The distinction between the neo-Freudians and the feminists here is admittedly somewhat arbitrary and refers more to their explication of the problems of motherhood than to other political concepts.

8. *See* neo-Freudians [chapter 4, note 7].

9. *See* feminists [chapter 4, note 7].

10. The psychoanalytic discourse is the subject of some brief development in chapter 6, which specifically focuses on the structure of the family—the context in which Mother is placed.

11. *See, e.g.,* de Beauvoir, Firestone [chapter 4, note 7].

12. de Beauvoir [chapter 4, note 7].

13. Deirdre Bair, *Simone de Beauvoir: A Biography* (New York: Simon & Schuster, 1990): p. 170.

14. *See, e.g.,* Nancy Rubin, *The Mother Mirror* (New York: Putnam, 1984): p. 263.

15. Barbara K. Rothman, *Recreating Motherhood* (New York: WW Norton, 1989): p. 260.

16. Ann Snitow, "Motherhood—Reclaiming the Demon Texts," *Ms. Magazine* (May/June 1991): p. 34.

17. *Id.*

18. This book, of course, is of that genre.

19. Snitow [chapter 4, note 6] p. 37.

20. *Ibid.*

21. *See, e.g.,* Katharine T. Bartlett and Carol Stack, "Joint Custody, Feminism and the Dependency Dilemma," 2 *Berkeley Women's Law Journal* 9 (1986); and Carolyn S. Bratt, "Joint Custody," 67 *Kentucky Law Journal* 271 (1979). For a counterview, *see* Jana B. Singer and William L. Reynolds, "A Dissent on Joint Custody," 47 *Maryland Law Review* 497 (1988); and Diane Post, "Arguments Against Joint Custody," 4 *Berkeley Women's Law Journal* 310 (1990).

22. *See* William Blackstone, *Commentaries,* Vol. I (London: W. Maxwell, 1869): pp. 452–453. In modern practice, this support obligation is fulfilled through child support payments without the father having actual physical custody of the children. James Schouler, *A Treatise on the Law of Domestic Relations* (Boston: Little, Brown, 1870).

23. *See* Michael Grossberg, *Governing the Hearth: Law and Family in Nineteenth-Century America* (Chapel Hill: Univ. of North Carolina, 1985): pp. 61, 233.

24. *See, e.g.,* Michael Grossberg, "Who Gets the Child? Custody, Guardianship, and the Rise of a Judicial Patriarchy in Nineteenth-Century America," 9 *Feminist Studies* 235, 239, 246, 254–55 (1983).

25. For a general description of the development of state supervision of parental duties, *see* Grossberg, *Governing the Hearth* [chapter 4, note 23] pp. 289–91.

26. For a discussion of the origins of the tender-years doctrine, *see* Jamil S. Zainaldin, "The Emergence of a Modern American Family Law: Child Custody, Adoption and the Courts, 1796–1851," 73 *Northwestern Univ. Law Review* 1038, 1072–74 (1979).

27. *Ibid.,* pp. 237–53; *see also* Robert J. Levy, "Custody Investigation in Divorce Cases," *American Bar Foundation Research Journal* 713 (1985).

28. This focus on conduct within the context of custody determinations endures in some jurisdictions today, even though there has been a retreat from fault-based divorce. Some of the states with express statutory grounds require that denial of custody on the grounds of conduct be based on a finding that the child is adversely affected by the behavior in question. For data supporting the proposition that women are treated more harshly than men in such instances, *see* Linda K. Girdner, "Child Custody Determination: Ideological Dimensions of a Social Problem." In *Redefining Social Problems,* Edward Seidman and Julian Rappaport eds. (New York: Plenum, 1986): pp. 165, 175–176.

29. Norma Basch, *In the Eyes of the Law* (Ithaca, NY: Cornell Univ. Press, 1982): pp. 179–80; *see also* Francis E. Olsen, "The Family and the Market: The Study of Ideology and Legal Reform," 96 *Harvard Law Review* 1497, 1530–35 (1983). It is also relevant to note that, at this time, there were few divorces,

particularly among middle- and upper-class couples, those most likely to be concerned with the content of family laws.

30. *See* Grossberg, *Governing the Hearth* [chapter 4, note 23] pp. 289–307 (discussing the role of the judiciary in imposing patriarchal law).

31. *See, e.g.,* WIS. STAT. ANN. §767.245(6) (1993); *Mo. St.* §452.377 (1993); *570 IL. C.S.* 5/609 (1993). *And see* Katherine C. Sheehan, "Post-Divorce Child Custody and Family Relocation," 9 *Harvard Women's Law Journal* 135 (1986) for a critical treatment of this policy.

32. *See, e.g.,* FL. ST. §61.13(3)(a) (1993) (in making custody determinations, the court shall consider which "parent . . . is more likely to allow the child frequent and continuing contact with the nonresidential parent"); *Egle v. Egle,* 715 F.2d 999 (5th Cir. 1983) (custody transferred to father because mother interfered with visitation).

33. Blackstone [chapter 4, note 22] pp. 458–59.

34. *See* Blackstone [chapter 4, note 22] who stated that such a practice discouraged marriage for which he saw "one main inducement . . . not only the desire of having children, but also of procreating lawful heirs." *Id.* at 454–455.

35. *See* R.H. Helmholz, "Support Orders, Church Courts, and the Rule of Filius Nullius: A Reassessment of the Common Law," 63 *Virginia Law Review* 431, 445; *see generally* F. Donald Logan, *Excommunication and the Secular Arena in Medieval England* (Toronto: Pontifical Institute of Medieval Studies, 1968): pp. 48–53.

36. *See* Helmholz, *see* [chapter 4, note 35] pp. 446–447.

37. Blackstone [chapter 4, note 22] p. 459.

38. Michael Grossberg, "Crossing Boundaries: Nineteenth-Century Domestic Relations Law and the Merger of Family and Legal History," *American Bar Foundation Research Journal* 799, 836 (1985).

39. Mary Ann Mason, *From Fathers' Property to Children's Rights: The History of Child Custody in the United States* (New York: Columbia Univ. Press, 1994): p. 25.

40. *Ibid.* pp. 25–26. Mason develops the laws in colonial America, placing them in context. For example, she notes that the records she found dealt exclusively with the children of women who were not free women. Many women came to the United States as indentured servants. The fate of their children was bleak; many were taken from their mothers and apprenticed as soon as feasible. *Ibid.,* p. 28. Interestingly, however, she also notes that the unwed mothers losing custody were treated no differently than poor widows and impoverished two-parent families, whose children were also taken and involuntarily apprenticed to "earn" their own way and relieve the public of their charge. *Ibid.,* p. 29.

In a bit of legalistic formalism (which may also be misleading), Mason also notes that, while children born to enslaved mothers were legally slaves and hence the property of the mother's owner to be disposed of at his will, in practice these mothers had a great deal more "power" than nonslave impoverished mothers in regard to young children:

> The practicalities of slavery gave the mother a certain degree of protection in maintaining physical, if not legal custody of her children until they were around ten years old. In fact, it may be argued that slave women had a somewhat better chance of holding on to their children than did mothers of illegitimate children, or impoverished widows, whose children were often "put out" after weaning to relieve the public of their charge. (*Ibid.*, p. 44)

Mason also notes there is evidence that the "economics of slavery" as well as the "moral pressure on masters to keep mothers and young children together" further strengthened the role of slave mothers in regard to their young children. *Ibid.*, p. 44.

41. Grossberg, *Governing the Hearth* [chapter 4, note 23] p. 219. Changes by many state legislators or by judicial decision were also made so that a subsequent marriage of the parents legitimated the child. In addition, children born of void marriages and marriages that were eventually annulled were no longer classified as illegitimate. Grossberg, *Crossing Boundaries* [chapter 4, note 38] p. 837.

42. Grossberg, *Crossing Boundaries,* at [chapter 4, note 38] p. 838. Grossberg states that "judicial innovations created a new legal household and bound it together. . . ." He quotes a panel of New York judges, which declared in 1807, "In the case of illegitimate children, and especially as to females, the mother appears to us to be the best entitled to the custody of them." *Ibid.*

43. The connection between mothers and children was manifested in the most pronounced and generalized way through changes in custody rules. The unwed mother came to have a right to custody theoretically limited only by the state's power to remove abused or neglected children. Grossberg, *Governing the Hearth* [chapter 4, note 23] pp. 208–209.

44. Grossberg, *Crossing Boundaries,* at [chapter 4, note 38] p. 839. Grossberg recognizes that change is only part of the story, however. He also notes that the autonomy and redefinition of women's roles and responsibilities evident in the new rights mothers won in custody of illegitimate children were tempered by the continuing influences of traditional factors. The desire of local officials to relieve the public purse of responsibility for poor children as well as deep-seated negative reactions to nonmarital sexual relations continue as stigmatizing and limiting burdens borne particularly by poorer women. *Ibid.*, pp. 839–40.

45. Grossberg, *Governing the Hearth* [chapter 4, note 23] p. 209.

46. One still-lingering common-law rule that symbolically underscores the extent of this principle is the presumption in many states, often irrebuttable, that the child of a married woman is also the child of her husband. Such a presumption makes the marriage of the mother (rather than the biological identity of the father) the legally significant event in the classification of the child's status. *See generally The Uniform Parentage Act* §4, which states the bases for a presumption of paternity as including the marriage of the mother and the putative father. This presumption has come under attack in part because genetic testing and other devices for determining paternity have been discovered and refined, allowing for more certainty in the validity of challenges. In addition, one should not underestimate the impact of the "horror story" of biological fatherhood denied and children's rights ignored that has emerged in the press and legal journals after the Supreme Court's decision in *Michael H. v. Gerald D; 491* U.S.110 (1989).

47. *See* Grossberg, *Governing the Hearth* [chapter 4, note 23] p. 227, where Grossberg reports that the new "orthodoxy" in refusing to hold unwed parents equally liable for support (the burden falling on fathers) was accompanied by the "conviction that men should be penalized as sexual predators and held accountable because of their assumed superior economic status."

48. *See* Chapter 5 for a detailed discussion of this rhetoric and the ideology it reflects.

49. *See* Nancy D. Polikoff, "Custody and Visitation: Their Relationship to Establishing and Enforcing Support" (1989) (unpublished manuscript, on file with author).

50. Joint custody is the most explicit suggested reform and is often cast as an ideal solution. *See, e.g.,* Holly L. Robinson, "Joint Custody: An Idea Whose Time has Come," 21 *Journal of Family Law* 641 (1983). Robinson quotes the court's definition of joint legal custody from *Beck v. Beck,* 432 A. 2d 63, 65–66 (1981: "[Joint] legal custody [means] the legal authority and responsibility for making 'major' decisions regarding the child's welfare—is shared at all times by both parents." *Ibid.,* p. 641. Robinson argues that joint custody is preferable because some of the harms suffered by children post divorce are linked "directly to the detrimental effects of parental conflict and the typical sole custody arrangement." *Ibid.,* p. 645. Robinson argues that studies indicate that joint custody does not lead to greater hostility than sole custody and may reduce the level of parental conflict. *Ibid.,* p. 652. She acknowledges that some parents will not be able to put their personal antagonism aside but urges this is not a reason to abandon joint custody, since they would be just as hostile in the sole-custody situation. She thinks behavior that "can be shown to result in feelings of insecurity and rejection, unwarranted self-blame, reduced cognitive performance, and sexual role identification problems in their children" should be considered mental

abuse or neglect. *Ibid.,* pp. 653–54 The courts should require parents to "seek constructive methods of dealing with continuing conflict between them." *Ibid.,* p. 655. The possibilities this raises for state intervention in private lives are frightening.

51. *See, e.g.,* Michael Raschick, "Wisconsin Non-Custodial Parents' Groups" (May 16, 1985) (unpublished manuscript, on file with author). For a discussion of the various ideological strains within the men's movement, *see* Michael Schiffman, "The Men's Movement: An Exploratory Empirical Investigation" (paper prepared for presentation at the Annual Meeting of the American Sociological Association, Washington, DC August 26–30, 1985) (draft on file with author), pp. 3, 4.

52. Janice Drakich points out that these fathers' groups have been supported by popular portrayals in the media, the movies, and even the comic strips. Fathers are portrayed as nurturing, legitimate caregivers and socializers. Janice Drakich, "In Search of the Better Parent: The Social Construction of Ideologies of Fatherhood," 3 *Canadian Journal of Women and the Law* 69. "Yet, for the majority of mothers, the image of the nurturing father is a myth. The anecdotal information is not supported by hard data." *Ibid.* at 70. She reviews several social science studies that portray fathers as actively participating in child care, exhibiting significant interest in the baby, and other positive images such that one might conclude "that if a child has an active father, he or she really does not need a mother. After all, the research shows that it is the father who is responsible for gender, cognitive, intellectual, and academic development." *Ibid.,* pp. 75–76. Drakich criticizes these studies for their failure to control for, or investigate, the mother's influence on the father-child relationship, the mother-father relationship, the father's actual participation in child care, and other relevant factors. *Ibid.,* p. 76.

   She noted that, in reality, fathers are participating only slightly more in routine child care and household duties than they were in 1967. Research indicates that in 1967 they spent 104 minutes a day on "family work"; in 1977 this had increased to 130 minutes a day. A 1980 study showed that wives with full-time jobs spend three times as much time on child care and housework as do their husbands; women employed part time average approximately five times as much time as their husbands. Fathers spend about 40 minutes a day with children under the age of 4, regardless of the mother's employment status, and about 15 minutes a day with teenagers. A 1985 study reported that 61.6 percent of mothers spend four or more hours a day in child care, whereas only 10 percent of fathers spend that much time. According to a 1988 study, employed women still spend twice as much time with child care and twice as much time on housework as do their husbands. *Ibid.,* pp. 83–85.

   See also Nancy Gibbs, "Bringing Up Father," Time (June 28, 1993): p. 53, in which men are portrayed as wishing to be more nurturing and more involved in their children's lives but are stymied by work requirements and frequently women's intransigence. Bosses don't want men taking paternity leave; women don't want them doing child care unless they do it "her" way.

53. *See* Jay Folberg, "Custody Overview," in *Joint Custody and Shared Parenting*, Jay Folberg ed. (Washington, DC: Bureau of National Affairs, 1984): pp. 3–10; *see also* Letter from Neal Skrenes, Secretary, Custodial Parents' Rights Coalition, Inc., Ft. Landerdale to Wis. Rep. Jeannette Bell, Chair, Special Legislative Committee, Custody Arrangements (on file with the author).

54. For an analysis of the tender-years doctrine under the Equal Protection Clause, *see Ex Parte Divine*, 398 So. 2d 686 (Ala. 1981), which held that the doctrine constituted unconstitutional gender discrimination. *See State Divorce Statutes Chart and Summary Sheet Introduction, Family Law Reporter*. (BNA) (March 25, 1986): pp. 5–6. The relevant Wisconsin statute reads: "In making a custody determination, the court . . . shall not prefer one potential custodian over the other on the basis of the sex of the custodian." *Wis. Stat. Ann.* §767.24(2) (West 1993).

55. *See, e.g.,* William J. Everett, "Shared Parenthood in Divorce: The Parental Covenant and Custody Law," 2 *Journal of Law and Religion* 85, 85–89 (1984).

56. *See* John Elster, "Solomonic Judgments: Against the Best Interest of the Child," 54 *University of Chicago Law Review* 1 (1987); Robert Mnookin, "Child-Custody Adjudication: Judicial Functions in the Face of Indeterminacy," 39 *Law and Contemporary Problems* 226, 289–91 (1975).

57. Quoted in Anne Marie Delorey, "Joint Legal Custody: A Reversion to Patriarchal Power," 3 *Canadian Journal of Women and the Law* 33, 43 (1989).

58. *Ibid.,* p. 33. Delorey notes that legal custody is power—power over the child and power over the parent who has primary caretaking responsibilities. The parent, usually the father, who is least actively involved in the day-to-day rearing of the child is given significant power to make decisions in contradiction to the mother's wishes. He thus has tremendous power (rights) with regard to the rearing of the child with no corresponding responsibility for the day-to-day care of the child. *Ibid.,* pp. 37–38. Giving veto power to the noncaretaker reduces the caretaker to a puppet, even though she is the one most fully involved with the child, and contravenes the "best interests of the child" standard. *Ibid.,* p. 41.

59. Grossberg states that the "most profound changes in the fate of illegitimate children occurred neither in the courtrooms nor legislative chambers, but rather through the gradual exertion of control over bastardy by social workers and welfare bureaucrats." Grossberg, *Governing the Hearth* [chapter 4, note 23] p. 231. He also notes that professional social workers were a "house divided"

when it came to reforms in regard to nonmarital children. On the one hand, some reformers argued that bastards be accorded the same legal rights as legitimate children, arguing that while there "may be illegitimate parents . . . there can be no illegitimate children." *Ibid., p. 230.* On the other hand, reforms assisting unwed mothers or benefitting their children were viewed as correspondingly threatening the sacred status of marriage. Grossberg quotes several reformers in the debate, including Emma O. Lundberg's 1926 assessment: "In practically all states, up to the present time, it has been held incompatible with the interest of the legal family to place the child of illegitimate birth upon an equality with the children born in wedlock with respect to his claims upon the father." *Ibid., pp.* 232–33.

Other reformers were less concerned with preserving the legal family and more focused on doing what they could given the realities. As Kate Waller Barrett stated: "If we cannot have the trinity which God intended—husband, wife, child—we can have the other trinity—mother, child, home—that has a mighty potency in it for good." *Ibid.* at 230.

These arguments track the debates heard today in regard to welfare reform. *See* chapter 5.

60. *See generally* Mary Kay Kisthardt, "Of Fatherhood, Families and Fantasy: The Legacy of Michael H. v. Gerald D.," 65 *Tulane Law Review* 585 (1991).

61. *Trimble v. Gordon*, 430 U.S. 762, 769 (1977).

62. *Family Law: Cases, Text, Problems* Ira Mark Ellman, Paul M. Kurtz and Katharine T. Bartlett eds. (2d ed., 1991): p. 960. On the development of federal constitutional protection generally, which the authors remind us is "only a minimum which the laws of many states already surpass."

63. 405 U.S. 645 (1972).

64. Parents were defined as the "father and mother of a legitimate child, or the survivor of them, or the natural mother of an illegitimate child, and . . . any adoptive parent." *Stanley* at 649. Unwed fathers were presumed unfit, and therefore the Stanley children were placed in state custody at their mother's death.

65. *Ibid.* at 652.

66. This term from *Caban v. Mohammed*, 441 U.S. 380, 389 (1979) refers to a unit of unmarried mother, father, and their child. This unit mimics the traditional, formally married heterosexual unit that forms the "foundation" of society in much legal and political rhetoric, a topic explored fully in chapter 6. In this case, the father's tie to the children came through this family group.

67. *Lehr v. Robertson*, 463 U.S. 248 (1983). *Lehr* requires an unwed father to have demonstrated "a full commitment to the responsibilities of parenthood" before a liberty interest attaches. *Ibid.* at 261. *See also Quilloin v. Wolcott*, 434 U.S.

246 (1978). *And see Caban, Id.* in which an unwed father had established a substantial relationship with his children, and his right to object to the adoption of the children by the mother's new husband was preserved. The language in *Caban* indicates that factors such as the father's having lived with the mother and their children as a "natural family unit" and having supported the child were significant. Paternal behavior, not biology, was crucial.

68. *Caban* [chapter 4, note 66].

69. *Caban* [chapter 4, note 66] at p. 388.

70. *Ibid.* at 397 (Stewart, J., dissenting). Justice Stevens was specifically concerned about adoption and recognized it was the mother who would more directly be dealing with questions of how to care for the child. *Ibid.* at 401 (Stevens, J., dissenting).

71. *See* Chapters 5 and 6 for more detail on this point.

72. John R. Hamilton, "The Unwed Father and the Right to Know of His Child's Existence," 76 *Kentucky Law Journal* 949, 1009 (1988). This author's view of fatherhood seems overly sentimental and either ignores the interests of the child beyond the realization of a tie to the father, or places those interests in a secondary position to the biological imperative of fatherhood.

73. The most notorious of these cases was that involving Jessica DeBoer, who was returned to her biological parents after several years of legal battles culminated in allowing the fact that the biological father lacked notice (due to the mother's misrepresentations) to undo the adoption. *In the Interest of B.G.C.*, 114 S. Ct. 11 (1993), application for stay in the Supreme Court of the United States denied July 8, 1993. The denial of the stay prompted Justices Blackmun and O'Connor to dissent. They described the case thus: "We have before us ... a child of tender years who for her entire life has been nurtured by the DeBoers. ... Now the biological father appears, marries the mother and claims paternal status" *Ibid.* at 11 (Blackmun, J., dissenting).

A more recent (and more outrageous) case is unfolding in Illinois, where the state supreme court ordered a boy removed from his adoptive parents, with whom he has lived since the age of four months, and "returned" him to his biological father, who has never seen him. The biological father had been told by the mother that the child died at birth. The case differs from that of Baby Jessica in that a "valid" adoption had occured and the adoptive parents had no clue of the biological father's claim until years after the legalities had been finalized. In both of these cases the unwed fathers asserted that their biological rights coupled with lack of notice in regard to the adoption mandated the adoptions be revoked. In the Illinois case, the Justice who wrote the opinion defensively stated in response to criticism: "If this case is a tragedy, then that tragedy is the wrongful break up of a *natural* family and the keeping of a child by strangers without rights" (emphasis added). Don Terry, "Storm Rages in Chicago Over Revoked Adoption," *New York Times* (July 15, 1994), p. A12. The adoptive parents, who do not consider themselves "strangers," are likely to appeal to the United States Supreme Court.

74. *See, e.g.,* the cover story by Nancy Gibbs, "In Whose Best Interest?" *Time,* July 19, 1993, p. 45, where the bold print introducing the story states, "The Courts viewed Jessica DeBoer more as property than as a person; now she must return to her biological parents." Later in the story, the author notes that the Iowa court deciding between adoptive parents and the rights of the biological father "declared that it could not and should not pay attention to the best interests of the child, that the only issue at hand in this case was the father." p. 49. The article concludes that the law is the real villain and mentions reform efforts following "public outcry" over such notorious cases.

In a case decided a few months later and covered in the media by contrasting it with the Baby Jessica case, joint custody of "Baby Pete" was awarded to his biological father, who had not had notice of the adoption, and his adoptive mother. In an editorial entitled "For Once, the Baby Won," the *New York Times* noted that "lawyers are already pointing to this agreement as a possible model for future squabbles over biological parents', adoptive parents' and children's rights." *New York Times,* September 1, 1993, p. A18.

75. The existence of women in law as practitioners, judges, and teachers, and the fledgling movement among some female legal academics to develop feminist legal theory, have yet to substantially alter the nature of legal discourse or the dominant legal concepts and constructs. An overriding commitment to the equality objective seems to preclude these feminists from conceptualizing and becoming proponents of a gendered analysis of the policy and politics of families in the United States. This is an essentially assimilationist stance that does not challenge existing structures of dominance and control.

76. *See* Fineman, *Illusion* [chapter 2, note 8].

77. For a detailed case study, in which these aspirations are documented by reference to feminist reform literature, *see* Fineman, *Illusion* [chapter 2, note 8].

5

The Deviant Mother

IN THE PRECEDING CHAPTER, I explored the contemporary assault on mother preference that has taken place under the banner of equality in divorce-law reform. The complementary development is the encroachment of egalitarian notions used to bolster the parental claims of unwed fathers. This transformation in law—from an appreciation of the socially differentiated and gendered nature of parenting to an equality model—was wrought by father-centered reforms in the divorce context and by the ascendance of the biological connection to give fathers increasing rights in the nonmarital context. Corresponding to these movements in legal doctrine has been the devaluation of the concept of Mother as a status worthy of any unique legal significance. The neutering of Mother and the granting of rights disassociated from caretaking or nurturing has important implications for mothers and their children in all contexts.

The process of reformulating and reinforcing the historic control of fathers over children and in families hinges on casting the practice of single motherhood as "deviant." The impetus for this designation seems to be that the existence of unstigmatized mothers successfully mothering outside of the traditional heterosexual family calls into question some of the basic components of patriarchal ideology. The very fact of their singleness is central to the construction of deviant mothers. Marital status is definitional—single motherhood is synonymous with deviant motherhood. This connection between singleness and deviancy is clear in the rhetoric used to generate and articulate the societal consequences associated with the increased numbers of single mothers.

While many single mothers in both the divorced and never-married categories are also poor and this contributes to the societal designation of them as "deviant," their real offense—the "true" indicia of their pathology—is their singleness. It is this demographic characteristic that embodies the challenge they present to the asserted necessity and inevitability of the hetero-sexual family in our society. The representation of single motherhood as pathological is inextricably linked to patriarchical ideology.[1] It is through this constellation of symbols and beliefs about what constitutes a "natural" or "normal" family that all motherhood discourses are processed. In fact, singleness is the official explanation for poverty.

Why has this casting of single motherhood as pathological, as a social disease, and as one of the core explanations of poverty, been so readily accepted? Why is it perpetuated in such a variety of contexts and by people who occupy a wide range of political viewpoints? It would seem evident to liberals that this stereotyping could be viewed as misogynist and racist.

Steeped in divorce discourses after completion of my last book on the rhetoric of reform in that area, I began to read poverty discourses. I was struck by both the similarity in the articulation of the "problem" (absent father) and in the creation of an ideal "solution" (bring him [back] into the family in some form). The ideological spaces occupied by the discourses of poverty and divorce, with their two unique categories of single mothers, were different enough so that the existence of a common articulation of problems and solutions suggested to me the need for further thought.

Perhaps the similarity in the creation and definition of problems and solutions should not have been surprising. Many single-mother families are created by divorce, and many of these mothers will eventually need state assistance. In poverty discourses, however, the single-mother family under consideration is not typically presented as the once-married, formerly mid-dle-class housewife and mom, who, with her children, now finds herself upon hard times as the result of divorce. The single mother constructed within poverty discourses is differentiated by race and by class from her divorced sister. Yet, despite these differences, the core and common problem facing mothers within each group is identified as the missing male. It follows, therefore, that the solution to the problem for both categories of single mothers lies in the legally coerced (re)establishment of a paternal presence, physically outside of, but metaphysically completing, the family structure.

As a result of this observation, I became interested in what I now call the phenomenon of "cross-over discourses." I define this phenomenon as the propensity for rhetorical images associated with being female in our culture, which are generated and perpetuated in one context, to spill over and define our understanding of women in other contexts. Any process in which "Mother" is explicitly the focus of attention generates images that ultimately are significant in shaping societal attitudes toward the regulation of motherhood through the creation of rules governing such things as reproduction, child custody, and other areas of the law in which the institution of "Mother" is implicated.

In other words, "Mother," as a socially defined and symbolic institution, has trans-substantive implications. The concept of "Mother," conceived of as "true" in poverty or divorce discourses, will inevitably be definitive in our understanding and grand construction of the institution of "Mother."

A critical examination of poverty discourse discloses that patriarchy as the dominant family ideology fixes the core concepts and images about motherhood. Patriarchy also facilitates, and even mandates, the crossover effect of such discourses. In this regard, the discourses that concern poverty and single motherhood are consistent with other stereotypes and myths fashioned under the influence of patriarchal ideology, in which the dominant family form is a male-dominated reproductive unit with defined gender roles.

As developed more fully in the next section, although the image of the traditional family has undergone some revisions in light of the modern concerns with gender equity and equality, the nuclear-family form, with a sexual affiliation between man and woman as the paradigmatic intimate associational bond, is still dominant.[2] The tendency of policy discourses about both divorce and welfare to reference and reify patriarchal images and ideas is directly related to the continued vitality of the ideology. Although our social circumstances have substantially altered, patriarchal concepts remain at the center of how we define and understand families in our culture.[3]

In this chapter, I discuss the articulation of the concept of deviancy in the context of welfare policy and the political rhetoric that accompanies it. I also consider how this concept of deviancy has been developed in contexts beyond "practical" objections associated with "welfare dependency" and political concern for the "taxpayer's purse" in both political and popular contexts.

The diffuse nature of the discourse of deviancy associated with single motherhood is also reflected in the rhetoric surrounding divorce, a process in which married mothers are rendered single. In this context, professional discourses and legal policy condemn resistance to continued patriarchal control. I argue that the extrapolation of the concept of deviancy to encompass all practices of single motherhood suggests that it is the characteristic of singleness itself and not any resulting manifestation that is considered deviant. The popular, professional, and political come full circle within the rhetoric of contemporary politicians who condemn single motherhood regardless of the economic, social, or racial context in which it occurs. The public interest is perceived to be in saving the traditional family, not in providing for poor children and their caretakers. The idea of inevitable harm to children and society has been popularly expressed in an article entitled "Dan Quayle was Right":

> The social-science evidence is in: though it may benefit the adults involved, the dissolution of intact two-parent families is harmful to large numbers of children. . . .
>
> Across time and across cultures, family disruption has been regarded as an event that threatens a child's well-being and even survival. . . . The social arrangement that has proved most successful in ensuring the physical survival and promoting the social development of the child is the family unit of the biological mother and father. Consequently, any event that permanently denies a child the presence and protection of a parent jeopardizes the life of the child.[4]

This extremely and highly questionable "family values" perspective is based on faulty and incomplete social science and disingenuously compares idealized nuclear families with those of single mothers already in trouble. Nonetheless, this panicked reactionary rhetoric is taking over the policy debate. Some responsible researchers do qualify their conclusions about harm to children living in single-parent households. Angel and Angel, for example, report that:

> Unfortunately, studies of the impact of divorce on children's mental health tell us little about the consequences of fatherlessness for children who never have a father figure in the home. Again in most studies of the impact of divorce on children's mental health, the effects of the emotional upheaval surrounding the disruption are confounded with the effects of the fathers' absences that follow divorce. It is simply impossible to determine from these studies the independent effects of divorce and family structure. Findings from studies of the children of divorce, therefore, cannot be generalized to the children of never-married mothers; there are simply too many differences between these types of families. For example,

for the children of divorced parents, the loss of the father's income can lead to poverty. This change in status, in conjunction with the emotional upheaval preceding the divorce, may contribute significantly to the emotional trauma they experience.

Families in which the father has never been present are often chronically poor, and it may be this poverty, rather than a rapid change in family structure or income, that accounts for any negative health consequences. Never-married mothers tend to be young and poor, and they are often ill-equipped to raise their children in an optimal manner. It is hard enough for an educated middle-class mother to deal with the burdens of raising a child alone. For a young woman with little education, few job skills, and no family support, the task can be truly daunting. The necessity of being both mother and father to her children while attempting to maintain a household beset by the disruptive forces of poverty can be an almost hopelessly difficult task.[5]

The authors also indicate that there are studies that find no effect on children's mental health from father absence.[6]

In regard to the "evidence" indicating some negative effect of father absence, Angel and Angel, unlike so many of their contemporaries, do not jump to simplistic and mean-spirited conclusions. They explicitly recognize the paucity of reliable information and the complexity of the problems. They indicate that a multiplicity of factors might be responsible for the well-being of mothers and children in single-parent homes.

What we would like to know is whether father absence has long-term health consequences for children and whether single motherhood has long-term health consequences for women. We would also like to identify the mechanisms through which any negative physical or mental health effects operate. Unfortunately, a more detailed understanding of these mechanisms must await longitudinal data on marital status, fertility, and health. We can be fairly certain, however, that any negative health consequences of single motherhood for children or adults result from complex interactions among poverty, emotional stress, and such factors as low education and inadequate social support. What remains for future research is to disentangle these complex interactive relationships and to identify those factors that are most responsible for any health deficits that single mothers and their children suffer.[7]

In spite of the example provided by such moderation, few commentators (and virtually no politicians) make qualified statements. They speak with great authority based on little information. As Judith Stacey has noted:

By endlessly repeating and cross-citing one another's views the [family value warriors] seem to have convinced most of the media, the public and Clinton that the superiority of the family values they espouse is . . . "a confimed empirical generalization." Their efforts paved the yellow brick road to the shockingly respectful response that Charles Murray, an American Enterprise fellow, has received to his punitive quest to restigmatize "illegitimacy" and to terminate "all economic support for single mothers."[8]

I. The Construction of Maternal Deviancy in Poverty Discourses

The concept of deviant motherhood that emerges in poverty discourses most clearly and unambiguously reflects the role of patriarchal ideology in the process of constructing Mother. One characteristic typical of a group of welfare recipients—being unmarried—has been identified and characterized by a wide variety of commentators as constituting the cause as well as the effects of poverty. In political and professional discourses, single-Mother status is defined as one of the primary predictors of poverty–predictor often being translated into cause.

This confusion of characteristic with cause has fostered suggestions that an appropriate and fundamental goal of any proposed poverty program should be the eradication of the status and practice of single motherhood. This goal is to be accomplished through appropriate coupling of the single mother with the child's father through the paternity proceeding. The father would thereby assume his "rightful" place in the family as its economic head and fulfill his financial obligations to the child. By his doing so, the paramount welfare reform objective—letting the state off the economic hook—will have been achieved.[9]

Although many commentators prefer sanctified mother/father relationships, the coupling of the single mother and financially-endowed male anticipated by such reforms need not be accomplished though the formation of a marital bond. The objective of such proposals is the creation of a legal tie between the male, who is presumed to be economically viable, and the dependent single mother and child. Through this legal tie, child support obligations can be established and enforced. Neither the mother's nor the father's wishes regarding the establishment of a legal tie are considered relevant.[10]

A. Popular Discourse

Michael Katz reports the comment of "an otherwise sympathetic radio talk show host," who told him: " 'I don't mind paying to help people in need, but I don't want my tax dollars to pay for the sexual pleasure of adolescents who won't use birth control.' "[11] Katz concluded that the host's "outrage summed up popular stereotypes about the relation among adolescent pregnancy, welfare, and the underclass."[12]

The actual statistics were summarized by Katz:

> [M]ost poor people in America do not live in families headed by adolescent mothers or even by women. In 1980, 37% of poor people lived in female-headed families. Poverty is not synonymous with single parents. Nor does adolescent pregnancy consume a large share of the social welfare budget or gross national product. In 1980, the money spent on AFDC represented only about 4% of all the costs of major public assistance and social insurance programs for the elderly, totally disabled, and all others, and only a fraction of AFDC payments go to adolescent mothers. In 1984, all means-tested cash transfer payments by federal, state, and local governments used 0.8% of GNP or two percent of the share of GNP spent by governments.
>
> Consider, next, the question of birth rates. Among blacks, adolescent birth rates have fallen; among whites they have increased. Between 1970 and 1980, the birth rate of unmarried black women dropped 13%, in contrast to a 27% increase among unmarried white women. Nonetheless, black marital fertility fell faster (38%), which means that the fraction of births occurring to unmarried women increased. Among just 15–19-year-old black women, the nonmarital fertility rate (births per 1,000 women) rose from 76.5 in 1960 to a peak of 90.8 in 1970 and has declined since then; by 1980 it had dropped to 83.0. Among whites, the rate, always lower than blacks', has risen steadily from 6.6 in 1960 to 10.9 in 1970 and 16.0 in 1980. In other words, between 1970 and 1980, the fertility of unmarried black 15 to 19-year-old women dropped almost 10%, while the rate for unmarried white women of the same age increased by 48%.[13]

Indeed, in the public's mind, and despite overwhelming evidence to the contrary, the face of poverty has increasingly become that of a single mother, particularly the African-American single mother. Recently, in poverty discourses emanating from a broad spectrum of groups, single mothers have now been lumped together with drug addicts, criminals, and other socially defined "degenerates" in the newly coined category of "underclass." The undeserving status of single-mother families in this context is established partly by their lack of relationship to the work force (either through their own jobs or through their attachment to a male breadwinner) and partly by their asserted role as mothers in the perpetuation of poverty.[14] Consider, for example, this set of assumptions and conclusions:

> The link between female headship and welfare dependency in the urban underclass is also well established, leading to legitimate concerns about the intergenerational transfer of poverty. At the root of this concern is the paucity of employment among welfare mothers and how this affects attitudes of their children toward work.[15]

After citing statistics on this point, the author continued:

> One does not require a deep sociological imagination to sense the attitudinal and behavioral consequences of growing up in an impoverished household where there is no activity associated with the world of work and a household that, in turn, is spatially embedded in a commercially abandoned locality where pimps, drug pushers, and unemployed street people have replaced working fathers as predominant socializing agents.[16]

It is significant that the authors' assumptions as to the composition of "work" is limited to that which is compensated by the market. Mothering, although considered a socially productive endeavor and also a lot of work in many other contexts, is typically excluded from the "world of work" in such rhetoric.

Also of interest is the fact that the category of underclass is defined not only by the perception that its designated members are the chronically poor but also by the belief that their poverty results from their own failings. Single motherhood is considered a sign of degeneration on the same level with crime and other social pathology. Single mothers are implicated by their asserted role in the intergenerational transmission of poverty through their complicity within a "culture of poverty."[17]

Many commentators assume not only that individual behavior causes poverty but also that choosing to make personal changes in one's life can solve the problems of this category of the poor. Consider, for example, the analysis of the problems of the underclass and the recommendations emanating from the American Enterprise Institute:

Today, for example, significant numbers of American adults are not demonstrating the behaviors expected of free and responsible citizens. Linked to poverty among an important fraction of the poor is a high incidence of dropping out from school, of failure to prepare themselves for future employment, of begetting children out of wedlock, of crime, of drug use, and of other visible disorders. Such persons—whose numbers appear to be growing—are the behavioral dependent, since their need for help from others springs in significant measure from their own behaviors. . . .

It is not entirely a mystery how many climb from poverty. Some specific behaviors empower them. The probabilities of remaining involuntarily in poverty are remarkably low for those who

—complete high school

—once an adult, get married and stay married (even if not on the first try)

—stay employed, even if at a wage and under conditions below their ultimate aims.[18]

Predictably, marital status is central to the self-help regimes proposed for the poor. Liberal commentators often share this concern with the marital choices made by the poor and consider marital status an appropriate objective to be fostered by public policy. William Julius Wilson writes:

Perhaps the most important factor in the rise of black female-headed families [is] the extraordinary rise in black male joblessness. . . . [T]he decline in the incidence of intact marriages among blacks is associated with the declining economic status of black men. . . . [B]lack women nationally, especially young black women, are facing a shrinking pool of "marriageable" (i.e., employed) black men. This finding supports the hypothesis that the sharp rise of black female-headed families is directly related to increasing black male joblessness.[19]

In poverty discourses, such as those set out above, the label "Mother" is modified by the woman's legal relationship (or lack thereof) to a male. Mothers (who are in "vertical" relationships with their children) are classified by whether they are single (or in "horizontal" relationships, a fact that is positioned as significant and even central to the discourses). Generally, recent welfare reforms assume as a normative matter that children should be firmly anchored (financially, morally, and legally) within the nuclear family.

The socially and economically based deprivations that poor children and their mothers suffer are thereby transformed into deprivations attributable to and based upon their deviant family form. Economic and social salvation will therefore come about through the restructuring of these families to conform as closely as possible to the "natural" (nuclear) family, thereby perpetuating traditional roles. The reforms are driven by the perceived compelling need to reestablish patriarchy, redefined for the contemporary context in which not only is divorce common, but increasing numbers of never-married women choose to become mothers.[20]

B. Political Discourse

The Family Support Act (FSA) of 1988 was the first major piece of legislation addressing poverty to pass Congress in several decades.[21] Although more reform is expected in 1995 from the current Democratic administration, the core concepts articulated in 1988 are likely to remain central to subsequent legislation. The 1988 legislation reflected the belief that welfare dependency is a significant societal problem that requires a dramatic reorientation of welfare policy. The FSA's primary objective was to link poverty with the lack of a work ethic, thereby attaching welfare recipients to a new workfare scheme. This was accomplished in two ways: first, by mandating that the single mother work (or train for work); and second, by establishing a system for substituting support from fathers for state support, or Aid to Families with Dependent Children (AFDC), thus transforming a child's primary source of support from public to private hands.

The Job Opportunities and Basic Skills (JOBS) program that resulted has been called the "new workfare" because, although it requires work, it also offers opportunities for education, job training, skill development, job counseling, and placement in the private sector, along with other supportive services such as extended child care and health insurance.[22] The JOBS program is thus workfare plus support services and replaced the Work Incentives Program (WIN)[23] that was initiated in 1967. The legislation's focus on reinforcing the work ethic and dominant individualistic norms of self-sufficiency through the imposition of "workfare" provisions for mothers of young children became the major emphasis of most commentators.

Prior to the passage of the Family Support Act, policy discussions emphasized research that highlighted the effectiveness of state-tested new workfare programs in moving people from welfare to work.[24] Many of these studies stressed that low-cost programs that emphasize work requirements are generally cost efficient and likely to provide considerable movement from welfare to work.[25] Some commentators, however, were less sanguine.[26]

Jencks and Edin argued that their research indicated that the increases in income produced by employment workfare programs were hardly a solution to the poverty problems of poor, female-headed families. If the earnings needed to enable these families to get out of poverty were considered, mothers would, on average, require jobs that paid approximately two to three times the minimum wage before they could reasonably be expected to leave welfare and cover their expenses, including child and health care. They argued that:

> The essence of the so-called "welfare trap" is not that welfare warps women's personalities or makes them pathologically dependent, though that may occasionally happen. The essence of the "trap" is that while welfare pays badly, low-wage jobs pay even worse. Most welfare mothers are quite willing to work if they end up with significantly more disposable income as a result. But they are not willing to work if working will leave them as poor as they were when they stayed home. . . . All these calculations lead to one inexorable conclusion. An unskilled single mother cannot expect to support herself and her children in today's labor market either by working or by collecting welfare. If she wants to make ends meet, she must either get help from someone else (usually an absent father, parent, or boyfriend) or she must combine work and welfare. At present, the only way she can combine work and welfare is to collect AFDC and then work without telling the welfare department.[27]

This more systemic approach was largely ignored on the political level in the 1980s and seems to be lost in today's virulent anti-AFDC rhetoric.

The drive toward reform is manifest across all political positions. Today, as in 1988, the fact that proposals for work requirements are coupled with greater supportive services for recipients than previous schemes has meant that liberals can comfortably conclude that reforms offer more than merely a state policy that discourages welfare.[28] Some feminists criticized the earlier workfare provisions, even those including training, as unwarranted and inappropriate, but their voices remained unincorporated into powerful public forums.[29]

In fact, the various experimental workfare programs likely to be influential in current national reform are not very different from those tried in the past, with one significant exception. Most of the previous programs exempted women who had young children at home from required participation. Current programs do not have this exemption.[30] The programs in Florida and Wisconsin are typical.

The Florida Employment Opportunity Act provides that an application for AFDC constitutes registration for employment or training in the program. All recipients of AFDC benefits are required to participate in the program, including mothers with children under the age of 3. Young mothers, i.e., those under the age of 20, must participate in educational activity if the child is 90 days or older.[31] The Family Transition Program[32] requires all AFDC recipients to participate in whatever "employability" plan the state designs for them. If the recipient is not otherwise employable, she can be required to attend "workfare"—a "skills training program, consisting primarily of unpaid work performed for a public agency."[33] South Dakota has a similar provision requiring the "obligor," the absent parent, to participate in a workfare program.[34]

Wisconsin requires all "appropriate individuals to register for manpower (sic) services, training or employment under the work incentive demonstration program."[35] A waiver is being obtained from the Federal Department of Health and Human Services to require participation of the parents of a child three months to six years.[36] Both Wisconsin and Florida also have "learnfare" provisions, which sanction the failure of school-aged children to remain in school by reducing the amount of aid received.[37]

But, as ill conceived and inappropriate as work requirements may have been or are,[38] it is the second type of provisions designed to achieve economic "independence" for the welfare mother, first so clearly articulated in the Family Support Act 1988, that is of particular significance to the themes developed in this book. On their face, the provisions mandating stricter enforcement of child-support orders, including wage-withholding and the establishment of child-support guidelines at first may seem benign, even progressive.[39] Under the 1988 FSA, the states are required to meet federal standards to establish the paternity of children born out of wedlock as a method of obtaining child support from absent fathers.[40] The Family Support Act also struck a blow for the "equality" of poor two-parent families with the mandate that all states adopt the AFDC-UP Program, which provides welfare benefits to impoverished families in which the principal wage earner is unemployed.[41]

On an ideological level, however, it is ominous that a major policy thrust is tied up with paternity actions and child-support provisions. These "remedies" for female and child poverty reflect the domination of and are derivative and dependent upon the traditional male-headed family model. State-established fatherhood is offered as the panacea for the economic needs of children. Even more disturbing on a symbolic as well as a policy level is the fact that the fatherhood solution is presented as foundational. Fathers are essential to the resolution of problems encompassed by and extending beyond child poverty. Fathers are economic providers and disciplinarians in patriarchal nuclear families—it is to a semblance of this institution that we must revert.

The vitality of the nuclear family as an ideological structure has operated as a constraint on our collective political imagination. This is evident in the political rhetoric surrounding the 1988 reforms. In addressing the Family Support Act in the Senate, for example, Senator Moynihan began his 1990 address by commending President Bush for his remarks at the United Nations World Summit for Children. He stated:

> One sentence [of President Bush's remarks is] especially notable. "We want to see the day when every American child is part of a strong and stable family." The importance of this statement is elemental. Unlike the problems of children in much of the world, age-old problems of disease, new problems of ecological disaster, the problems of children in the United States are overwhelmingly associated with the strength and stability of their families. Our problems do not reside in nature, nor yet are they fundamentally economic. Our problems derive from behavior.[42]

After establishing his basic premise (that behavior, not nature or economics) accounted for the plight of America's poor children, Moynihan continued with a Karl Zinmeister quote:

> There is a mountain of scientific evidence showing that when families disintegrate, children often end up with intellectual, physical, and emotional scars that persist for life. . . . We talk about the drug crisis, the education crisis, and the problems of teen pregnancy and juvenile crime. But all these ills trace back predominantly to one source: broken families.[43]

Moynihan's rhetoric simplistically views family form as the "cause" of our nation's children's problems and signifies that the "cure" is the reestablishment of the traditional nuclear family. He thereby attributes the problems of the poor to marital status and furthers the misogynist tendency in poverty discourses to categorize mothers according to their relationship with men. The very existence of single mothers is generally deemed to present potential social problems, problems for which they alone are largely responsible.[44] Single mothers are still being blamed for much of societal ills. If we could just get "them" to stop having babies everything would be just fine. Prime among these voices is that of Charles Murray of the American Enterprise Foundation, who believes that "illegitimacy is the single most important social problem of our time—more important than crime, drugs, poverty, illiteracy, welfare, or homelessness, because it drives everything else."[45] Murray states that single women with children are a drain on a community's resources and "in large numbers . . . must destroy the community's capacity to sustain itself."[46] Therefore, he reasons, we should not give any economic support to single mothers.

Mothers who cannot support their children will be forced to enlist the support of others, be forced to give the child up for adoption, and be stigmatized (as the anger of the community is roused by having to help her) as an example to others. If all else fails, the children can be placed in orphanages. These extreme punitive measures are necessary because "the brutal truth is that American society as a whole could survive when illegitimacy became epidemic within a comparatively small ethnic minority. It cannot survive the same epidemic among whites."[47]

Murray should not be dismissed as an ultraconservative with no influence. In an editorial entitled "Veering Off-Center on Welfare," the *Washington Post* indicated that Congressional Republicans[48] are revising their welfare plan to incorporate many of his punitive ideas.[49] And even Bill Clinton views, with qualified approval, various state governments' implementation of a variety of experimental programs, at least somewhat consistent with Murray's proposals.[50] New Jersey, Wisconsin, and Georgia already have legislation that eliminates incremental payments for additional children,[51] and Maryland is considering such a proposal.[52]

Misperceptions and erroneous images of mothers are incorporated into political debates. Alexander Cockburn, discussing a paper written by Mike

Males of Occidental College, addressed the myth of widespread, out-of-control teen births:

> The whole notion of a (black) teenage sex epidemic, born of teenage "irresponsibility," is utterly bogus. . . .
>
> [L]ess than one-eighth of all "teenage" births and one-fifth of all births to school-age girls match the myth of "children having children." In only about 20,000 births annually—less than 4 percent of all births among teenage girls, or 1 percent of the total births in the United States—are both partners minors under the age of 18. . . .
>
> Births among teenage girls peaked in 1958, declined through the mid-1980s and have since risen, for reasons of youth poverty. Among all age and race groups, higher rates of poverty provoke higher rates of birth. Poverty, not age, is the problem.[53]

Another misperception is the view that the rise in nonmarital births is a new phenomenon, unique to modern times, and linked to a decline in morality. Some recent research calls this belief into question. This research indicates high rates of pregnancies among pre-twentieth-century unmarried women and the social acceptance of sex before marriage and pregnancy out of wedlock. One author notes that approximately 40 percent of her sample of "106 babies born to first-time mothers between 1785 and 1797" were to single women.[54]

The popular characterization of single mothers as "bad" or lazy resonates in the larger political currents that classify the poor as either "deserving" or "undeserving." This classification feeds the public's perception that the impoverished individual is poor either because of her personal choices and actions, *or* as a result of forces beyond her control.[55] This ideological distinction between deserving and undeserving has concrete, material implications attached to its categories. Public policy is built upon such distinctions, and the way that one becomes a single mother often dictates the source of public assistance to which one may turn. Women who have become single mothers due to the death of their spouses are generally excused from the condemnation so frequently cast at their never-married sisters. These mothers are sympathetically considered worthy as widows even if they have not worked or do not work. Widows are typically entitled to generous Social Security benefits, whereas, in contrast, mothers who are divorced or who never marry are left to the variability of the child support system or AFDC.

Ironically, Senator Moynihan, one of the prime architects of the "single motherhood as deviant and pathological" analysis, is also one of the predominant voices objecting to these disparate subsidies for children to which his own analysis has contributed. In arguing for the Family Security Act, the Senator noted the inequities in financial support services for children, and pointed out that although Survivors Insurance Benefits have increased by 53 percent, AFDC benefits were down an average of 13 percent. The result is that children receiving Social Security benefits get over twice the benefits of those relying on AFDC. The Senator questioned the equity of this situation, noting that "these are identically situated children. They are children living in a single-parent, female-headed household. . . . There is no way you can distinguish these children excepting one brutal reality: The majority of the children receiving Survivors Insurance are white, and the majority of the children receiving AFDC are non-white."[56] Racism is certainly a significant factor in this process.[57]

Such distinctions, therefore, go beyond social stigma (which, in and of itself, is significant); they have a real impact on the material future of a large number of single mothers and their children. The ideological ramifications of this view are expressed by Stuart Butler and Anna Kondratas:

> The typical AFDC parent today is not the "worthy widow" envisaged in the original legislation but a divorced, deserted, or never-married woman. Regardless of extenuating circumstances behind any particular out-of-wedlock birth or the justification for any particular divorce, the fact remains that illegitimacy and divorce have an element of personal choice and responsibility that widowhood does not. . . . Regardless of how difficult it is for individuals to pay for making irresponsible or unfortunate choices, that does not absolve those individuals of dealing with the consequences as best they can, before society is asked to step in to support them and their children. . . . Social assistance has always been based on social norms and expectations. One of the assumptions underlying AFDC was the idea that a mother has an important role to play in the upbringing and socialization of her children. It was the humane intention of the program in 1935 [designed for widows] to enable a mother to take care of her children—in other words, to encourage what was left of a family to stay together. It was, in today's parlance, a "pro-family" measure. But now the program finances a subculture whose citizens argue . . . that they want children but not marriage, because "you don't want the commitments" and "male figures are not substantially important in the family."[58]

This quote lumps together divorced and never-married mothers as objects appropriately condemned. This tendency continues even in more liberal policy rhetoric as societal judgments about these women's status cross over from the welfare context to divorce. In some quarters, however, poor women who become single mothers because of divorce are more likely to be included within the category of "deserving."[59] Parsimonious treatment of poor women who choose to become mothers without marrying is socially justified because they can be stigmatized as the undeserving poor.[60]

The absence of the formal legal tie to a male is far more than just a descriptive term or classifying category. It has powerful ideological implications. In addition to providing a basis for determining who is undeserving in our culture, the rhetoric constructs single motherhood as dangerous and even deadly, not only to the single mothers and their children but to society as a whole. The moral imperative as well as the social policy is that the practice be curtailed. The following quote from Marge Roukema in opposition to the Family Support Act illustrates how political rhetoric can integrate a narrow definition of what constitutes work, the fear of taxpayer anger, and moralizing about stereotypical welfare mothers:

> This bill, if enacted, will trigger the law of perverse effects. There exists the potential that this bill will make it more attractive to go on welfare and stay on welfare. . . . [It] provides that a welfare mother does not have to have training or take on a job if she has a child three years or younger.[61]

After citing statistics that 50 percent of working women have children under one year of age and announcing that the proposed bill was inconsistent with present economic and social realities, she continued:

> Imagine this: A welfare mother could actually continue to have a child every two years and never have to work at all. That's wrong. And not only will that mother not have to work, but her children, born into impoverishment, will have little hope for their own futures. And the cycle of poverty and dependency continues. I ask: how much longer do you think the two-worker couple will tolerate the welfare state and its cost to them in taxes to support that welfare mother? . . . The answer is that they should not have to.[62]

This casts the single mother not as a victim but as a calculating individual who lives lavishly off the poor, victimized taxpayer. She is demonized into the "bad" mother.

Whatever the status of divorce discourse, the imagery surrounding welfare remains laden with moral and normative judgments that are founded on stereotypical assumptions about single mothers in the poverty context. A woman's decision to become or remain a single mother is the decisive consideration for determining whether she is to be considered a "good" mother. If she is not single as a result of death (or, perhaps, divorce), she is deemed a "bad" mother. Her conduct is considered to have "earned" her this designation, and stereotypes about her motivations and behavior abound.[63]

II. The Construction of Maternal Deviancy in the Context of Divorce

The popular rhetoric attending single-mother families resulting from increased instances of divorce is not so clearly focused on the pathology of the mothers—at least not initially. Of course, the tremendous increase in the number of divorces that has occurred over the past several decades is viewed as a social dilemma, but since men were once present as husbands and fathers, single motherhood can be understood as not the woman's "fault."

This doesn't mean that divorced single mothers have escaped negative characterizations, however. To be sure, some commentators blame feminist aspirations and no-fault divorce rules and maternal custody norms for making it too easy for women to leave marriages, but for most observers the "real" problems have to do with women's desire to be the dominant parent after divorce. What has come to be seen as deviant behavior in regard to divorcing mothers is their demands for sole custody and insistence on retaining primary control over their children. This situation, which was the norm in doctrine and practice only a few decades ago, is now cast as pathological by helping professionals and legal commentators alike.[64]

While the links may not be as obviously drawn as they are in poverty discourses, it seems clear that society constructs divorced mothers as deviant and potentially dangerous. If divorced mothers are dangerous, it is a moral and political imperative that they be contained. The legal tools to accomplish this task are different than in the poverty situation—joint custody and shared parenting, rather than the paternity proceeding—but the objective is the same. The remedy is the reinstitution of the paternal to provide mediation within the family. Father and the patriarchal family are designated as the only appropriate solutions for the societal problems generated by changing patterns of mothering.

The metaphors reflected in new custody rules illustrate the nature of new definitions of maternal deviancy. We valorize the "most generous parent" as the one who should have custody and ignore the differences in actual child care performed by mother and father. In this context, most generous parent does not mean the one who provides more material, psychological, or emotional benefits. Nor does it indicate the parent who sacrifices job, career, or individual desires to the needs of the children. Rather, "most generous parent" refers to the parent most likely to encourage an ongoing relationship with the noncustodial/absent parent.[65]

Fathers, as a group, do not have an impressive record when it comes to continuing relationships with, or meeting responsibilities for, their children postdivorce.[66] That fact notwithstanding, they are increasingly portrayed as in need of more rights to their children at divorce (and in nonmarital custody cases).[67] In fact, the poor record fathers have for payment of child support is used to justify giving them increased control and more access to their children.[68]

As a corollary, mothers are being portrayed as liars who will do anything to get custody of their children, including fabricating claims of paternal abuse. There is a widely held perception that a large number of unwarranted maternal allegations of child abuse (particularly sexual abuse) by fathers have been made in the context of divorce. One popular fathers' expert, Richard A. Gardner, repeatedly reiterates his view that allegations of sexual abuse during custody litigation are highly suspect.[69] Citing no authority (other than himself), Dr. Gardner implies that many of these allegations are fabricated by mothers intent on obtaining custody of the child. Though allegedly reluctant to generalize, he notes, "We sometimes hear about the typical personality patterns of mothers who support or even initiate a child's fabrication of sex abuse. . . . What I present are tentative conclusions, held by many who examine such mothers."[70] Strangely, the "many who examine such mothers" are never identified.

Gardner constructs "clues" to help identify such mothers. He notes that one way to identify the "fabricating" mother is that she "will seek only 'hired gun' mental health evaluators."[71] This suggestion seems anomalous. While it may be true generally that a parent will seek only experts who support his or her position,[72] in a custody case involving allegations of child sex abuse, the state will have become involved. In that instance, the parents will have little, if any, control over who is evaluating the child.

Gardner has woven an entire family drama that he speculatively plays out. He asserts that one "Very Valuable Differentiating Criteria" to distinguish valid from invalid accusations of sexual abuse is the degree of shame felt by the mother. If the abuse is real, the mother may "downplay" or even "deny" the abuse or "tolerate it silently," according to Gardner. Mothers who (or whose children) are fabricating the story, Gardner claims, "would tell the world, if they could, to destroy, humiliate or wreak vengence on their husbands."[73] On its face this conclusion seems questionable. It seems more likely (or at least as likely) that women freed by the process of divorce are also finally free to confront the abuse and the abuser of their children. If that is so, what a traumatic situation it would be for mother and child who have finally gotten the courage and the opportunity to resort to the court to be met with "experts" like Dr. Gardner or judges and social workers who adopt his biases.[74] Reading Gardner, one is left with an impression that many mothers contesting custody are vengeful, lying, vindictive, malicious, scheming and willing to do anything to win.

In sharp contrast to Gardner are the conclusions of Sandra Morris, an attorney who has worked with intact-family and divorce incest cases. Morris asks:

> Are we on another witch hunt? Has the accusation of child sexual abuse become the divorce litigant's nuclear weapon of the eighties? Although there is anecdotal evidence of false reporting based on either fabrication or misperception, the overwhelming body of scientific investigation and literature would answer the above question, "No."[75]

Morris reports that figures from a long-range study done by the Association of Family and Conciliation Courts with the American Bar Association revealed that out of a sample of 9,000 dissolution cases nationwide, only 2 percent reported child sexual abuse. Furthermore, persons other than the mother made these allegations in 55 percent of the cases. Observers who independently reviewed the allegations concluded that only 33 percent were "probably" false, and, of these, slightly more than one-half were based on a misinterpretation of the child's statement. Thus, 86 percent of the allegations of abuse in the study were believed "to be sincerely made."[76]

In a review of her most recent cases, Morris reports that in those cases where the allegations were supported by physical evidence, the male perpetrators generally exhibited rigidity, lack of empathy, impulsiveness and difficulty in controlling outbursts, and hostility. Mothers exhibited only one universal characteristic: independent-mindedness. While the characteristics exhibited by the fathers were consistent with the general literature, the independent-mindedness of the mother contrasted sharply with the norm of the "passive mother found in most intact incest families"[77] and as described by Gardner.[78]

Mothers' use of children for their own evil purposes is also the story behind the recently fabricated "Munchausen Syndrome by Proxy."[79] This "newly discovered" syndrome is a variation on the "Munchausen Syndrome," first diagnosed in 1951 and named after Baron von Munchausen, who liked to spin "tall tales." Patients exhibiting the original syndrome would either pretend to be sick or actually self-induce symptoms of illness to attract attention from doctors and hospital staff. The Munchausen Syndrome by Proxy uses these ideas of pretense and inducement, but applies them to mothers who are suspected of lying about or having created suspect symptoms of illness in their children.[80] Of particular significance is the fact that women generally perceived to be "good" mothers can thus be cast as abusive.

In fact, given the premise of Munchausen Syndrome by Proxy, model motherhood may be suspect in and of itself. One commentator noted that "the typical 'Munchausen mom' is a housewife who works hard in constructing for herself the image of the perfect mother.[81] Another "specialist," one Dr. Schreier, stated: "So what we have here are mothers who look to all the world as the most incredible good mothers."[82] Dr. Schreier continued, " 'Munchausen moms' are very, very hard to detect." One can no longer tell the good mothers from the bad.[83] "Nice mother? Nice mother that might just be a monster."[84] This diagnosis, allowing ordinary women to be portrayed as dangerous to their children, is terrifying. Other specialists accepting the validity of the syndrome speculate that most persons suffering from it suffered child abuse themselves. These experts are more charitable in their conclusions, indicating that when these mothers "view their children . . . as having something seriously wrong with them," they were relating to this past abuse.[85]

III. Abusive Mothers

As many of the quotes in this chapter indicate, single motherhood is widely perceived as not only a threat to patriarchal society but also as damaging to individual children.[86] In a significantly expanding area of deviancy discourse, single motherhood is increasingly conflated with abusive motherhood— single mothers are presumed to be abusive. This tendency seems apparent in popular literature and is also reflected in social welfare literature, in which "profiles" of potentially abusive families emerge. The abusive characterization attaches whether the single status is the result of divorce or because the mother never married.

A particularly stunning example of this tendency is that provided by Joanne Jacobs, a columnist for the San Jose, California, *Mercury News*. Jacobs wrote an article in 1990 entitled "Illegitimacy Biggest Killer of Our Babies," in which she furthered the assertion that the *leading killer* of young children in America is not drugs, cancer, or accidents, but illegitimacy.[87]

This article is offensive beyond the author's use of the antiquated term "illegitimate," a term that suggests that the marital status of the child's mother has implications for the quality of the child. It also shows the ways in which conservative and reactionary responses to changing patterns of behavior have been uncritically absorbed and then regurgitated by the press. Jacobs reported the results of a study by Nicholas Eberstadt of Harvard's Center of Population Studies and the American Enterprise Institute. In so doing, she popularized and publicized the rather amazing belief that the high death rate for "illegitimate" children was not related to the mother's age, race, education, or income, but was due to "the lack of care that leads to illegitimacy [and that] also leads to poor care for the kids."[88]

Jacobs dutifully lists, although ultimately disagrees with, Eberstadt's harsher conclusions. She considers, along with similar proposals made by another comentator, Nicholas Davidson, the suggestion that the alleged lack of maternal care warrants such drastic action as the denial of welfare benefits to mothers who "deliberately give birth to and raise a fatherless child."[89]

The divorced mother is also a target of this rhetoric. Jacobs tells the reader that she rejects Davidson's suggestion to alter the law "to grant divorce only for cause [such as] adultery, abuse or desertion—and to deny women custody of their children," thereby removing the "incentive" to divorce provided by easy no-fault divorce, maternal custody, and mandatory child-support payments.[90] But she nonetheless concludes the column with her own normative observation that "we've become way too accepting of an alternative lifestyle in which fathers are dispensable. It's bad for kids."[91]

One of the most common factors listed as a "predictor" of child abuse is the marital status of the mother.[92] However, little if any data exist to support the belief that single mothers are essentially or potentially more abusive than any other mothers (or fathers, for that matter). Studies conducted in this area find it extremely hard to predict who will abuse children. Profiles developed by social service agencies have resulted in a significant number of false assertions.[93] According to Emily Campbell, while some of the identified "characteristics" of child abusers, such as youth and low self-esteem, are shared by some single mothers, the traits are not universal for abusers nor are they confined to single mothers.[94] As Campbell points out, these characteristics are found in nonabusive parents as well as abusive ones, an observation that calls into question the whole process of classifications and prediction.[95]

The image of single mothers as presumptively "bad mothers" fits within other aspects of our cultural consciousness. According to Marie Ashe, "The 'bad' or 'unfit' mother has been a powerful figure in both Western law and Western literature, which identify the 'bad mother' as the woman whose neglectful, abusive, reckless, or even murderous behaviors threaten or destroy her children."[96] The "bad" mother is evident in several Greek figures such as Medea and Jocasta, mother of Oedipus. She is found in the biblical Solomon story, willing to allow her child to be killed rather than relinquish her claim to it.[97] While it is certainly true that mothers do abuse their children, and some mothers are, in fact, bad mothers, Ashe suggests that the "bad" mother stereotype may create "badness" where none exists.[98]

IV. Conclusion

The popular characterizations of single motherhood noted in this chapter are crude echoes of the images of the single mother prevalent in political, legal, and professional discourses that speculate freely about the impact of single motherhood on the institution of the family and ultimately on the fate of our society. We speak of the "broken" family, the "disintegration" of the family, the "crisis" in the family, the "unstable" family, the "decline" of the family, and, perhaps inevitably from some perspectives, the "death" of the family. Underlying such labels is the specter of single motherhood—statistically on the upswing—pathological and disease-like, contaminating society, contributing to its destruction and degeneration.[99]

With this perspective so pervasive, it is little wonder that many reformers urge efforts to curb the practice of single motherhood. Even liberal commentators such as Irwin Garfinkel, formerly of the Institute for Poverty Research—now at Columbia University—are mindful of the role of deterrents and incentives in welfare reform. Garfinkel states that "the problem with providing more aid to single-parent families is that doing so creates incentives for the formation and preservation of single-parent families."[100]

Unlike some conservative commentators, Garfinkel recognizes that single-parent families are not necessarily bad:

> Of course, it is possible that society is better off—or at least not worse off—as a result of whatever additional single-parent families are created by more favorable treatment of those groups. Not all marriages are made in heaven. Some men beat their wives and children. In some of these cases, all the parties may be better off separate rather than together."[101]

Nonetheless, he concludes that "despite the fact that increases in single parenthood may not be socially pernicious, prudence would suggest that in the face of ignorance we should seek to minimize incentives for single parenthood."[102]

Single motherhood has been designated as the source of other social phenomena such as crime and poverty. Single motherhood represents both the cause and the result of the disintegration of the family and society; it is a demographic category filled with political and moral significance, and as such is viewed as having both explanatory and predictive powers. This is true not only in popular discourse[103] but also in more "reflective" areas of discourse such as the social sciences, policy, and law.[104]

When one considers the relationship between motherhood and patriarchy, it seems that motherhood has always been, and continues to be, a colonized concept—an event physically practiced and experienced by women but occupied and defined, given content and value, by the core concepts of patriarchical ideology. Single motherhood as a social phenomenon should be viewed by feminists as a practice resistive to patriarchal ideology, particularly because it represents a "deliberate choice" in a world with birth control and abortion. As such, the existence of single motherhood as an ever-expanding practice threatens the logic and hold of the dominant ideology.

However, even though society may now be grudgingly forced to accept single-mother households as an unfortunate by-product of the social and economic dislocations that characterize the latter part of this century, they are seldom treated as an acceptable, let alone a desirable, family form. In expressions of popular culture, as well as in public policy, single motherhood may be perceived, at best, as requiring an uneasy accommodation with the dominant ideology. The societal aspiration, however, remains to complete the "family" by the addition of a man.

Notes

1. *See* Chapter 2.

2. Patriarchal ideology may have adapted to twentieth-century shifts in expressions of sexuality and redefinitions of gender roles, but the fundamental composition and nature of the core images remain constant. Mother and child are defined by their relationship to the patriarch.

3. As developed in Chapter 2, the ideology of patriarchy is the most instrumental force in the creation and acceptance of discourses about Mothers in our society. *See also* section 3 for the development of concepts of the private family, the natural family, the sexual family, and the sacred family.

4. Barbara Defoe Whitehead, "Dan Quayle Was Right," *The Atlantic Monthly* (April 1993): pp. 47, 48–49.

   In May 1992, Vice-President Dan Quayle attacked the television character Murphy Brown (played by Candice Bergen) for having a baby out of wedlock on her television show. "Hollywood thinks it's cute to glamorize illegitimacy, . . ." Quayle told reporters. "Hollywood doesn't get it." John E. Yang, Ann Devroy, "'Hollywood Doesn't Get It' Administration Struggles to Explain Attack on TV's Murphy Brown," *Washington Post* (May 21, 1992): p. A1.

   This attack opened the floodgates to the debate on "family values" later espoused by the Republican Convention and to a full-scale attack on single mothers. Numerous articles appeared in national magazines and journals, blaming single mothers for everything from drug abuse to the failure of the liberal state. Representative samples include the following:

> The core question about births to never-married women that the British (like the Americans) have to answer is how important marriage is? . . .
>
> Marriage is indispensable. When the portion of children born to single women rises above a certain point, there will be a cascading effect on crime, unemployment, and the overall civility of social interaction that will eventually make a liberal society unsustainable.

(Charles Murray, "No Point Fiddling with Welfare at the Margin," *Sunday Times,* [July 11, 1993]).

> Childbearing by unmarried women adds significantly to the costs of the nation's social and welfare programs, to the already strained budgets of state and federal governments. . . . It is a major cause of poverty, a significant reason why decades of anti-poverty programs have had only limited success. It is linked to poor health in children, beginning with the increased risk of low birth weight, and to a range of behavior and emotional problems. Children in single-parent homes have a higher risk of school problems and failure than other youngsters.
>
> Certainly the absence of strong, active caring fathers in the lives of children and in the neighborhoods where large numbers of single mothers live is a big factor in the high rates of crime, drug dealing and gang activity.

(Joan Beck, "Nation Must Stem the Tide of Births Out of Wedlock," *The Times-Picayune,* [March 6, 1993] p. B7.)

> "[There are] two different types of poverty. . . . One is material—the family has an income below the official poverty threshold."
>
> The second is "behavioral poverty, [which] includes a cluster of pathological behaviors: out-of-wedlock birth, prolonged welfare dependence, eroded work-ethic, lack of educational aspiration, criminal activity, drug and alcohol abuse, and family desertion."

(Robert S. Stein, *Investors' Business Daily,* June 24, 1993: p. 1, quoting Robert Rector, senior policy analyst with the Heritage Foundation.)

5. Ronald Angel and Jacqueline Angel, *Painful Inheritance: Health and the New Generation of Fatherless Families* (Madison: Univ. of Wisconsin Press, 1993), 104–105.

6. *Ibid.,* p. 104. For a critique of the methodology of these studies in the context of divorce *see,* Fineman, *Illusions* [chapter 2, note 8] Chapters 6 and 7.

7. *Ibid.* at 183.

8. Judith Stacey, "The New Family Values Crusaders," *The Nation,* July 25/ August 1, 1994, pp. 119, 120. Stacey also notes "these new family values warriors have already achieved astonishing influence over the Clinton Administration. It took scarcely a year to convert Clinton from a proud icon of a single mom's glory into a repentant Quayle acolyte. *Newsweek* published the President's revised family credo last December: 'Remember the Dan Quayle speech? There were a lot of very good things in that speech. . . . Would we be a better-off society if babies were born to married couples? You bet we would.' " *Ibid.,* p. 119.

9. The paternity proceeding is the legal process through which this tie is accomplished. Increased reliance on this process has been a mainstay of recent welfare reforms. It is an essential step in assuring that the family, and not the state, takes responsibility for children. *See Family Support Act* of 1988, Subtitle B, *Establishment of Paternity.*

10. *See,* Chapter 5, notes 33 and 34, *Family Support Act,* (requiring paternity proceedings for all nonmarital children of mothers receiving benefits) and *Wisconsin Stat.* 767.45 (6m) (1993) (requiring paternity proceedings for all nonmarital children regardless of whether the mother is receiving benefits).

11. Michael B. Katz, *The Undeserving Poor: From the War on Poverty to the War on Welfare* (New York: Pantheon, 1989): p. 215.

12. *Id.*

13. Katz continues, "Although the black rate remained more than five times as great as the white, adolescent pregnancy is not an issue just for blacks." (*Ibid.,* pp. 216–17)

    For a debunking of a variety of "welfare myths," *see* Marion Wright Edelman, *Families in Peril: An Agenda for Social Change* (Cambridge: Harvard Univ. Press, 1987): pp. 68–74.

14. *See, e.g.,* Sara McLanahan and Irwin Garfinkel, "Single Mothers, the Underclass, and Social Policy," 501 *Annals* 92, 94 (1989). In defining the socioeconomic classification of the "underclass," the authors assert that "weak attachment to the labor force" is one characteristic possessed by this group. The authors ultimately conclude that a small but significant percentage of single mothers (less than 5 percent) falls within their definition of underclass (a pejorative term), but only after excluding those who are single mothers as a result of the death of a spouse:

    > Disabled workers, widows, and married homemakers may be indirectly attached to the labor force either through their personal work history or through the current or past employment history of their spouse. In the case of disabled workers and widows, the primary source of household income comes from social insurance, which is linked to the past

work history of the individual and the individual's spouse, respectively. In the case of married homemakers, the primary source of income is the partner's current earnings. *Id.* at 94.

15. John D. Kassarda, "Urban Industrial Transition and the Underclass," 501 *Annals* 26, 44 (1989). In noting the worsening of the "economic and social plight" of urban blacks, Kassarda also states that "persistently poor ghetto dwellers [are] characterized by substandard education and high rates of jobless-ness, mother-only households, welfare dependency, out-of-wedlock births, and crime." *Ibid.*, p. 27. The author asserts that one reason that poor urban blacks do not succeed in starting their own businesses as other ethnic groups do is because blacks lack the strong extended families of other ethnic groups. He concluded that the black "fragmented family" cannot pool its resources for labor, childcare, and funds as can other groups with extended families. *Ibid.*, pp. 42–44.

16. *Ibid.*, p. 45.

17. In a recent issue of *Signs,* Maxine Baca Zinn asserts that there are two models that have been used to describe the urban underclass: cultural and structural. Maxine Baca Zinn, "Family, Race, and Poverty in the Eighties," 14 *Signs: J. Women, Culture & Soc'y* 856 (1989). The cultural model first gained recogni-tion with the "culture of poverty" theory popularized by Moynihan in the late 1960s. Daniel P. Moynihan, *The Negro Family: The Case for National Action,* in *Moynihan Report and the Politics of Controversy* Lee Rainwater and William L. Yancy eds. (Cambridge: M.I.T. Press, 1967): pp. 39–132. Zinn concludes that the cultural model blamed welfare for the disintegration of the family, for providing disincentives to work, and for encouraging a lifestyle in which women have children out of wedlock and depend on the system to support the children, thus allowing men to avoid financial responsibility for children.

Loäc Wacquant and William Julius Wilson distinguish their articulation of the development of the underclass from the culture of poverty reasoning. In recounting the statistical data in support of their assertion that "social condi-tions in the ghetto . . . are scaling new heights in deprivation, oppression, and hardship," they note that black communities in Chicago's South Side and West Side have experienced an increase in the number and percentage of poor families, an increase in the outmigration of working and middle-class house-holds, stagnation of income, unemployment, and that "over two-thirds of all families living in these areas were headed by women." Loäc Wacquant and William Julius Wilson, "The Cost of Racial and Class Exclusion in the Inner City," 501 *Annals* 8, 11 (1989). The thrust of their article is that the underclass is a product of the spacial concentration and isolation of the most socially excluded and economically marginal members of the dominated racial and economic group, not a new breed of individuals molded by an all-powerful culture of poverty. *Ibid.*, p. 25. The authors assert that a variety of factors—class, gender, race—contribute to the marginalization of groups who are concentrated into neighborhoods. Social, political, and economic structures are built up around these marginalized groups in such a way that they perpetuate their oppression. Female-headed households, however, although not blamed for the decline, are used as evidence that a decline has occurred.

18. *Working Seminar on Family and American Welfare Policy, the New Consensus on Family and Welfare: A Community of Self-Reliance* (Washington, DC: American Enterprise Institute for Public Policy Research, 1987): pp. 4, 5.

19. William Julius Wilson, *The Truly Disadvantaged: The Inner City, the Underclass, and Public Policy* (Chicago: Univ. of Chicago Press, 1987): pp. 104–105.

20. In a contemporaneous article summarizing the statistics of the 1980s, Myron E. Wegman noted:

> During the past decade, an increasing proportion of all births has been to unmarried women; in 1987 the birth rate to this group increased on the order of 5%. In fact, the whole increase in births and birth rates for the year is approximately equivalent to the increase to unmarried women. By contrast, both number of births and birth rates to married women were less than 1986 levels. The increase in births and birth rates among unmarried women has been relatively continuous since 1980 and the proportion has increased from less than one fifth in 1980 to nearly one quarter in 1987.

Myron Wegman, Annual Summary of Vital Statistics—1988, 84 *Pediatrics* 944–45 (1989).

Wegman's figures showed that "[d]ifference in the races continued to be great; almost one-fifth of all white births were to unmarried women, but more than three-fifths of black newborns had unmarried mothers. On the other hand, since 1980, there had been a large, 40 percent increase in the birth rate per 1000 unmarried white women age 15 to 44 years, to a level of 24.6, whereas the increase among the black population was only 2%, to 84.7 in 1987 as against 82.9 in 1980." *Ibid.*, p. 945.

The most recent census figures show a continuation of this pattern, with the largest percentage increase in never-married motherhood occurring among women with some college education. *See* Amaru Bachu, *Fertility of American Women: June 1992, Current Population Reports, U.S. Department of Commerce, Bureau of the Census.* The Bachu report reviewed the 1990 census data for women between the ages of 18 and 44 who had never been married and found that 24 percent of those women had become mothers—as opposed to 15 percent in the 1980 census. The rate of births for unmarried women who had at least one year of college increased from 5.5 percent to 11.3 percent; for women in professional or managerial positions, it rose from 7 percent to 8.3 percent.

A great deal of media attention has been devoted to this development. *See, e.g.,* Joan Beck [chapter 5, note 2]; Jason DeParle, "Big Rise in Births Outside Wedlock" (*New York Times,* July 14, 1993): p. A1; Richard Whitmire, "Number of Never-Married Moms Stretches Across Income Lines" (*Gannett-News Service,* July 13, 1993); Richard Cohen, "Judging Single Mothers" (*Washington Post,* July 16, 1993): p. A19; Katha Pollitt, "Bothered and Bewildered" (*New York Times,* July 22, 1993): p. A23; and "Single But Mothers by Choice," a combined article about middle-/upper-class single mothers by Carol Lawson, "'Who Is My Daddy?' Can Be Answered In Different Ways," and Anne Lamott, "When Going It Alone Turns Out to Be Not So Alone at All" (*New York Times,* Aug. 5, 1993): pp. C1, C10.

21. *Family Support Act* of 1988, Pub L. No. 100–485, 102 Stat. 2343 (codified in scattered sections of 42 U.S.C.).

22. The Job Opportunities and Basic Skills Training Program component in Title II, 42 U.S.C. §602 (hereinafter JOBS program), of the reform legislation represents the latest instance in the long history of welfare to promote work and discourage welfare dependency among the poor. The term "workfare" is generally reserved for the requirement that recipients work for their benefits, usually by accepting some form of community work assignment. *See* Lawrence M. Mead, "The Logic of Workfare: The Underclass and Work Policy," 501 *Annals of the American Academy of Political and Social Science* 156 (1989).

23. WIN, Title IV, Parts A & C of *SOCIAL SECURITY ACT* of 1967, 42 U.S.C. §602 (1967).

24. *See* Judith Gueron, Reforming Welfare With Work (1987) (occasional paper Number Two, Ford Foundation Project on Social Welfare and the American Future); Lawrence M. Mead, *Beyond Entitlement: The Social Obligations of Citizenship* (New York: Free Press, 1986); Lawrence M. Mead, "The Potential for Work Enforcement: A Study of WIN," 7 *Journal of Policy Analysis and Management* 264 (1988); Michael Wiseman, "Workfare and Welfare Policy," 9 *Focus* #3, 1 (1986).

25. Mead [chapter 5, note 24] p. 164.

26. *See* Christopher Jencks and Kathryn Edin, "The Real Welfare Problem," 1 *American Prospect* 31 (1990).

27. *Ibid.,* pp. 43–45.

28. *See, e.g.,* "Welfare, Reform or Replacement? (Child Support Enforcement—II): Hearing Before the Subcomm. on Social Security and Family Policy of the

Senate Comm. on Finance," 100th Cong., 1st Sess. (1987) (statement of Irwin Garfinkel, professor at the University of Wisconsin).

29. *See, e.g.,* Mimi Abramovitz, "Social Disservice: Why Welfare Reform is a Sham" (*The Nation,* V. 247, Sept. 26, 1988): p. 221 (officials running the workfare program in California [the GAIN program] calculated that graduates needed a minimum of $11.00 per hour to stay off the welfare rolls—yet graduates averaged only $6.50 an hour); Joan Walsh, "Take This Job or Shove It" (*Mother Jones,* September 1988): p. 30, 32 (noting that a 1986 study found that low wages pushed 43 percent of educational training graduates back onto welfare, so program officials imposed a wage floor requiring that training contractors place women in jobs paying at least $6.00 an hour).

30. *See, e.g., Cal. Civ. Code, Welfare and Institutions* §11310(b)(6)9A)(1985) (persons caring for child under the age of three were exempt from participation in Greater Avenues for Independent Action [GAIN]). The current law provides that this exemption shall be applicable only once during any period of continuous eligibility. If subsequent children are born, the recipient will be exempt from participation only for four months after the birth or adoption of the child. *Cal. Civ. Code, Welfare and Institutions* §11310(b)(5)(A)(1993).

31. *Fl. Stat.* §409.029 (8)(a) & (b) (1993).

32. Created by Chapter 93–136 *Laws of Florida,* codified at *Fl. Stat.* §409.924 *et seq.* establishes demonstration districts to move AFDC recipients into jobs and off the welfare rolls.

33. In addition to requiring custodial parents to work, the law provides that absent parents can be required to participate in training or work for up to forty hours per week. *See* chapter 93–136 *Laws of Florida,* Section 11.

34. *So. Dak. Stat.* §25–7–51 (1993).

35. *Wis. Stat.* §49.50(7)(a) 4(am)(1993).

36. *Ibid.* at 7(f). Wisconsin, Florida, Colorado, Iowa, and Vermont have received federal waivers from the Department of Health and Human Services to cut off AFDC benefits after a set period. New Jersey's family cap program has also been approved. *See* Baker [chapter 3, note 5]. *See also* Jason DeParle, "States' Eagerness to Experiment on Welfare Jars Administration" (*New York Times,* April 14, 1994): p. A1 (discussing concern that states may be going too far with their reforms. "Do the programs represent responsible social science or a backdoor war on the poor?")

37. *Wis. Stat.* §49.50(7)(g) and (h) (1993); Chapter 93–136 *Laws of Florida,* Section 13. These programs can be problematic. A 1990 audit of the Wisconsin learnfare program found that 84 percent of the orders imposing sanctions were overturned by an administrative judge "because of errors in record-keeping

by either the schools or the welfare agency." Paul Taylor, "Welfare Policy's 'New Paternalism' Uses Benefits to Alter Recipients' Behavior" (*Washington Post,* June, 8, 1991): p. A3.

38. These proposals are "innovations" offered in the context of a history that shows similar proposals have failed. As required by the Family Support Act of 1988, Florida, like most states, already has a JOBS program in place, which serves 21 percent of the state's AFDC population. From fiscal year 1987–88 to fiscal year 1991–92, the program placed an average of 25,000 recipients per year. (In November 1992, there were 252,276 families and 684,088 individuals receiving AFDC in Florida, and 7,150 families and 27,966 individuals receiving AFDC-Unemployed benefits.) "Approximately 67% of the participants [were] still on the job 90 days after placement. . . . Limited funds prevent full implementation of Project Independence. Lack of case management and support services (child care) prohibit participants from engaging in education and training activities that lead to employment." *See* Committee Report on Chapter 93–136 *Laws of Florida,* at 3. Considering the current state of the economy and the trend toward lower taxes, one is forced to wonder how much better funded or how successful the new programs are going to be. Estimated figures for Clinton's welfare reform are $1 billion in 1996, $6 billion in 1999, and nearly $15 billion over the five year period from 1994 to 1999. Child care for the working poor will cost $5 billion over those same five years, and child care and other services for those in transition from welfare to work will cost nearly $8 billion. *See* William Claiborne, "Clinton Gets Panel Report on Welfare; Detailed Plan Leaves Funding Unspecified," *Washington Post,* March 23, 1994, p. A13. How much are we really willing to spend? *See also* Stanford F. Schram, "Finding New Ways to Blame the Poor," *Star Tribune* (MS), March 14, 1994, p. 13A, reviewing studies of earlier welfare reform efforts.

39. *Family Support Act* 1988, Title I—*Child Support and Establishment of Paternity,* Pub. L. No. 100–485, 102 Stat. 2343, 2344. Subtitle A, entitled *Child Support,* provides in section 101 that the wages of an absent parent are subject to withholding in enforcing payment of child-support orders and that the Secretary of Health and Human Services will conduct a study to determine the feasibility of requiring immediate income withholding of all child-support awards in a state. Exceptions are allowed where both parties agree to other arrangements or one party shows good cause why income should not be withheld. *Ibid.* at 2344–46. Section 102 provides that the first $50.00 of each child-support payment to a family receiving public assistance will not be counted against their entitlement, even if that payment is made more than once in a single month, e.g., payments made for prior months. *Ibid.* at 2346. Section 103 requires that the state establish support payment guidelines and provides for a judicial "rebuttable presumption" that such guidelines are cor-

rect. This presumption may be overcome by showing that enforcement of such standards would be "unjust or inappropriate in a particular case." *Id.*

Subtitle C, entitled *Improved Procedures for Child Support Enforcement and Establishment of Paternity,* provides various standards for state support programs, *id.* at 2351, including that states establish time limits for responding to requests for investigations and for when payments of support money collected by the state must be made. The Act also requires that states set up an automated data-processing and information-retrieval system or an equivalent alternative system. Section 125 states that "each State shall require each parent to furnish to such state . . . the social security account number . . . issued to the parent unless the State (in accordance with regulations prescribed by the Secretary) finds good cause for not requiring the furnishing of such number." *Ibid.* at 2353–54. Section 126 establishes a Commission on Interstate Child Support to make recommendations to Congress to improve interstate child support and to hold at least one conference on the issue to assist in formulating these recommendations. *Ibid.* at 2354–55. Section 128 requires that the Secretary of Health and Human Services "conduct a study of the patterns of expenditures on children in 2-parent families, in single-parent families following divorce or separation, and in single-parent families in which the parents were never married, giving particular attention to relative standards of living in households in which both parents and all of the children do not live together." *Ibid.* at 2356. The Secretary also is required to submit policy recommendations based on this study.

40. *Id.* Subtitle B—*Establishment of Paternity.* Section 111 imposes standards of state compliance requiring that as of 1991 each state's "paternity establishment percentage for such fiscal year equals or exceeds" a requisite amount. *Id.* at 2348. The "paternity establishment percentage" is the ratio of the total number of children born out of wedlock who receive some form of public assistance and for whom paternity has been established, to the total number of children born out of wedlock who receive some sort of public assistance. This section also requires that the child and all other parties in contested paternity cases submit to genetic tests, except where good cause has been shown that this is not in the best interest of the child. Those who do not receive AFDC may be charged for such tests. The statute encourages the states to adopt simple civil procedures for voluntary acknowledgement of paternity and for establishing paternity in civil cases.

41. Family Support Act, Part A—*Aid to Families with Dependent Children,* 42 U.S.C. §602. The "UP" refers to unemployed parent. In enacting this requirement into state law, the Louisiana Legislature expressed its intent thus:

Section 3. The legislature finds that, effective October 1, 1990, Louisiana will be required to provide welfare to two parent families under the federal

Family Support Act of 1988, including families in which the parents are not married. The legislature finds that couples who do not at least show a commitment to their needy children through marriage, should not be eligible for government cash assistance. The legislature finds that the AFDC eligibility requirements for this program should reflect such basic societal values and should not promote illegitimacy. (LSA-R.S. 46–238).

42. 136 *Cong. Rec.* S14416, S14417 (daily ed. October 3, 1990) (statement of Senator Moynihan).

43. *Id.* at 14418 (quoting Karl Zinmeister, "Raising Hiroko," *Am. Enterprise*, March–April 1990: pp. 52, 53). For similar analyses, *see Senator Moynihan Discusses Children in Poverty*, 134 *Cong. Rec.* S16919 (daily ed. October 19, 1988) (statement of Sen. Glenn, introducing to the record an article by Sen. Moynihan); *The Family Security Act*, 134 *Cong. Rec.* S7730 (daily ed. June 14, 1988) (statement of Sen. Specter); *The Need for Cooperation on Welfare Reform*, 134 *Cong. Rec.* S4712 (daily ed. April 26, 1988) (statement of Sen. Cochran); *Welfare Reform—The Need to Attack Family Dependency*, 134 *Cong. Rec.* S3069 (daily ed. March 25, 1988) (statement of Sen. Cochran).

44. *See generally* Marthan L. Fineman, "Images of Mothers in Poverty Discourses," *Duke Law Journal* 274 (1991); Thomas Ross, "The Rhetoric of Poverty: Their Immorality, Our Helplessness," 79 *Georgetown Law Journal* 1499 (1991); Lucy A. Williams, "The Ideology of Division: Behavior Modification Welfare Reform Proposals," 102 *Yale Law Journal* 719 (1992); and Evelyn Z. Brodkin, "The Making of the Enemy: How Welfare Policies Construct the Poor," 18 *Law & Social Inquiry* 647 (1993), reviewing Joel F. Handler and Yeheskel Hasenfeld, *The Moral Construction of Poverty: Welfare Reform in America* (Newbury Park, CA: Sage, 1991).

45. Charles Murray, "The Coming White Underclass," *Wall Street Journal* (October 29, 1993), p. A14.

46. *Ibid.*

47. *Ibid.*

48. In *The Republican Platform*, 1992, the Republican Party expressed a belief "in the value of every human being from the very young to the very old." *Ibid.* p. 2. It touted the traditional family, in which parents would teach their children "the importance of honesty, work, responsibility, and respect for others . . . built on solid spiritual foundations." *Ibid.* p. 3. The Party wanted to protect "family formed by blood, marriage, adoption, or legal custody" (*Ibid.*, p. 4), from governmental intrusion; and deplored Democratic attempts "to redefine the traditional family." *Id.* It promised to "promote whole, caring families" (*Ibid.*, p. 5), by changing the tax code, reforming the foster-care

system, and by "[urging] State legislatures to explore ways to promote marital stability." *Id.*

49. March 11, 1994, p. A24. *See also* William J. Bennett, "The Best Welfare Reform: End It," *Washington Post* (March 30, 1994): p. A19, replying to that editorial: "American society cannot withstand this much longer. The evidence is in: illegitimacy is the surest road to social decay and poverty. The 1991 median family income for two-parent families was $40,137. For divorced mothers, it was $16,156, and for never-married mothers $8,758. Welfare subsidizes and sustains illegitimacy. The most humane policy is to end it for those who have children out of wedlock."

50. These welfare "reforms" are designed to change the behavior of recipients. *See* chapter 5, note 44.

51. *See* Judy Mann, "Punishment is not a Contraceptive," *Washington Post* (March 2, 1994): p. E15. Mann discusses these "family caps" and then tells us: "States with the highest birth rates for 18–19-year-old mothers have benefits below the national median, while those that boast the lower birth rates for that age group have benefits above the national median." This suggests that higher grant amounts do not correlate with higher birth rate.

52. Graciela Sevilla, "NAACP for Welfare Overhaul: Bid to Tighten Rules Gets Surprise Support," *Washington Post* (March 6, 1994): p. B1. For other articles illustrating the popular view of the problem, *see* Jason DeParle, "Clinton Target: Teen-Age-Pregnancy," *New York Times* (March 22, 1994): p. B6; William Raspberry, "Out of Wedlock, Out of Luck," *Washington Post* (February 25, 1994): p. 21; and Edward Walsh, "As At-Risk Children Overwhelm Foster Care, Illinois Considers Orphanages," *Washington Post* (March 1, 1994): p. A9. For contrary views, *see* Alexander Cockburn, "Beat the Devil, Clinton and Teen Sex," *The Nation* (1994): p. 259; Stephanie Mencimer, "The Welfare Mommy Trap: Want the Poor to Have Fewer Kids? Fund Abortions," *Washington Post* (January 9, 1994): p. C1; and James P. Donahue, "The Fat Cat Freeloaders: When American Big Business Bellys Up to the Public Trough" *Washington Post* (March 6, 1994): p. C1. Donahue points out that taxpayers, through the federal government, will spend "$51 billion in direct subsidies to business and lose another $53.3 billion in tax breaks for corporations" compared to "$25 billion for food stamps and $15 billion for AFDC."

53. Cockburn [chapter 5, note 52].

54. Abigail Trafford, "Unwed Motherhood—Insights from the Colonial Era," *Washington Post* (January 8, 1991): p. Z6, writing about Laurel Thatcher Ulrich's *A Midwife's Tale—The Life of Martha Ballard, Based on Her Diary, 1785–1812.*

55. In his analysis of the concept of the "underclass" that developed in the mid-1980s and the imagery that this new category evoked about the poor, Michael Katz states:

> The very poor evoked two different images among affluent Americans. When they appeared pathetic, they were the homeless; when they seemed menacing, they became the underclass. Although membership among the homeless and underclass overlapped, public discourse implicitly divided them by degree of personal responsibility for their situation. As long as they remained supplicants rather than militants, objects of charity rather than subjects of protest, the homeless became the new deserving poor. (Katz [chapter 5, note 11] pp. 185–86).

56. 134 *Cong. Rec.* S14250, (June 13, 1988) (statement of Sen. Moynihan). He questioned why this situation developed and answered himself: "Very simply it came about because the welfare program has become stigmatized as a program for people who did not work in a world where others did." *Id.* Although he recognizes this as a stigma, he concluded that "[it] also reflects a certain reality," and argued that to change the public's unwillingness to adequately fund these programs would require the adoption of a program that is primarily a jobs system with supplemental income assistance. *Id.*

57. *See* two articles by Dorothy Roberts: "Punishing Drug Addicts Who Have Babies, Women of Color, Equality, and the Right of Privacy," 104 *Harvard Law Review* 1419 (1991); and "Racism and Patriarchy in the Meaning of Motherhood," 1 *American University Journal of Gender and the Law* 1 (1993).

58. Stuart M. Butler and Anna Kondratas, *Out of the Poverty Trap: A Conservative Strategy for Welfare Reform* (New York: Free Press, 1987): pp. 138–39.

59. The argument that divorced mothers are also "worthy" is based on recent changes in the norms concerning marital dissolution. These changes are epitomized by the advent of no-fault divorce, a legal reform built upon the popular perception that the failure of a marriage is a joint responsibility. Divorce reform has generated its own system of "pathology," however. Although the insistence that there be a designated villain and victim between the spouses may have declined, children are portrayed as innocent victims of divorce—of their parents' selfishness and hostility during divorce—and worthy mothers suppress all their own needs and desires in the interests of children and a newly crafted stable post-divorce nuclear family.

    The villain and victim imagery continues to exist in divorce discourses, but it is not directed at the decision to divorce. For example, the contemporary divorce discourse of the helping professionals often casts mother with custody as a villain who wrongfully interferes with her ex-husband's relationship with his child (both of whom are cast as victims). For a fuller exposition of this rhetoric, *see* Martha Fineman, "Dominant Discourse, Professional Language, and Legal Change in Child Custody Decisionmaking," 101 *Harvard Law Review* 727 (1988).

60. This distinction between categories of poor seems inevitable. As Paula Roberts and Rhonda Schulzinger noted, the principles established through the legacy of the English poor laws affected American thinking:

> First, the poor could be divided into two categories. The "worthy poor" were impoverished through no fault of their own (e.g., the sick and the aged) or because they could not find work. "Paupers," on the other hand, were those who refused to work. Paupers represented a moral pestilence and had to be controlled, put in the poor house, and made to work.

Paula Roberts and Rhonda Schulzinger, "Toward Reform of the Welfare System: Is Consensus Emerging?" 21 *Clearinghouse Review* 3 (1987).

61. 133 *Cong. Rec.* H11515 (daily ed. December 16, 1987) (statement of Rep. Roukema).

62. *Ibid.*, p. 11516.

63. Some of the recent welfare reforms are attempts to remedy this by providing incentives to single mothers receiving AFDC to get married. For example, the Family Transition Program in Florida disregards the income of a stepparent whose needs are not included in the AFDC grant, and expands the benefits for two-parent families. This could substantially increase the family income of a mother who is receiving AFDC. Other states including New Jersey and Wisconsin, have enacted these so-called "Bridefare" provisions. *See* Schram [chapter 5, note 38].

64. I explore this phenomenon fully in Fineman, *Illusion* [chapter 2, note 8].

65. Some states have enacted so-called friendly parent provisions. *See, e.g.,* Cal. Civ. Code §4600(b)(I) (West 1993); *COLO. REV. STAT.* §14-10-124(I-5)(f) (1993); *FLA. STAT.* §61.13 (3)(a) (1993); *ME. REV. STAT. ANN.* tit. 19, §752.5H (1993); *MICH. COMP. LAWS. ANN.* §722.23(j) (1993).

66. *See* Lenore J. Weitzman, *The Divorce Revolution: The Unexpected Social and Economic Consequences for Women and Children in America* (New York: Free Press, 1985): pp. 283–307; Nina J. Easton, "Life Without Father: As More and More American Men Disconnect From Family Life, Society Suffers the Consequences," *Los Angeles Times Magazine,* June 14, 1992, at 14. Fathers generally are less consistent with visitation as well. According to a study done by Eleanore E. Maccoby and Robert H. Mnookin, children who reside with their mothers see their fathers less as time passes. Children who reside with their fathers see their mothers more. Eleanore E. Maccoby and Robert H.

Mnookin, *Dividing the Child: Social and Legal Dilemmas of Custody* (Cambridge: Harvard Univ. Press, 1992): pp. 197–98.

67. *See generally* Karen Czapanskiy, "Volunteers and Draftees: The Struggle for Parental Equality," 38 *U.C.L.A. Law Review* 1415 (1991).

68. *See* David Miller, "Joint Custody," 13 *Family Law Quarterly* 345 (1979).

> Most supporters of joint custody contend that it significantly improves parental cooperation. The need to reach an agreement on all major child rearing decisions, combined with equalized parental power, fosters an atmosphere of detente rather than hostility. . . . (364)
>
> Joint custody is said to reinforce and facilitate several modern social trends. It is consistent with the movement for sexual equality and its many corollaries, such as the right of the individual to determine his or her own lifestyle. . . . Increasingly, fathers are sharing child rearing and nurturing responsibilities. All of these developments are perfectly conducive to joint custody arrangements in the event of divorce. . . . (365)
>
> There is also evidence that joint legal custody makes default on child support payments less likely. Several practitioners believe that the involvement in family affairs due to joint custody results in fathers paying child support more readily. (*Ibid.*)

69. Richard A. Gardner, "Differentiating Between Bona Fide and Fabricated Allegations of Sexual Abuse of Children," 5 *Journal of the American Academy of Matrimonial Lawyers* 1, 11, 17, 20 (1989). In the article he cites his previous work, Richard Gardner, *The Parental Alienation Syndrome and the Differentiation Between Fabricated and Genuine Child Sex Abuse* (Cresskill, NJ: Creative Therapeutics, 1987)

70. *Ibid.*, p. 17.

71. *Ibid.*, p. 18.

72. Gardner also notes a defining characteristic of "fathers who have abused their children" is a reluctance to accept impartial evaluation. *Ibid.*, p. 21.

73. *Ibid.*, pp. 17–18.

74. *See* Mahoney [chapter 3, note 18] (discussing the difficulties associated with leaving battering situations).

75. Sandra Joan Morris, "Sexually Abused Children of Divorce," 4 *Journal of the American Academy of Matrimonial Lawyers* 27 (1989).

76. *Ibid.*, p. 28.

77. *Ibid.*, pp. 30–31.

78. "The mothers of children who have been involved in incestuous relationships with the father are more likely to be passive, incapacitated, disabled. . . . In contrast, the mothers of fabricating youngsters are more likely to be aggressive and outspoken." Gardner [chapter 5 note 69] at p. 19.

79. *See* Isabela M. C. Araujo, "Munchausen Syndrome by Proxy (or the Making of Monster Mommies)" (1993) (manuscript on file with the author. Araujo reviews three depictions of this syndrome: Jonathan Kellerman, *Devil's Waltz* (New York: Bantam, 1993); the April 8, 1993, *Larry King* show on CNN; and Allen J. Palemer, M.D., and G. Joji Yoshimura, M.S., "Munchausen Syndrome by Proxy," *Journal of the American Academy of Child Psychiatry*. Araujo notes that although this syndrome occurs in both men and women, these sources "pervasively" focus on mothers: "The criminal profile: model mommy, often charming and personable, with a background in medicine or a paramedical field." *Id.* quoting at 6, from *Devil's Waltz*. For cases discussing this syndrome, *see In the interest of M.A.V., a child*, 425 S.C. 2d377 (Ga. App. 1992); *Matter of Jordon*, 616 N.E.2d 388 (Ind. App. 1993); *State v. Lumbrera*, 845 P.2d 609 (Kan. 1992).

80. *Id.*

81. *Ibid.*, p. 3.

82. *Ibid.*, p. 5, quoting Dr. Schreier from the *Larry King Show*.

83. *Ibid.*, p. 9.

84. *Ibid.*, quoting *Devil's Waltz* [chapter 5, note 79]. *See also*, "Decades Later, Mother Held in Children's Deaths," *New York Times*, March 25, 1994, p. B2, detailing story of mother who killed her children being described as "an extreme case of Munchausen's syndrome by proxy," and follow-up, Lindsey Gruson, "A 25-Year Trail to 5 Murder Charges," *New York Times* (March 29, 1994): pp. B1, B2.

85. Araujo [chapter 5, note 79] pp. 5–6.

86. In one article that might have predictive potential of the shape and direction of President Clinton's promised welfare reforms Donna Shalala—then Chancellor of the University of Wisconsin at Madison, now Secretary of Health and Human Services—was reported as stating that unwed teen pregnancy is "an issue that threatens the future of Milwaukee and is as dangerous and crippling to young lives as polio." Describing the enormity of the problem as "frightening," Shalala warned that "the stakes are very high. The stakes are our future, not only in Milwaukee, but our future as a state." "Teen Pregnancy Called Issue That Threatens State," *Milwaukee Sentinel* (May 1, 1990): p. 1.

87. Joanne Jacobs, "Illegitimacy Biggest Killer of Our Babies," *Wisconsin State Journal* (Feb. 9, 1990): p. 11A, col. 6.

88. *Id.*

89. *Id.*

90. *Id.*

91. *Id.*

92. *See* Emily Campbell, "Birth Control as a Condition of Probation for Those Convicted of Child Abuse," 28 *Gonzaga Law Review* 67, 81, 82 (1992). Accurate statistics on the incidence of child abuse are extremely hard to find. It is even more difficult to know who is responsible. *See, e.g.,* Ellen Creager, "Child Abuse Strikes Every Sort of Family," *Detroit Free Press* (March 13, 1994): p. 4J, in which Creager notes that statistics from the National Committee to Prevent Child Abuse are "appallingly incomplete." These statistics demonstrate that "23 percent of child abuse is committed by [a] 'parent (or) substitute living in the home,' 8 percent by a 'paramour,' with nearly 70 percent of perpetrators unknown or unspecified. Michigan's 1992–93 stats [sic] show 81 percent of abuse committed by a parent in the home and 5 percent by a stepparent, boyfriend or girlfriend." The statistics do not distinguish between sexual abuse and other physical abuse. *See also* Deborah Rissing Baurac, "Programs Try to Help Parents Keep Their Cool," *Chicago Tribune*, May 16, 1993, *Womanews* 1, who notes that because reporting methods are not uniform from state to state, data on how many parents deliberately harm or kill their children are unavailable.

93. Campbell [chapter 5 note 92] p. 80 (focusing on women, while noting one case in which a man was required not to father additional children, *Howland v. State,* 420 So. 2d. 918 (Fla. Dist. Ct. App. 1982)). Interestingly, when there is a finding of abusive motherhood, one "innovative" punishment fashioned by judges is requiring single mothers to use birth control, including the implantation of Norplant so they will not become mothers again. For a discussion of cases in which the judge ordered defendants either to use contraception or not to get pregnant (obviously women), *see* Stacey L. Arthur, "The Norplant Prescription: Birth Control, Woman Control, or Crime Control," 40 *U.C.L.A. Law Review* 1, 24 (1993). *See also* Roberts [chapter 5, note 57]; Dorothy E. Roberts, "Motherhood and Crime," 79 *Iowa Law Review* (1994): p. 1.

    Furthermore, it is more than a little ironic that mothers are being held responsible for the rise in child abuse committed by men. The notion of "derivative abuse" explains why mothers are blamed when the abuse comes from another source.

94. *Ibid.,* p. 81.

95. *Ibid.,* p. 85.

96. Marie Ashe, "The 'Bad Mother' in Law and Literature: A Problem of Representation," 43 *Hastings Law Journal* 1017, 1019 (1992); Marie Ashe and Naomi

R. Cahn, "Child Abuse, A Problem for Feminist Theory," 2 *Texas Journal of Women and Law* 75 (1993).

97. Ashe, *The "Bad Mother"* [chapter 5, note 96].

98. *Ibid.*, p. 1021. *See also* Carol Sanger, "Seasoned to Its Use," 87 *Michigan Law Review* 1338, reviewing Scott Turow, *Presumed Innocent* (New York, Farrar, Straus, Giroux, 1987), and Sue Miller, *The Good Mother* (New York: Harper & Row, 1986), in which she discusses the perception that a sexual mother is a bad mother, and the conflict between the erotic and the maternal.

99. *See* text accompanying Chapter 5, notes 42 and 43 (statement of Sen. Moynihan).

100. Irwin Garfinkel, "The Role of Child Support in Antipoverty Policy" 12 (1982) (Institute for Research on Poverty, Discussion paper, #713–82) (on file with author).

101. *Id.* It seems incongruous that Garfinkel uses the married mother who becomes single as a result of misbehavior by her husband in this example, given that he subsequently condones measures designed to lessen "incentives" for single parenthood. Incentives in this context are best understood as economic subsidies, widely believed to provide the impetus for leaving marriage or never marrying in the first place.

102. *Id.*

103. *See, e.g.,* Peter Passell, "Economic Watch: Forces in Society, and Reaganism, Helped Dig Deeper Hole for the Poor," *New York Times* (July 16, 1989): p. 1A. The article reports the release of a document from the House Ways and Means Committee that shows a decrease in income for the poorest one-fifth of Americans and an increase in income for the wealthiest one-fifth between 1979 and 1987, and asks: "Why is the gap widening?" The author responds:

> Frank Levy, a professor at the University of Maryland, cites the growth of households headed by single parents who lack the skills and motivation to earn a decent living. The figures bear him out: from 1979 to 1987 the number of single parent families living below the poverty level rose by 46%. p. 20.

Ibid. at 20. The article proceeds to cite several other factors, such as the increasing number of women competing for jobs in the work force, foreign competition, and changes in tax laws. However, it is significant that the immediate response was to look to the increase in single motherhood as responsible for the increase in poverty.

104. The preeminence of the demographic category over material and structural circumstances, even when both factors are considered significant, is evident in the work of Renee Monson and Sara Mclanahan. "Most analysts agree that

the proximate causes of poverty in mother-only families are: (1) the low earning capacity of single mothers; (2) the lack of child support from non-resident fathers; and (3) the paucity of public benefits." Renee Monson & Sara McLanahan, *A Father for Every Child: Dilemmas of Creating Gender Equality in a Stratified Society*" (unpublished paper) (available from author). Nonetheless, as they uncritically note: "The Family Support Act of 1988 attempts to redress [the first two] of these cases." *Id.* The authors identify as "a major weak link in the current child support system [the] failure to establish paternity for children born to never-married mothers." *Id.* The Act attempts to remedy this by "requiring states to (1) increase the proportion of AFDC cases with child support awards; (2) obtain social security numbers from both parents in conjunction with the issuance of birth certificates; and (3) require all parties in contested paternity cases to take a genetic test." *Id.* The Act also urges states to simplify civil paternity proceedings and gives incentives for states to set up programs to track down out-of-state fathers.

Feminist critiques in this area are often poorly received. Monson and McLanahan complain, for example, that instead of supporting new child-support legislation as "creating a partnership between the family and the state that would help ensure the adequate care of children," feminists have objected to the new law as an intrusion "on women's privacy and sexual freedom." *Ibid.,* p. 7.

PART 3

The Sexual Family

THIS SECTION IS RELATED to the two preceding chapters and describes aspects of what I refer to as the sexual family. Attention to the ideological role of the family is central to the reconsideration of motherhood, which is defined and practiced in the context of this family. Transformation of the concept of motherhood has been, and continues to be, impeded by our idealized notions about the nuclear family and our societal belief in the inevitability and desirability of its form.

The sexual family is the traditional or nuclear family, a unit with a heterosexual, formally celebrated union at its core. I use the term "sexual" to modify "family" to emphasize that our societal and legal images and expectations of family are tenaciously organized around a sexual affiliation between a man and woman. This is the primary intimate connection. Of course, it reflects the reproductive imperative, but this basic biological fact also has important ideological ramifications. The sexual family is considered the "natural" form for the social and cultural organization of intimacy, its form ordained by divine prescription and perpetuated by opinion polls. The sexual family is an entity entitled to protection—granted "privacy" or immunity from substantial state supervision.

Historically, in order to qualify as the foundational family relationship, a heterosexual union had to be legally privileged through marriage. There is a great deal of current agitation to eliminate this formality. "Liberals" seek to expand the traditional nuclear-family model, urging the recognition of informal heterosexual unions within the definition of family. There are also calls for acceptance and legal legitimation of same-sex relationships in the form of proposed domestic partnership laws.

But these reforms merely reinforce the idea of the sexual family. By duplicating the privileged form, alternative relationships merely affirm the centrality of sexuality to the fundamental ordering of society and the nature of intimacy. The nexus or affiliating circumstances of these "alternatives," although not the traditional "conjugal family," is still the sexual connection. The adult sexual affiliation remains central; indeed, its very existence is the basis for arguing that these nontraditional unions should be included within the formal legal category of family. By analogy, these nontraditional unions are equated with the paradigmatic relationship of heterosexual marriage.

Formal, legal, heterosexual marriage continues to dominate our imagination when we confront the possibilities of intimacy and family. This domination is evident in the language we use to describe the end of the relationship through divorce, when we speak of the "broken" family. It is also evident in the way we characterize the growth of unwed mother-child units as constituting a threat to the family.

Chapter 6 addresses the construction of the concept of the sexual family both outside of and inside law. In drawing conclusions about society, human nature, and the interests to be expressed in law, lawmakers reference information produced and framed by specific disciplines and methodologies such as science, history, religion, logic, philosophy, and sociology. They may also just derive answers from their own past experiences and present intuitions. All methods for production of knowledge produce some controversial conclusions and quite often there is conflicting, unclear, or dubious information about any specific "fact" or conclusion.

Often choices must be made from among competing assertions or interpretations as amorphous social and cultural concerns and areas of real and potential conflict are reduced to law. Shared beliefs, social and cultural "metanarratives," shaped in accordance with dominant ideology, influence what is chosen from among competing and contradictory facts and conclusions. The law that is built around such choices, more than being just another specific articulation of societal interest, operates as a potentially coercive or punitive force in the lives of people whose circumstances or preferences do not conform to the norms.

The reflection of the sexual family that is ensconced in law may be a distortion or a mere fragment of social reality, but that legal image constitutes the legal reality and forms the basis for state regulation. Because this legally constructed image expresses a vision of the appropriately constituted family, it defines the normal and designates the deviant. As discussed in chapter 7, the characterization of some family groupings as deviant legitimates state intervention and the regulation of relationships well beyond what would be socially tolerated if directed at more traditional family forms.

6

The Sexual Family

IN THIS CHAPTER, I want to elaborate on some of the core assumptions inherent in our current social and cultural narratives about the family as an institution. These assumptions have tremendous significance in the political and legal definition of the family and, hence, for the fate of mothers. The legal story is that the family has a "natural" form based on the sexual affiliation of a man and woman. The assumption that there is a sexual-natural family is complexly and intricately implicated in discourses other than law, of course. The natural family populates professional and religious texts and defines what is to be considered both ideal and sacred. The pervasiveness of the sexual-family-as-natural imagery qualifies it as a "metanarrative"—a narrative transcending disciplines and crossing social divisions to define and direct discourses. The shared assumption is that the appropriate family is founded on the heterosexual couple—a reproductive, biological pairing that is designated as divinely ordained in religion, crucial in social policy, and a normative imperative in ideology.[1]

I. Structuring Intimacy

The dominant components of the metanarrative—that the family is sexual—mean that the family is experienced as an institution of primarily "horizontal" intimacy, founded on the romantic sexual affiliation between one man and one woman. Intergenerational relationships—vertical lines of intimacy—may be temporarily accommodated, such as when children are "underage," or uncomfortably maintained, such as when an ill, elderly parent has to be fitted into the sexual family. The dominant paradigm, however, privileges the couple as foundational and fundamental. Children achieve adulthood and go on to form their own discrete, primary, horizontal and sexual connections, drawing boundaries between this new unit and their childhood families. Parents are shipped to nursing homes or eventually die, and the sexual family reverts to its natural state.[2]

The image of horizontally organized intimacy is a crucial component of contemporary patriarchal ideology in that it ensures that men are perceived as central to the family. Politicians, as well as religious leaders, extol the marriage relationship as sanctified, the core of the family. Alternatives to the nuclear family are cast as threatening and dangerous to society, destructive to cherished values. This view was explicitly and forcefully expressed in a speech by California Governor Pete Wilson. Speaking over a chorus of chants protesting his veto of a bill outlawing employment discrimination against homosexuals, the Governor made a plea for a return to the values more common in the 1950s—a time he characterized as when the family was cherished as a "sacred union born from romantic love" and "hard work was rewarded."[3]

In addition, marriage is constructed as essential, not only the foundational relationship of the nuclear family but the very basis of society itself. As Chief Justice Waite wrote over a hundred years ago in a case condemning plural marriage:

> Marriage, which from its very nature is a sacred obligation, is . . . a civil contract, and usually regulated by law. Upon [marriage] society may be said to be built, and out of its fruits spring social relations and social obligations and duties, with which government is necessarily required to deal.[4]

As this quote illustrates, in our society, marriage has historically been so venerated as to become a "sacred" institution, the archetype of legitimate intimacy.[5] In popular culture, sexual expression (particularly heterosexual expression as traditionally realized through marriage) is portrayed as the indication of maturity, completeness, success, and power. Historically, deviance from the formal heterosexual paradigm of marriage has brought with it condemnation in the discourses of psychology, social work, and medicine. In law, marriage traditionally has been designated as the only legitimate sexual relationship.

States have punished extramarital sexual relationships through laws making cohabitation, fornication, and adultery criminal.[6] Contemporary laws and prosecution policies in some states continue to treat these configurations as illegal or extralegal and, therefore, deserving of criminal and/ or civil sanction.[7] The nuclear family remains the only form universally protected and promoted by our legal institutions.[8]

However, the law has been altered somewhat in response to changing patterns of behavior, offering at least the promise of a more relaxed and expandable legal model of the family. Nonmarital sexual behavior has been decriminalized in many states in recent years.[9] So-called "alternative" family arrangements have even been afforded some specific affirmative protections in the few municipalities and several states that recognize them as having quasi-family status for some limited purposes.[10]

These legal changes reflect and reinforce challenges to the hegemony of the nuclear family and are part of an "evolutionary dialogue" associated with cultural negotiation. The social changes upon which they are based have not proved to be revolutionary, however. To a large extent, the new visions of the family merely reformulate basic assumptions about the nature of intimacy. They reflect the dyadic nature of the old (sexual) family story, updating and modifying it to accommodate new family "alternatives" while retaining the centrality of sexual affiliation to the organization and understanding of intimacy. This process of reiteration and reformulation reveals the power of the metanarrative about sexual affiliation and the family. The paradigm structures and defines the rhetoric and directs the debate about alternatives.

While a great deal of emotionally charged rhetoric in family law is directed at children, the primary focus is still on maintaining the traditional heterosexual family model. In the rhetoric of those espousing children's rights, children's problems are deemed to be created by the fact that they are "trapped" in a "deviant" family situation, "prisoners" or "victims" of a family that is often "broken" through divorce or "pathological" in that it was never sanctified by marriage. Attention and concern initially directed at children too often is deflected to the adults with whom they live who have failed to form or maintain a sexual connection. The sexually affiliated family is the imposed ideal and, as such, it escapes sustained, serious consideration and criticism. The nuclear family is "natural"—it is assumed. The dominance of the idealized sexual family in social and legal thought has restricted real reform and doomed us to recreate patriarchy.

As a result and in spite of the real and perceived ideological shifts in what is socially and legally considered to be an acceptable family formation, single motherhood can comfortably continue to be considered deviant. It is deviant simply because it represents the rejection of the primacy of the sexual connection as the core organizing familial concept. In fact, the threat in its practice is implicit in the language we use to discuss the status. The very label "single mother" separates some practices of motherhood from the institution of "Mother" by reference to the mother's marital situation. Mother, as constructed and defined in the discourses about "single" mothers, is modified by her relationship (formal and legal) to the father—she is single.[11] By contrast, the institution of motherhood when practiced in its "normal" form is not analogously modified. No one speaks of a "married mother"—the primary connection of husband and wife is assumed in the unadorned designation of "Mother."

It is only the "deviant" form of motherhood that needs qualification and, by implication, justification. Furthermore, in this process of distinguishing the deviant variation of motherhood from the married norm, a complementary cluster of stereotypical designated family roles are also resolved. Husbands and wives, as well as mothers and fathers, are created by the nuclear family. These roles are valued according to contemporary images of the ideal family.

That the relationship between women and men has been at the core of our perception of family is evident when we see how it has defined other family members. For example, the historic characterization of children as "legitimate" or "illegitimate" depended on whether their parents were married. While children of unmarried parents are more apt today to be labeled "nonmarital," the focus is still the same—the child is defined by the relationship between the parents.

The privileging of the sexual tie stands as an eloquent statement about our understanding of the nature of family and intimacy. It also impedes the development of solutions to real family problems. One negative consequence flowing from the obsession with sexual affiliation, for example, is that in policy and reform the inevitable focus seems to be on "doing justice" between sexually affiliated adults. Given the contemporary hostility between the sexes and the status of equality as the dominant legal framework for discussions about fairness and justice, the potential divisive effects of this focus are apparent. As we face high divorce rates and the organization of women and men into gendered interest groups when confronting issues of intimacy, we should not be surprised that legal rules are considered prizes by competing factions. Law provides an arena for public, symbolic as well as real competition between groups of women and groups of men.

Furthermore, in the process of regulating intimacy, the coalescence of antagonistic interests along gendered lines is probably inevitable. The sexual family represents the most gendered of our social institutions, and this remains true even after decades of an organized women's movement. While other, nonfamily transformations have fostered male-female competitiveness, the family is the one area where tensions generated by perceived changes in the status and position of women are registered most clearly.

To the extent that today's society has developed a system of easy access to divorce and provided some economic security for women, a woman now can combine private and public roles or reject the imposition of an historically defined "female" role altogether. She may choose both work and family or decide to become a mother without becoming a wife. Women can choose to end a marital relationship or never formally establish one and need not fear that their own or their children's futures in such circumstances will involve total impoverishment and social condemnation. In fact, a recent nationwide poll of teenagers suggests that a substantial number of very young women do not see their futures inevitably including marriage. In response to the question, "How likely is it that you will get married?" only 65 percent of the teenage girls surveyed indicated it was "very likely." Six percent chose "not likely at all," while 29 percent equivocated, designating "somewhat likely." Sixty-three percent indicated they would still be "happy" and not feel they had "missed" part of meaningful life if they didn't get married.

Also significant were the gender differences in the expectations for marriage and the projected resort to alternatives should these expectations be unmet. Most of the girls interviewed were adamant about their plans to have a career and an egalitarian marriage. But many of the boys expressed firm convictions that a woman's place was in the home. Furthermore, the girls surveyed were overwhelmingly committed to having careers but far less dedicated to the idea of making and maintaining a marriage. One young woman said:

> I think a career is the most important thing, then children, then marriage. . . . I've always wanted to succeed in a work field, maybe something like being a marine biologist. I know I will work. If I get married,

> I would want it to be with someone who did as much of the housework as me. I think girls are more liberated and guys are going to have to compromise. If they say they want their wives at home, I think it's because they want more power in the relationship.

This sixteen-year old, like 55 percent of the girls surveyed, said she would consider becoming a single parent if she did not marry: "If I weren't married, I could imagine being a single mother. I know it's hard, but it's worth it. I just know I want children."[12]

Taking advantage of emerging possibilities to live outside conventional norms, living change, is not undertaken without substantial costs, however. Change hurts many. Some women articulate the feeling that the changes in family law have been detrimental—burdensome and expensive for many women while benefiting only a few. Others question whether such changes actually have been advances for anyone, arguing that they universally operate to further reassert, albeit in different forms, the power men implicitly enjoyed within the context of indissolvable marriage and traditional patriarchy. Patriarchy has not been displaced, and its beneficiaries (female as well as male) are displeased. The norm of the male-defined and male-headed family, with heterosexual union at its core, is threatened by the changes that have occurred. Consequently, we see the desire to contain and moderate, even undo, the reforms.

II. The Sexual or Natural Family as Sacred

The sexual family simultaneously exists in our social imagination both as a legal institution and as a cultural ideal with divine credentials. The nuclear family has an assumed "naturalness," venerated in law, institutionalized as the appropriate form of intimacy and secured against defamation or violation by unsanctified alternatives. Our legal ideal is built upon a specific religious tradition that presents only one view of what constitutes a true family. In that regard, the family is an explicitly sacred ideal. I have, however, a broader notion of sacred in mind when referring to the veneration of the sexual or natural family.

A. The Merger of Sacred and Secular

Contemporary political and academic discussions typically assume that, as an entity, the family has a natural configuration, based in the first instance on a formalized sexual tie between a man and woman, reinforced by the later biological event of parenthood. The naturalness of the sexual family is central to a variety of discourses in secular society. As a secular concept the family is sanctified because it is viewed as essential and inevitable. This notion of natural family is reiterated in the ways in which we construct reproductive and sociological imperatives. The sexual family is also viewed as functionally efficient from an economic perspective and necessary for appropriate or individual psychological development.[13] In its social and cultural presentations, the sacred status of the nuclear family as the most powerful ideological symbol of social order and structure is reinforced.

1. Deep Structure and Metanarratives

I have argued that law is but one institution in which cultural and social meanings are produced and, for the most part, that law is more reflective than constitutive of social norms. Social and cultural institutions outside of law reflect the primacy of sexual affiliation. Even more significant (and ominous, in regard to the prospects of any ideological restructuring project) is the fact that some version of the natural nuclear family pervades discourses across disciplines—it is found in every area and typically presented as a privileged institution. In other words, there are transdisciplinary assumptions about the optimal structure of the family.

Scholarly disciplines have many different emphases and modes of discourse in assessing the ideological role of the family. Some dwell on the symbolic significance of the family, others consider it from a practical or functional perspective, still others attempt to measure its value to individual family members and society. The disciplines have different methods of proof also; for example, the family narrative that surfaces in social science case studies is illuminated and buttressed by so-called "scientific" and therefore presumed "objective" means.

These stories about the family have different forms—some are "horror stories," others are more like "sentimental visions"—but they usually seem to offer explanations both for the status quo as well as normative directions for the future. What interests me are the unifying threads of the family stories representing core notions about the family that transcend disciplines—revealing that there is a "deep structure" to the ways in which we think about the institution: a metanarrative.[14]

The narratives of socially significant disciplines, such as psychology, anthropology, economics, and history, consistently cast women in complementary and supporting family roles. A detailed discussion of such disciplinary presentations is beyond the scope of this book, but some summary treatment will suffice to support the general point that the nuclear family is unquestionably accepted.

Psychoanalytic discourse is particularly relevant. This discourse, as initially constructed by Freud and elaborated upon by his disciples and popularizers, centers on a "family drama" in which the Oedipal complex is the script. Attachment to, or desire for, the Mother locates the male child in the presocial stage. In order for the male child to become a full or realized social being—to achieve selfhood—the Mother must be surpassed. The male child, in struggling with the father over his love for Mother, resolves the Oedipus complex, evidenced typically by the male child's identification with the father and "temporary" renunciation of Mother. The Mother is "rediscovered" (transformed) in the male child's adult sexual object.[15]

For the "postmodern" psychoanalyst, Jaques Lacan, the Oedipus relationship and dilemma operates within the same nuclear family structure. However, the drama is cast at the level of language or the symbolic. Lacan shifts the psychological inquiry from biological drives (Freud's conception) to the allocation of meaning through language. In order to gain entry into the "symbolic order," the child must ascend into subjectivity. He cannot be an "I" while still dependent upon and attached to Mother. Thus Mother comes to represent the presymbolic or inarticulate stage. In Lacan's view, the father introduces the principle of "the law," in particular the law of the language system. Initially, the infant is bound to his mother, the presymbolic, who is herself bound to the phallus. In Lacanian theory (and crucial to the thesis of this book), Mother is conceptualized as "deficient." Because she lacks a phallus she is the site of the negative—she represents "the lack" and cannot alone assist her child to ascend into subjectivity. Lacan and his followers attempt to degender the drama with assertions that women can represent the phallic—that a "phallic" mother is possible.[16]

Lacan considered castration important because of its relationship to paternal law.[17] Rather than desiring the mother, the child understands what the mother desires, and wants to be what the mother desires, which is the imaginary phallus.[18] The phallus becomes symbolic when the child recognizes that "desire cannot be satisfied."[19] The phallus thus represents the law of the father (the third term) and is that which breaks the mother-child dyad.[20] This "moment of division," represented by the phallus, "re-enacts the fundamental splitting of subjectivity itself."[21]

Object relations theory, the third major branch of contemporary psychoanalytic discourse, also identifies and centralizes the struggle of the child to differentiate himself from the Mother. This process of separation or differentiation is the crucial event of gender-identity formation. Object relations theory, however, permits *mutual* recognition between mother and child, building the basis for an idealized dyadic relationship. In positing the necessity for separation, object relations theory is similar to, but not identical with, Lacanian "castration" experience.[22]

The psychoanalytic discourses all are based on a family that is self-contained, nuclear in form. The psychic drama takes place in this triangular unit and each player has her or his role. The drama is drawn in terms of the child's experience. Mother as obstacle is taken for granted, and it is the search of the child for identification with father that is the center of the story. As that which is left behind, Mother is constituted as a derivative form of masculinity in the psychoanalytic paradigm—she does not see, she is seen; she does not write, she is written.[23]

In anthropology, the structure of the family and its sexually affiliated base are subjects of inquiry. Claude Lévi-Strauss, in a classic work published in 1956, described family formation and the role of the universal taboo against incest. In discussing the taboo, Lévi-Struass analogized it to the sexual division of labor, a device to "make the sexes mutually dependent on social and economic grounds, thus establishing clearly that marriage is better than celibacy."[24] Male and female are complementary to each other; their relationship is symbiotic in nature due to differentiated specialization; men hunt and war, women reproduce and nurture. Together, their complementary roles constitute a whole.

Similar gendered dramas in which Mother is cast as supporting actor to the main (male) characters in the family are played out in economic models of the family. The University of Chicago's Gary Becker, who won the Nobel Prize for his work on economic theories of family roles, analyzes role divisions that systematically disadvantage woman in the public sphere and concludes that they are "efficient." This work updates Lévi-Strauss with a bit of sociobiology thrown in for good measure. Women assume the burdens of family and intimacy because market inequities and social rules inevitably distribute a major share of child care and housework to them. Pay differentials for women's work outside the home become the justification for a continued unequal division of labor within the family and for the maintenance of rigid gender roles.[25] This version of economics is often bolstered by sociobiology establishing that women have a stronger "preference" for children. It is their preference and the choices based upon it which contribute to their ultimate status as unequal.[26] Women, so cast, need and want men just as they need and want the nuclear family, and they get what they want (and deserve): inequality.[27]

In history, many texts on the family assume its nuclear form, although there is debate about how porous it is, particularly to extended kin. In fact, one important family historian postulates that early families in the colonial United States were "not fundamentally different from the pattern of our own day: a man and a woman joined in marriage, and their natural-born children. The basic unit was therefore a 'nuclear' one, contrary to a good deal of sociological theory about premodern times."[28] Other historians disagree about the centrality of the sexual unit, noting that the family extended beyond this core. In general, there is evidence to support a variety of historical theories. A central historical inquiry, however, is into the role and function of the nuclear family form and its relationship to the larger kin grouping or the society as a whole. The emphasis is on understanding the genealogy of this structure.

To my surprise, I encounter strong assumptions about the inevitability and desirability of the sexual family even in so-called "oppositional" discourses operating within established disciplines such as feminism. Political theorists such as Susan Moller Okin resort to the (reformed) sexual family as the institution in which to socialize children to notions of "justice" and "equality." In assessing what policies should be encouraged, she concludes that "only children who are equally mothered and fathered can develop fully the psychological and moral capacities that currently seem to be unevenly distributed between the sexes."[29] What about single mother families or lesbian families? Injecting a mandatory component on the theme of sharing of complementary strengths, Okin states "only when men participate equally in what have been principally women's realms of meeting the daily material and psychological needs of those close to them . . . will members of both sexes be able to develop a more complete human personality."[30] One wonders how she would compel such masculine participation. What legal regulations would attend her compulsory heterosexual family ideal?

Feminist psychoanalytic literature also emphasizes the importance of men. In discussing the process of personal and positional identification, Nancy Chodorow theorizes that it is a significant problem that men do not mother.[31] Girl children identify with mothers who are present as caregivers. Boys, by contrast, have more difficulty with the identification process because the male adult is not present.[32] Masculine identification is based on cultural images of masculinity. Mothers are seen to represent regression and lack of autonomy and boys learn to disassociate themselves from Mother—they learn they must "reject dependency and deny attachment and identification."[33] Becoming a man is therefore based on the discovery and rejection of difference—"masculine identification processes stress differentiation from others, the denial of affective relation, and categorical universalistic components."[34]

The pervasiveness of similar assumptions about the inevitability of the nuclear family shows the tenacity and rigidity of our views about intimacy—rigidity that ultimately affects how we constitute and understand what is an "appropriate," "essential" family form and structure. This type of secular reification of the natural family is paralleled in law, where the meta-narrative about what constitutes a natural family directs the discussions as well. The idealization of the natural nuclear family is preserved through constant reiteration and recitation of family ideology in political and legal rituals, in which variations from the ideal family are labeled deviant and considered abnormal. The increasing visibility of nontraditional families in society has generated discussions about possible ways to remedy or compensate for these perceived defective, unnatural, or profane units.[35]

B. Legal Challenges to the Natural Family

Even though the sexual or nuclear family is designated as "sacred," it would be hard to argue that this family is a totally untarnished icon.[36] This may be particularly true for those interested in law and law reform. In fact, there has been a great deal of conflict and social agitation over the performance of the nuclear family. This discussion has tended to be reformist in nature, often generated by legal feminists interested in some modifications. There have been some shifts in the explicit rhetoric of families in feminist legal theory and some questioning of the success of the nuclear or sexual family as an exclusive institution.[37]

For example, the lines between what have historically been called the "public" and the "private" spheres have become less clear in recent decades. Our ideas about family and marriage have been challenged by evolutions in legal thought that focus our attention on individuals, not entities; and by the spread of grand legal principles, such as equality and freedom, to reform efforts directed at the family. Tensions are generated on many different levels. These tensions erupt in legal and cultural institutions as well as in specific families, provoking heated debates about the need for and extent of possible reforms. There is the perception of change, and change generates fear.

Fears for the future of the traditional, heterosexual, hierarchical (patriarchal) family as a privileged institution in law, though greatly overreactive, are not totally unfounded. For over twenty-five years the American family has been the object of so-called "second-wave" legal feminist criticism and attack.[38] Most of this criticism has been reformist, but occasionally specific problems have mandated a more radical approach. One area where this has been true is "domestic" violence.[39] The family constructed in this discourse sometimes has been cast as a potentially violent and dangerous social institution, marred by long-standing power imbalances and the specter of gender domination.[40]

These feminist critiques of the family have had some significant impact on recent law reforms. No longer can violence between intimates easily remain invisible and ignored. Laws explicitly forbid child abuse, marital rape, and other violence historically considered "normal"—or at least inevitable and excusable—because it was "domestic." In addition, and affecting all families, the veil of privacy has been partly pulled aside, revealing the hierarchical nature of the family and its conceptual core of common-law inequality. In response to feminist agitation (and after much time and effort), the language of the law regulating the domestic has changed.

In some states, marriage is no longer formally an appropriate defense to a charge of rape, and battering one's spouse is technically punishable by law. These challenges to the traditional family confront some of the foundational myths that provide the contemporary, secular-ideological underpinnings of the nuclear family. The sentimental designation of the nuclear family as a haven, a refuge from the cold and cruel world, has become harder to maintain when social movements such as feminism and child advocacy have brought to light the very real exploitative and abusive behavior within some families.[41]

These arguments focus on the individuals within families, affording the entity no independent deference *per se*. Tearing the veil of privacy from the traditional family has revealed that, even if not abusive, the family often fails to perform the social and psychological functions that were the justifications for its privileged position. Indeed, ultimately such revelations about family practices call into question the whole concept of the nuclear family as a legally privileged unit that is entitled to special status as an essential form of social organization. The sacred family can be obscene!

This type of challenge, when understood as an attack on structuring intimacy around sexual pairing, could set the stage for a systematic reconsideration of the historic nature and continued desirability of the traditional family as a social institution.[42] Unfortunately, however, the functional (or dysfunctional) critiques more characteristically focus on specific families or individuals as "dysfunctional" and generate discussions about the causes of such deviation from the ideal. These critiques spawn proposals for "cures" that reinvent the natural family for contemporary circumstances.[43] This process, referencing more of the same in terms of the family, is a reconstruction of the assumed natural family, not a re-visioning of what should be viewed as natural.

1. The Egalitarian Family as a Challenge

A companion and perhaps related development to the "discovery" of domestic violence within the haven of the family is the structural linguistic reformulations of marriage as an institution. Marriage has been recast to present an egalitarian idea.[44] Grand aspirations about equality are manifested in the terms we now use to discuss family relationships—"partnership" substituted for marriage; "shared parenting" substituted for mothering and fathering; "interdependency" and "contribution" substituted for need and obligatory domestic labor. On a formal legal level, issues may no longer be resolved according to explicitly patriarchal assumptions.

Tasks and responsibilities associated with families have ceased to be allocated in law on the basis of gender, with the husband deemed the "head" of the household with obligations to support a wife and children over whom he exercises control and who correspondingly owe him obedience and, on the wife's part, sexual and domestic other services.[45] Female subservience is no longer assumed, and females' "inherent incompetence" for the business and market world is not seriously asserted and used as a basis for exclusion. Indeed, wives and mothers are now equally responsible for the economic well-being of their families and no longer presumed by virtue of their sex to be the preferred parent in custody disputes. On an abstract level, the law has adopted a "gender-neutral" stance. Our rhetorical model is now based on the marital "partnership" of husband and wife. Gone from our formal, official discourse is the hierarchical organization of the common-law marriage described so graphically by Blackstone under the doctrines of "unity" and "merger." The old common-law hulk has been refashioned into the "egalitarian family."

This egalitarian reconstruction of the family narrative—initially undertaken largely in response to women resisting their historically assigned roles as wives and mothers—has the potential to undermine the hierarchical nature of the sexual family. Perhaps because it deals with day-to-day realities, family law has been responsive to some of the undercurrents of upheaval, and a considerable amount of it has already been rewritten in an attempt to reflect more "contemporary" notions about the family.

Indeed, family-law language is now remarkably gender neutral in statutes and cases. In substantive terms, dependency is no longer assumed to be the justification for allocation of marital wealth to women; rather it is the contribution they have made to the family that justifies their partnership share at dissolution. The whole way in which marriage is discussed at divorce has changed substantially in the past few decades.

In considering the language of the formal laws governing marriage and divorce, for example, it is no longer clear what constitutes appropriate family role behavior—who is, or has, acted as a "good" wife and mother or husband and father, fulfilling the well-defined roles in the nuclear family.

In fact, it is no longer clear these are even appropriate questions for the legal system to ask.

The laws governing divorce have replaced normative assessments that took conduct into account through consideration of "fault" with a system of default rules such as no-fault divorce and preferences for joint custody, making the process more administrative than judgmental.[46] Each spouse is considered capable of providing and caring for her or himself, and any children are shared responsibilities. The ideal is of spouses voluntarily joined, interdependent—separate yet united. This is a deviation from the traditional nuclear family in that it is not a hierarchical model (some would say, therefore, it is also not patriarchal).

Specific suggestions focus on the need for a reorganization of existing gendered roles within the confines of the traditionally populated family unit—fathers would be expected to share more in the domestic tasks as modern mothers spend more time and energy in market endeavors. The marital partners simply would rework the parameters of their relationship that, nonetheless, would continue to serve as the anchor defining and giving content to other family associations.

But in spite of such reform, the family continues to be defined as an entity, built on and arising from the sexual affiliation of two adults.[47] This heterosexual unit continues to be considered as presumptively appropriate and it has ongoing viability as the core family connection. At worst, heterosexual marriage is viewed as merely in need of some updating and structural revisions, and we seem caught in an "equality trap" in discussions about these revisions.

As I discussed earlier, equality as an overarching goal continues to have severe limitations, both practical and theoretical—particularly in the context of the family. Feminist legal reformers naively assumed that sharing could and would happen. They believed that with the egalitarian aspiration ensconced in law women would be free to develop their careers, and men would be unconstrained in choosing nurturing over other endeavors. This reform vision was a particularly narrow one to begin with. It considered only some family actors in its reconstituted vision. Thus, while the roles of husband and wife were restructured in regard to child care and vaguely described household domestic tasks, little thought has been given to the demands on domestic time and labor represented by the less attractive specters of caring for the elderly, the ill, or the disabled.[48] The egalitarian family was structured around sexual affiliation—the assumed inevitability of heterosexual pairing and its association with reproductive destiny were expressed in family form.

Finally, and perhaps most basically, in a society in which the divorce rate approached fifty percent and never-married motherhood was on the rise, the reforms unrealistically continued the notion of husband and wife as a couple forming the basic family core. The heterosexual family was essential to the structure of "reform." Perhaps this was understandable, given the dominance in feminist discussions about inequality between the sexes in the "public sphere." The interaction between male and female in the family was symbolically central and inevitably became the focus of the reformers' concern. The identified problems of male dominance and control directed the reformist energy toward hammering out the relationship between prototypes, even when the nurture or care of others, such as children, was the ostensible topic of inquiry. This focus on sexual affiliation is a limiting paradigm and family theory built upon it is inadequate.

However, to analyze the resilience of traditional family behavior in the face of an idealized egalitarian role reassignment, we must look beyond the failure of a radical vision or the excessive naivete of feminist reformers to the public role of the natural family. While the egalitarian family they envisioned may have had radical potential, the societal context in which it was launched ensured it would offer little hope for more than symbolic, rhetorical changes. We must go further and consider the *structural* position of the family—the role it plays within the larger society—which influences us even today in our reform efforts.

In this assessment, we move away from preoccupation with the roles of *individuals* within the family and concentrate on the institution of the family in regard to *its role and interaction* within the state. It is important to remember that the family is first and foremost a social institution. As such, it is given social content and definition by systems of belief or knowledge more significant than, and with coercive potential far exceeding, that of law. In this regard, the family as an institution embedded in social practice and understanding should also be understood to be resistant to easy redefinition.

Furthermore, individual understandings about family are shaped by societal forces that manifest them. None of us are exempt from the implications of the culture in which we live—it influences our actions, our aspirations, our politics, and what we can see as possibilities. So, while one may "choose" to live outside of the conventional norms, one does not escape them totally, and the challenge presented is apt to be slight.

III. The Undeveloped Dependency Discourse

In part, the failure of changes based upon an equality model in the family arena have to do with the nature of the initial attacks on the family. The liberal legal feminist calls for equality within the larger society prompted a reconsideration of the institution of the family, yet this reconsideration left relatively undisturbed the core concept of what constituted a "family." The feminist notion of the "new" family was as a supportive institution that facilitated market participation, and their rhetoric continued to reflect an idealized image of the family core as a couple.[49]

The natural family is the social institution we depend on to raise the children and care for the ill, the needy, the dependent in our culture. In its idealized form, the family will be a self-contained and self-sufficient unit in accomplishing those tasks—located within the larger society, complementing the state that protects it, but not demanding public resources to do so.

A. Inevitable and Derivative Dependencies

Assumptions about the natural sexually affiliated family are related to inter-dependent assumptions about the role of family in the larger society. The idea of the family as natural coincides with the idea that it is the repository for "inevitable dependencies." The ideal of the natural family—the unit to which responsibility for inevitable dependency is referred—establishes a relationship between "public" state and "private" family. Dependency is allocated away from the state to the private grouping. These ideas of natural and privatized dependency reinforce one another on an ideological level. They perversely interact so that the societal tasks assigned to the natural family inevitably assume the role differentiation that exists within that sexually affiliated family.

Privatizing dependency mandates that in order to be "successful," natural families as entities must shoulder the burdens of caring for inevitable dependency. To do so, the burdens or costs must be allocated within the family. As we all know, this allocation is typically *gendered*. In other words, the way we perceive the family as a social institution facilitates the continuation of gendered role divisions and frustrates the egalitarian ideal.

Equality rhetoric and family law reforms aside, the burdens associated with intimacy and its maintenance have always been and continue to be disproportionately allocated to women.[50] This allocation is supported by extralegal norms; given the cultural, ideological, and market structures built and dependent upon this fundamental, unequal division of family labor, the pattern is going to be very difficult to alter. There are no obvious answers as to why these burdens continue predominantly to be borne by women, but it is clear any inquiry cannot be limited or confined to the language of law or the traces and fragments of legislative history that remain in the wake of reform. If we were really serious about redistributing the burdens of intimacy or family maintenance, it would require an ideological and structural reorientation of society, the rewriting of academic disciplines, and a major reallocation of social resources, none of which seem likely anytime within the near future.

As a definitional note, "burden" is *not* the same as oppression. I use the term to clearly signify that there are costs associated with what women typically do as caretakers in society. These labors may provide "joy," but they are also burdensome and have material costs and consequences. Not to recognize them as "burdens" is to ignore the costs to women and to continue to make women's labor invisible, as well as to condone that it is also uncompensated.

A second definitional point is that dependency is "inevitable" in that it flows from the status and situation of being a child and often accompanies aging, illness, or disability. In this sense, dependency always has been and always will be with us. Furthermore, caretakers are dependent too—a derivative dependency flowing from their roles and the need for resources their caretaking generates.[51]

Once dependency is seen to be natural and inevitable—as inherent in the status of infancy, illness, certain disabilities, and, quite often, age—we can begin to see the implications and the historic (and contemporary) significance of assignment of dependency to and within the family. Women, wives, mothers, daughters, daughters-in-law, sisters are typically the socially and culturally assigned caretakers. As caretakers they are tied into intimate relationships with their dependents. The very process of assuming caretaking responsibilities creates dependency in the caretaker—she needs some social structure to provide the means to care for others. In a traditional family, the caretaker herself, as wife and mother, is dependent on the wage-earning husband to provide for her so she can fulfill her tasks.

In this regard, the notion of the natural family has important ideological and political currency. Its existence as an ideological construct masks inevitable but unacknowledged dependency and perpetuates our official and public rhetoric, allowing it to be spun out in terms of ideals of capitalistic individualism, independence, self-sufficiency, and autonomy. It is significant that these ideals operate on two levels—they construct an ideal family as well as the ideal individual within our culture. But, caretakers with their charges do not stand alone; they cannot pretend to meet the individualistic ideal and often find themselves outside of traditional families.

Family narratives generally assume certain standard configurations and place the family members into roles. These assigned roles reflect an assumed division of family labor into complementary specializations. The component roles are perceived as making necessary but differentiated contributions to the "whole." The structure of the nuclear family with its interdependent, well-defined roles—with women's roles typically subservient to the greater whole—is one of its harmful legacies.[52]

A consideration of individuals' roles within the cooperative interactive endeavor labeled family focuses attention on the specific functions assigned to the family by society. The historic family-role divisions have profound practical and ideological implications for the organization of society as a whole. The creation of these family roles is related to what are considered to be essential social functions for the institution.[53] Some of the implications of assigning (sometimes confining) certain societal tasks to families have been explicitly recognized and theorized, particularly in critical scholarship.[54] The societal implications of other assigned or assumed family functions seem less well-developed, however, and are often concealed.

That the nuclear family has functioned on an ideological level in our society as the repository of dependency should be central to feminist theory. This important (some would say essential) societal function assigned to the nuclear family is seldom considered in discussions about the structure's persistence as an ideological and political ideal. However, it is extremely important from a contemporary policy perspective, and has many implications. The fact that the allocation of inevitable dependency to the family is premised on its having a specific structure—the continuation of the historic, essential division of labor within the family—should be of central concern.[55] Given current social realities, the historic model of the family can no longer be considered viable.

B. The Failure of the Family

While the dominant aspirational story for the past decades has been one of spousal "equality," great gender inequality in the allocation of the burdens and costs associated with family operation continues to affect how this story is played out in real lives.[56] Society has not kept pace with the formal egalitarian impulses of the law—and in spite of the rhetorical reforms, the family continues to operate as the most gendered or role-defined of our institutions, allowing for and justifying pervasive, ingrained, and persistent patterns of gender inequality in the larger society. In spite of the introduction of a radical alternative and well-articulated equality model, the unequal, gendered expectations and distribution of the burdens of dependency have not shifted.

I believe we must focus our attention on how well the traditional family is performing certain functional tasks structurally assigned to it. I am specifically concerned about how the assignment of managing dependency to the traditional family influences contemporary political discourse on child poverty, divorce, and welfare reform. Given such phenomena as increasing rates of divorce, the increase in the number of never married mothers, and the increase in life expectancy (particularly for women), the family seems doomed to fail in its historic task of managing and masking certain dependencies.[57] Two contemporary situations currently labeled as "problems" really are situations that call into question the viability of the caretaking capacities of the private-natural family. The first problem is in the tension generated by the wide acceptance among elites of the notion of the egalitarian family. The second problem is the sense of crisis (discussed in chapter 5) surrounding the increase in the number of women from all classes and races becoming single mothers as a result of either our high divorce rate or because they never married in the first place.

The very existence of these "problems" and our inability to respond to them within the confines of our family ideology are strong evidence of the failure of the nuclear family. They illustrate that the private-natural family is no longer viable as the sole, or even primary, institutional response to dependency.

The egalitarian family as an articulated ideal is premised on the couple-based family unit. As such, it generates tension insofar as one of the goals to be attained by the partners is equal career or market proficiency. Equality in ambition in nonfamily members leaves the two-parent family an institution with potentially NO available caretakers.

The case of the never-married or divorced single mother presents a version of the same dilemma. Not having a designated "partner," if she devotes her time to market work to support her child she will not be available as a caretaker. However, since she is single, if she fulfills her assigned obligations for the burdens of dependency, then with no wage earner to support her she will starve or "go begging to the state." In either case, her family has not privately dealt with its dependencies.

Both of these situations reveal to me the inherent flaws in the concept of the sexual-natural family. The tasks assigned to this family as the private repository of inevitable dependency necessitates a two-parent family unit with role differentiation and division of labor. This family will assume the traditional natural form almost inevitably.

Of course, the rhetorical resolution for the potential dilemma of no caretaker in the egalitarian couple family has been to share "caregiving." But, rhetoric aside, empirical information indicates sharing is not happening. The figures are overwhelming; not much has changed in terms of who does domestic labor, even when both partners are employed. Further, when it is necessary that one career be temporarily put aside, there are strong economic incentives that guide the choice. Equality fictions in the family may abound, but the reality of continuing market inequalities, with prevailing lower wage rates for women, typically dictates that the woman is the one "selected" when a family member is needed to accommodate caregiving.

Equality can be sacrificed (and it often is) or women can settle for less. Women can forego having children. Not infrequently, the "solution" when dependents need care leads to the "exploitation" of other women's nurturing labor. An egalitarian family typically hires someone to care for the children (or other dependents).[58] This hardly seems an acceptable feminist solution, however, given that caretaking is undervalued and underpaid in the "commercial" context as well as within the family. All too often, it is women of African American or Hispanic descent who are called upon to subsidize the middle-class woman's ideal of equal partnership in marriage. The expectation that caretaking is a private matter means that someone's (some woman's) labor will be undervalued even if it is compensated.

Furthermore, in addition to this gross economic structuring, centuries of social and cultural conditioning operate to shape the ways women understand the nature and scope of their "choices" in defining their own family role. Family failures in regard to children, evidenced in even minor deviations from an unattainable ideal, are most likely to be placed at a Mother's feet. It is mothers in the work place that elicit fears of generations of children abandoned to neglect and the horrors of day-care regimentation and potential abuses. The social assignment of dependency is even more pronounced (and less challenged) when it comes to care for the elderly or ill. It is daughters to whom the elderly parents look for expected accommodations.

In the case of single mothers, whether they are divorced or never married, the inadequacies of the private family are not capable of resolution by pretenses toward equality within the natural or nuclear unit. As chapter 5 demonstrates, these mothers are stigmatized and labeled as "deviant" and "pathological" as a result, blamed for their inability to achieve the nearly impossible economic "self-sufficiency" outside of the private, subsidized family.[59]

Notes

1. *See, e.g.,* Martha Minow, "'Forming Underneath Everything that Grows': Toward a History of Family Law," 1985 *Univ. Wisconsin Law Review* 819 (discussing the development of family law through an exploration of the social history of the family). Essentially a modernist concept, a meta- or public narrative is understood to be the story or "narrative," which both legitimates and controls knowledge in the western world. The modernist attempts to characterize the world as ultimately unpresentable while relying on a form of narrative presentation that is familiar or recognizable and that offers the reader or listener a degree of comfort. In contrast, postmodern theories accept the disappearance of

metanarratives and focus instead on the existence of local, interlocking language games that replace the overall structures. Jennifer Wicke, "Postmodern Identity and the Legal Subject," 62 *Univ. Colorado Law Review* 455, 462 (1991). *See generally,* Fredric Jameson, *Postmodernism* (Durham, NC: Duke Univ. Press, 1991); Willem van Reijen and Dick Veerman, "An Interview with Jean Francois Lyotard," 5 *Theory, Culture, and Society* 277, 301–302 (1988).

2. This "natural" state is reinforced in subtle ways as well, for example in mother-in-law jokes that convey the message that parents should not interfere with the sexual family. The recent trend of adult children "returning home" is infringing on this concept, however. *See, e.g.,* Eda Leshan, "Life Over 60: Senior Class Adults Back in the Nest," *Newsday* (January 30, 1988): p. II–7; Darrell Sifford, "When Grown Children Move Back In," *Philadelphia Inquirer* (May 2, 1991): p. C6; Joan Kelly Bernard, "Bringing up the 20-Somethings Until They're Settled into Adult Lives: Even Grown Children Need A Certain Amount of Parenting. Here's How to Walk the Fine Line Between Too Much and Too Little," *Newsday* (February 5, 1994): p. II–21.

3. Daniel M. Weintraub and Scott Harris, "Gay Rights Protest Disrupts Wilson Speech," *L.A. Times* (October 2, 1991): p. 1A.

4. *Reynolds v. United States,* 98 U.S. 145, 165–66 (1878).

5. In *Loving v. Virginia,* 388 U.S. 1, 12 (1967), the Court stated: "Marriage is one of the basic rights of man [sic], fundamental to our very existence and survival." This view was reiterated in *Boddie V. Connecticut,* 401 U.S. 371, 375 (1971): "As this Court on more than one occasion has recognized, marriage involves interests of basic importance in our society." The foundational role of the family in our society was noted by Judge Bork:

> The reason for protecting the family and the institution of marriage is not merely that they are fundamental to our society but that our entire tradition is to encourage, support, and respect them. . . .
>
> Fundamental rights are usually grounded in the existence of a tradition of respect for the cultural institution in question. The majority notes that there is no comparable tradition of respect for the bond between a child and his non-custodial parent.

Franz v. United States, supplemental opinion, 712 F.2d 1428, 1438 (D.C. Cir. 1983) (Bork, J., concurring and dissenting).

More recently, in determining that inmates should be allowed to marry, Justice O'Connor, writing for the Court, stated:

> [M]arriages are . . . expressions of emotional support and public commitment. These elements are an important and significant aspect of the marital relationship. In addition, many religions recognize marriage as having spiritual significance . . . the commitment of marriage may

be an exercise of religious faith as well as an expression of personal dedication. . . . [M]arital status often is a precondition to the receipt of government benefits (e.g. Social Security benefits), property rights (e.g. tenancy by the entirety, inheritance rights), and other, less tangible benefits (e.g. legitimation of children born out of wedlock).

Turner v. Safley, 482 U.S. 78, 95–96 (1987).

6. *See* Martha L. Fineman, "Law and Changing Patterns of Behavior: Sanctions on Non-Marital Cohabitation," 1981 *Wisconsin Law Review* 275 (describing the use of the criminal cohabitation statute in Wisconsin, and attempts to repeal it, which were finally successful.) *See also* Note, "Fornication, Cohabitation and the Constitution," 77 *Michigan Law Review* 253 (1978).

7. *See* Fineman, *Illusions* [chapter 2, note 8]. *See also State v. Jones,* 205 A.2d 507, 508 (Conn. Cir. 1964), in which Jones was convicted of lascivious carriage after being found in bed nude with a woman not his wife. The judges' words are illustrative of the attitude toward marriage and morality at that time:

> The status of the moral standards of our society is such that sexual intimacy is not forbidden. However, the standards of society are such that sexual relations or lascivious actions by persons who do not have the benefit of marriage to one another are regarded as obscene, unchaste and immoral. Whether or not they are committed openly or publicly or in the privacy of the bedroom makes them none the less lewd, immoral or unchaste.

Although Connecticut repealed the law making adultery a crime, adultery can still be used coercively to maintain the nuclear family. *See, e.g., Mason v. Mason,* 1991 WL 24027 (Conn. Sup. Ct. 1991) (discussing the impact of adultery on divorce, alimony, and custody) and *Silver v. Silver,* 1992 WL 157489 (Conn. Sup. Ct. 1992) (holding that wife must answer questions on deposition relating to adultery because, although no longer a crime, it was relevant to the issue of divorce, alimony, and child custody). *See also Farris v. Farris,* 532 So. 2d 1041 (Ala. 1988) (wife's adultery justified denial of alimony and custody to wife); *Adams v. Adams,* 374 S.E. 2d 450 (N.C. 1988) (husband's adultery was grounds for requiring him to pay alimony).

The state, through its regulatory mechanisms (be they the criminal justice system, child welfare laws, tax codes, or other regulatory civil laws) defines and secures for the nuclear family a privileged, if not exclusive, position in regard to the sanctified ordering of intimacy.

8. *See generally* Edward Shorter, *The Making of the Modern Family* (New York: Basic Books, 1975) (exploring the history and development of the nuclear family); Lawrence Stone, "The Rise of the Nuclear Family in Early Modern England:

The Patriarchal Stage," in *The Family in History* Charles E. Rosenberg ed. (Philadelphia: Univ. of Pennsylvania Press, 1975): p. 13.

　See also Lee E. Teitelbaum, "The Legal History of the Family," 85 *Michigan Law Review* 1052, 1053–54 ("Book Review") (discussing the relation of the patriarchal family to the commonwealth in the eighteenth and nineteenth centuries).

9. For example, in 1962, the Model Penal Code recommendations included the repeal of sodomy statutes; in the years since these recommendations, approximately one-half of the states have eliminated their prohibitions against sodomy, the most recent occurring in Wisconsin in 1983. *See* Nan D. Hunter, "Life After Hardwick," 27 *Harvard Civil Rights Civil Liberties Law Review* 531, 541 (1992). However, of the states that retain sodomy laws, most do not limit the reach of the laws to same-sex or extramarital relationships. *See* Julie A. Morris, Note, "Challenging Sodomy Statutes: State Constitutional Protections for Sexual Privacy," 66 *Indiana Law Journal* 609, 615 (1991).

10. *See* Note, "Looking for Family Resemblance: The Limits of the Functional Approach to the Legal Definition of Family," 104 *Harvard Law Review* 1640 (1991). *See also* Craig A. Bowman and Blake M. Cornish, Note, "A More Perfect Union: A Legal and Social Analysis of Domestic Partnership Ordinances," 92 *Columbia Law Review* 1164, 1267 (discussing recent proposals for legally recognized domestic partnership agreements).

11. Single motherhood could become the basis for arguing for a reordering of social subsidies and a recognition of equal family status to the form of intimate, nonsexual organization. *See* Chapter 9.

12. Tamar Lewin, "Poll of Teenagers: Battle of the Sexes on Roles in Family," *New York Times*, July 11, 1994, pp. A1, B7.

13. *See, e.g.*, David L. Chambers, *Making Fathers Pay: The Enforcement of Child Support* (Chicago: Univ. of Chicago Press, 1979); David J. Rothman, *The State As Parent: Social Policy in the Progressive Era*, in *Doing Good: The Limits of Benevolence* Willard Gaylin, Ira Glasser, Steven Marcus, and David J. Rothman eds. (New York: Pantheon Books, 1981): pp. 67–95; Eli Zaretsky, *The Place of the Family in the Origins of the Welfare State*, in *Rethinking the Family: Some Feminist Questions* Barrie Thorne and Marilyn Yalom eds. (New York: Longman, 1982).

14. The notion of the metanarrative assumes some sort of hierarchy of cultural representations and cultural values. Since the Enlightenment, for example, the central western metanarrative has been that of progress, reason, and revolution, a public narrative of Darwinian evolution and class struggle. Metanarratives provide grounds for collective identities, allowing for a linear interpretation of historical forces. Thus, for instance, the notion of a unitary metanarrative has

been used to establish public law adjudication as the paradigm of all adjudication, as a system of adjudication that is furthermore governed by a single set of principles whether the enterprise is common-law adjudication, statutory construction, or constitutional adjudication. For a critique of this position, *see* Melvin Aron Eisenberg, *The Nature of the Common Law* (Cambridge: Harvard Univ. Press, 1988): pp. 8–13.

In contrast, post modernist theories that call for the disintegration of the notion of metanarratives, as seen in the work of Frederic Jameson and Jean-Jacques Lyotard, understand cultural referents to be a closely knit weave of interconnections without any single exclusive or overpowering identity. *See* Wicke [chapter 6, note 1]. *See generally,* David Kolb, *The Critique of Pure Modernity: Hegel, Heidegger, and After* (Chicago: Univ. of Chicago Press, 1986); Richard M. Thomas, "Milton and Mass Culture: Toward a Post-Modernist Theory of Tolerance," 62 *Univ. Colorado Law Review* 525 (1991); Richard M. Unger, *Law in Modern Society: Toward a Criticism of Social Theory* (New York: Free Press, 1976): pp. 37–43, 134–37.

15. *See Feminism and Psychoanalysis: A Critical Dictionary* Elizabeth Wright, ed. (Cambridge, UK: Blackwell, 1992): p. 266; Charles Rycroft, *A Critical Dictionary of Psychoanalysis* (New York: Basic Books, 1968): p. 105.

16. *See* Bice Bienvenuto and Roger Kennedy, *The Works of Jacques Lacan: An Introduction* (New York: St. Martin's, 1986): pp. 126–41. *See also* Jessica Benjamin, *The Bonds of Love* (New York: Pantheon, 1988), especially Chapter 3.

17. Jacques Lacan, *Feminine Sexuality* (Juliette Mitchell and Jacqueline Rose eds.); Jacqueline Rose translator (New York: W.W. Norton, 1982), Introduction-2, 29

18. *Ibid.,* p. 37.

19. *Ibid.,* p. 38.

20. *Ibid.,* p. 38–39.

21. *Ibid.,* p. 40. In his later work, Lacan used the *object small a [object a]* to represent the lost object that symbolized desire. In relating to this object, man realizes that his sexual relations are a fantasy. This reduces woman to nothing— a being in a "fantasmic place." *Ibid.,* p. 48. In other words, woman as an "absolute category . . . is false." *Id.* Courtly love is a way of elevating woman "into a place where her absence or inaccessibility stands in for male lack. . . . [H]er denigration [is] the precondition for man's belief in his own soul. . . . [W]oman . . . stand[s] for both difference and loss: '[she] . . . is produced, precisely as what he is not . . . sexual difference, and . . . as what he has to renounce, . . . *jouissance*.' " *Ibid.,* pp. 48–49.

Because she is the negative, she becomes "a total object of fantasy (or an object of total fantasy), elevated into the place of the Other and made to stand for its truth." The Other and the *object a* (the cause of desire) are joined and fantasized as truth. The " 'Otherness' of the woman . . . serves to secure for the man his own self-knowledge and truth." However, Lacan did not believe in the category "woman" or that there could be an 'Other of the Other.' Thus he was led to challenge the myths of 'knowledge' and 'belief.' *Ibid.* at 50.

"The Other . . . stands against [masculine] knowledge . . . [and] therefore stands against the phallus—its pretence to meaning and false consistency." The phallus seeks the authority [of knowledge] from the Other and is refused. *Ibid.*, p. 51.

Lacan insisted that "femininity can only be understood in terms of its construction. . . ." *Ibid.*, p. 53. Subsequently, other members of the École Freudienne, Michele Montrelay and Luce Irigaray, raised the issue of women's relationship to language. They would remove woman "from the dominance of the phallic term and from language at one and the same time . . . [and assign her] to a point of origin." Presymbolic differentiation and law. *Ibid.*, p. 54. This gives women "access to an archaic form of expressivity" outside language. "This point of origin is the maternal body, an undifferentiated space . . . in which the girl child recognizes herself. . . . [S]he fully *knows* herself in the mother." *Id.* To line up with the phallic order, she must devalue that recognition. *Ibid.*, p. 55.

22. *See* Bienvenuto and Kennedy [chapter 6, note 17] pp. 172–83.

23. *See* E. Ann Kaplan, *Motherhood and Representation—The Mother in Popular Culture and Melodrama* (New York: Routhledge, 1992).

24. Claude Lévi-Strauss, *Man, Culture and Society,* (New York: Oxford Univ. Press, 1956): pp. 276–78.

25. *See* Gary S. Becker, *A Treatise on the Family* (Cambridge: Harvard Univ. Press, 1981): pp. 14–37.

26. *See, e.g.,* Richard A. Posner, "An Economic Analysis of Sex Discrimination Law," 56 *Univ. of Chicago Law Review* 1311 (1989); Richard A. Posner, *Sex and Reason* (Cambridge: Harvard Univ. Press, 1992); Fuchs [chapter 2, note 21].

27. To some extent women marry for economic reasons. *See generally* Heidi Hartmann, "Capitalism, Patriarchy, and Job Segregation by Sex," in Zella R. Eisenstein, *Capitalist Patriarchy and the Case for Socialist Feminism* (New York: Monthly Review Press, 1979): pp. 206, 208 (job segregation by sex enforces lower wages for women in the labor market, encouraging women to marry and thereby keeping them dependent on men; once married, the expectation that women will perform domestic chores weakens women's position in the labor market); Barbara Ehrenreich, *The Hearts of Men* (Garden City, NY: Anchor/

Doubleday, 1983), who argues that "women need men more than the other way round" from an economic perspective. *See also* Jane E. Larson, "The New Home Economics," 10 *Constitutional Commentary* 443 (1993), reviewing Richard Posner [chapter 6, note 26]. There is also some indication that men marry primarily for sex. *See, e.g.,* George Gilder, *Men and Marriage* (Gretna, LA: Pelican, Pub. 1986).

28. John Demos, "Images of the American Family Then and Now in Changing Images of the Family." Virginia Tufte and Barbara Myerhoff eds. (New Haven: Yale Univ. Press, 1979): p. 47.

29. Okin [chapter 2, note 25] at 107. Okin does concede much later in her book that single-parent families, among other nontraditional arrangements, are "more complicated." *Ibid.,* p. 178.

30. *Ibid.,* p. 107.

31. Chodorow [chapter 4, note 77].

32. Both boys and girls have negative feelings toward the mother during the Oedipal phase, but these feelings are resolved very differently. A boy comes to feel contempt for the mother, which frees "him not only from his mother but also from the feminity within himself." *Ibid.,* p. 182. (Freud bases this contempt in the boy's knowledge of his mother's "castration." *Ibid.* Karen Horney bases it in a fear of "maternal omnipotence [resulting] from their early caretaking and socialization by women." *Ibid.,* p. 183.) Girls resolve it more through feelings of fear and hostility. A girl cannot feel contempt for the mother, because the mother is herself. The "normal" outcome for a girl is "acceptance of her own feminity and identification with her mother." *Ibid.,* p. 182. This mother-daughter identification and relationship explains why it is that women and not men are mothers.

33. *Ibid.,* p. 181. Chodorow believes that this rejection means that a boy will repress those qualities he takes to be feminine inside of himself and reject and devalue women and the feminine in the social world. *Ibid.*

34. *Ibid.,* p. 176.

35. *See, e.g.,* "Speeches from the Federalist Society Fifth Annual Lawyers Convention: Individual Responsibility and the Law, Discussion," 77 *Cornell Law Review* 1012, 1016 (1992) (arguing that "the nuclear family has been the norm since the very beginning of human history" and that the "current pattern—where 40% of all American children now live apart from one or both of their biological parents" is the "aberration").

36. I am referring both to the extensive work done by feminists to expose and critique the traditional family as both unequal and oppressive for women and to the members of the community who either by choice or circumstance do not

live in traditional families. *See, e.g.,* Rubin [chapter 7, note 43]; Jed Rubinfeld, "The Right of Privacy," 102 *Harvard Law Review* 737, 799–802 (1982); Michael Sandel, "Moral Argument and Liberal Toleration: Abortion and Homosexuality," 77 *California Law Review* 521 (1989). The existence of such people challenges community acceptance of tradition behavioral norms as the "natural." Nevertheless, the family continues as the most explicitly gendered of our social institutions. This is related to the ways in which its idealized and realized functions are mandated by the ideology of American families.

37. *See, e.g.,* Katharine T. Bartlett, "Rethinking Parenthood as an Exclusive Status: The Need for Legal Alternatives When the Premise of the Nuclear Family Has Failed," 70 *Virginia Law Review* 879, 944 (1984) (criticizing law's continued reluctance to recognize child-parent relationships that arise outside the nuclear family); Mary P. Trenthart, "Adopting a more Realistic Definition of 'Family,'" 26 *Gonzaga Law Review* 91, 97 (1991) (asserting that "many people subscribe to a broader definition of family than those used by most courts and legislatures"); Kris Franklin, Note, "'A Family Like Any Other Family': Alternative Methods of Defining Family Law," 18 *N.Y.U. Review of Law and Social Change* 1027, 1062–64 (1991) (advocating reformulation of legal definition of family to reflect existing pluralities of family types); *See* Note, "Looking for a Family Resemblance" [chapter 6, note 10] at 1640 (asserting that "the traditional nuclear family is rapidly becoming an American anachronism").

38. For examples of feminist work that critique the doctrine of family privacy as more often a cloak for violence against women and children, *see* Sue E. Eisenberg and Patricia L. Micklow, "The Assaulted Wife: 'Catch 22' Revisited," 3 *Women's Rights Law Report* 138, 138–39, 146 (1977); Elizabeth Schneider, "The Violence of Privacy," 23 *Connecticut Law Review* 973 (1991); Amy Eppler, Note, "Battered Women and the Equal Protection Clause: Will the Constitution Help Them when the Police Won't?" 95 *Yale Law Journal* 788, 800–01 (1986).

39. The term "domestic violence" is itself problematic since it locates violence against women (and children) in the domestic or family or private sphere. Private violence is, or should be, of public concern. *See generally* the collection of papers addressing, in part, the need to recast this formulation of violence in *The Public Nature of Private Violence: Women and the Discovery of Domestic Abuse* Martha Fineman and Roxanne Mykitiuk eds. (New York: Routledge, 1994).

40. At the turn of the century similar criticisms were made of the family only to be forgotten and ignored as the idealized nuclear family form came to dominate the American imagination during the middle part of the twentieth century.

41. *See* Schneider [chapter 6, note 38] (asserting that legal notion of family privacy has encouraged and reinforced violence against women). *See generally, Domestic Violence on Trial: Psychosocial and Lead Dimensions of Family Violence* Daniel

J. Sonkin ed. (New York: Springer, 1987); Leonard Karp and Cheryl L. Karp, *Domestic Torts: Family Violence, Conflict, and Sexual Abuse* (Colorado Springs, CO: Shepards/McGraw Hill, 1989); *see also* Elizabeth H. Pleck, *Domestic Tyranny: The Making of Social Policy Against Violence from the Colonial Times to the Present* (New York: Oxford Univ. Press, 1987): p. 254.

42. *See* Martha Fineman, "Intimacy Outside the Natural Family: The Limits of Privacy," 23 *Connecticut Law Review* 955 (1991).

43. For a recent example of the idea that single-parent families are somehow "pathological," *see* Frank E. Harper, "To Kill the Messenger: The Deflection of Responsibility Through Scapegoating (A Socio-Legal Analysis of Parental Responsibility Laws and the Urban Gang Family)," 8 *Harvard Blackletter Journal* 41, 59–60 (1991) (locating the source of teenage gang activity in gang-concentrated communities as the predominance of single-parent, low-income Black and Latina households).

44. *See Kirchberg v. Feenstra,* 450 U.S. 455 (1981) (wives must be equally allowed to participate in the management of community property as husbands); *Wengler v. Druggist Mutual Ins. Co.,* 446 U.S. 142 (1980) (female wage earners must receive same worker's compensation benefits as male wage earners); *Orr v. Orr,* 440 U.S. 268 (1979) (the duty to support one's spouse must not be applied only to men); *Califano v. Goldfarb,* 430 U.S. 199 (1977) (Social Security survivors' benefits must provide female wage earners with the same protection for their spouses as male wage earners); *Stanton v. Stanton,* 421 U.S. 7 (1975) (female children of divorced parents are entitled to support for the same length of time as male children so that they too may pursue a post secondary education); *Weinberger v. Weisenfeld,* 420 U.S. 636 (1975) (a husband must receive the same survivor's benefits upon the death of his wife as the wife would upon the death of her husband); *Frontiero v. Richardson,* 411 U.S. 677 (1973) (women in the military must receive the same benefits for their families as men); *Reed v. Reed,* 404 U.S. 71 (1971) (wives must be equally eligible as husbands to administer their deceased relatives' estates).

45. Consider the way domestic violence, marital rape, and child abuse were dealt with in the past:

Domestic violence: The rule of thumb established the guideline for wife beating: it provided that a man could legally beat his wife so long as the rod used was no thicker than his thumb. *See* Terry Davidson, "Wifebeating: A Recurring Phenomenon Throughout History," in *Battered Women: A Psychosociological Study of Domestic Violence* Marie Roy ed. (New York: Van Nostrand Reinhold Ltd, Toronto Canada, 1970): pp. 18–21.

Marital rape: Lord Matthew Hale is credited with incorporating the marital rape exemption into the common law. In the seventeenth century he wrote, "The husband cannot be guilty of a rape committed by himself upon his lawful wife, for by their mutual matrimonial consent and contract the wife hath given up herself in this kind unto her husband, which she cannot retract." Matthew Hale, *History of Pleas of the Crown* 629 (London: E. & R. Nutt & R Gosling, 1736): p. 629.

Child abuse: On the issue of disciplining a child, John Demos notes that during the colonial period, which ended around the 1820s, "Magistrates and local officials [c]ould thus compel a married couple 'to live more peaceably together' or to alter and upgrade the 'governance' of their children. This, too, is the context of the famous 'stubborn child' laws of early New England, which prescribed the death penalty for persistent disobedience to parents." Demos [chapter 6, note 28].

46. *See, e.g.,* Herma H. Kay, "An Appraisal of California's No-Fault Divorce Law," 75 *California Law Review* 291, 299–304 (1987) (examining the policy underlying no-fault divorce as a step toward an egalitarian vision of marriage). *But see* Richard Ingleby, "Matrimonial Break-down and the Legal Process: The Limitations of No-Fault Divorce," 11 *Law and Policy Review* 1, 13 (arguing that despite the value of the policy of no-fault divorce, its aims may be unattainable); Lynn D. Wardle, "No-Fault Divorce and the Divorce Conundrum," 1991 *Brigham Young Univ. Law Review* 79, 97–112 (asserting that the adoption of no-fault divorce grounds failed to accomplish the purposes for which they were enacted).

47. In *Lester v. Lester,* 195 Misc. 1034, 87 N.Y.S. 2d 517, 519 (1949), Justice Panken stated:

> Man enters a marital relationship to perpetuate the species. The family is the result of the marital relationship. It is the institution which determines in a large measure the environmental influences, cultural backgrounds, and even economic status of its members. It is the foundation upon which society rests and is the basis for the family and all its benefits.

48. No one was arguing over who got to take care and credit for caring for "grandma" in the development of the rhetoric of the "new man" in the reconstructed family story.

49. *See, e.g.,* Mary Ann Glendon, *Abortion and Divorce in Western Law: American Failures, European Challenges* (Cambridge: Harvard Univ. Press, 1988); Weitzman [chapter 5, note 66]; and Okin [chapter 2, note 25].

50. For a view that disputes that male dominance is universal and demonstrates that caring for family members is not necessarily "women's work," *see* John Noble Wilford, "Sexes Equal on South Sea Isle," *New York Times* (March 29, 1994): p. C1.

51. To point out that the costs of caregiving associated with these dependencies continue to be allocated to women in our society should not be misunderstood to be an argument about essentialism. The allocation is accomplished and reinforced by the culture and our ideology of the family as a functioning institution. Nonetheless, to label something as a social construct does not mean it will be easy to change.

52. This may also shed some light on why divorce law discourse as enlightened policy fails at the implementation stage.

53. Three family roles come to mind: sexual/reproductive; emotional/psychological; and economic—production/consumption. For centuries, the formal family stood alone as the only institution of condoned sexual intimacy, a cultural monopoly currently under attack. *See* Minow [chapter 6, note 1] at 842; *see also* Teitelbaum [chapter 6, note 8] pp. 1055–57 (discussing historical views of family law).

54. *See* Lee E. Teitelbaum, "Intergenerational Responsibility and Family Obligation: On Sharing," 1992 *Utah Law Review* 765, 773–80 (discussing the ethics and recognition of family and dependency).

55. This gendered division of labor, the dominant casting script for family stories, is built upon gender ideology that historically confined women to the "private" or family sphere, thus making them directly bear the burdens of intimacy and dependency in our society; men, as fathers and husbands, may have the corresponding responsibility of economic support.

56. *See generally* Fineman, *Illusion* [chapter 2 note 8]; Fuchs [chapter 2, note 21].

57. *See, e.g.,* James D. Weill, "Child Poverty in America," 24 *Clearinghouse Review* 336, 345–348 (1991) (Special Issue) (arguing that the 1970's demographic shift toward single-parent families was the dominant force that pushed child poverty up).

58. This may also come with its own set of political problems for some moms, as indicated by the Zoë Baird and Kimba Woods incidents.

59. As discussed in other chapters of this book, punitive and harsh measures designed to stigmatize those who deviate from the failed norm seem to be preferred by many policy makers.

7

The Limits of Privacy—
The Public Family

SECTION 2 WAS SPECIFICALLY CONCERNED WITH the political and legal responses to increases in single motherhood, whether the result of women divorcing or not marrying in the first place. In chapter 6, I considered the development of societal presumptions and assumptions underlying the concept of the sexually affiliated or natural family, referred to as the "traditional" family—composed of a husband, a wife, and their child[ren].

In this chapter, I consider the concept of "privacy"—an important legal corollary to the concept of the natural or sexual family. There are other sets of legal doctrines and rules that benefit traditional families, conferring special treatment on them or protecting the interactions of their members, that are also important in implementing societal preference for the natural family.[1] In fact, the whole area of family law establishes special rules that govern the relationships between family members and monitor the interaction of the family with outsiders.

The traditional families that are the subjects of family law are not only entitled to legal protection but also receive significant social and economic subsidies without generating the type of negative comment found in the welfare context. These benefits are not the focus of this chapter. Instead, my concern here is the concept of privacy that surrounds traditional families.

I. The Discourse of Intervention

There is a presumption with constitutional dimensions that natural families have a right to be free of state intervention and control. They are also presumed to have a right to make demands upon the larger society for certain kinds of accommodation and support. Threats to this family are taken seriously. These presumptions that cushion traditional families are eroded when single mothers make similar or parallel demands. Single mother families fall outside of prevailing ideological constructs about what (or who) constitutes a complete or real family—they may be thought of as "public" families, not entitled to privacy.

As developed in chapter 4, the prevailing presumption for these families is that the absence of a father creates a void, one that is appropriately filled by the state—by the bureaucrats who populate the many institutions, including legal ones, that deal with single mothers. Here, intervention and supervision are the norms, not privacy and the presumption of adequacy. Coercive proceedings inquire into sexual histories of AFDC mothers, who must also document other significant aspects of their lives, opening up minute details for official inspection.

Divorced mothers also are highly supervised. They are typically precluded from leaving the state with their children without paternal or state consent. They can be threatened with the loss of their children in modification proceedings post-divorce in which the state assesses their mothering under the elusive and ill-defined "best interest of the child" test.[2] The assumption of official and unofficial monitors of single mothers is that they are incompetent and in need of supervision. Single mothers have become the explicit objects of punitive and deeply suspicious public and political discourses that characterize them as dangerous to their children and, derivatively, to the rest of us as well.

Against this background consider the legalistic arguments about intervention into families. The fact that single mothers face greatly disproportionate social censure and state supervision in their mothering puts this abstract issue in perspective. Some commentators have recently questioned whether the doctrine of privacy really provides much (or even any) protection for families. Intervention (that thing that privacy supposedly prevents) is an amorphous concept. Interjection of state personnel into families does not necessarily result in "harm," and state intervention is sometimes necessary to prevent harm to individual family members.

Another aspect of the debate about intervention involves those who insist that, concepts of privacy aside, intervention is already the norm. For example, Frances Olsen has attacked the distinction constructed by many legal scholars between state intervention versus nonintervention into the family.[3] She asserts that such distinctions are artificial and incoherent, for the state *always* intervenes if it recognizes families in any form. To Olsen the real legal or policy question is merely what values the state is choosing to enforce. She notes that state intervention arguments often attempt to distinguish between "protective intervention" and intervention that is not protective of families and, for that reason, considered unacceptable.

> The protective intervention argument justifies state intervention in the family to protect children from abuse or serious neglect. State officials can remove children from their families if the children have been physically or sexually abused. In cases of child neglect, the state may send social workers into the children's homes or remove the children, temporarily or permanently, for their protection. Such state protection can include ordering medical care, even against the parents' religious scruples. These policies are generally considered to be a form of state intervention in the family, but accepted as intervention that is justified, indeed necessary.[4]

Olsen refutes the distinction by her assertion that inaction is also "intervention." The state is never neutral—a coercive vision of family is incorporated into inaction as well as action. The state, having chosen not to act on the child's behalf in regard to an allegation of abuse or neglect, for example, upholds the parent's rights against the child's.[5]

While I recognize that Professor Olsen is attempting in her analysis to provide protection for women and children within the context of the traditional patriarchal family, I find this line of reasoning disturbing, as it leaves the impression that there are no qualitative distinctions to be made between situations typically labeled as instances of state intervention and those deemed nonintervention. In fact, Olsen seems to concede this point in a discussion of the abstract principle from the perspective of the poor single mother:

> The assertion I have made—that the concepts of state intervention and nonintervention in the family are essentially meaningless—might ring hollow to an impoverished mother struggling to keep the state from taking her children away from her. More tragically, my assertion could sound absurd or seem totally meaningless to many innocent children who live in fear of the juvenile authorities. Hundreds of youngsters, the quality of whose lives has already been diminished by poverty and neglect, have been forced into silence and concealment. The specter of state intervention in the family denies to many of them even the partial relief they might get from sharing their pain and humiliation with a friendly neighbor

or sympathetic teacher. Many such children exist, and to them state
intervention can seem real and frightening.[6]

The "specter" is corporal in the sense that how we feel about intervention
can make a "real" difference to specific families. State intervention not only
"can seem" frightening—it quite regularly *is* frightening.

Perhaps even more important, privacy, as a legal deterrent to zealous
intervention, can often be significant from the perspectives of those who
seek to regulate families and the courts that are often called on to assess
their actions. So, while it is true that privacy does not draw an airtight line
around a space in which state coercive action is prohibited, it does set
up barriers that deter action. If nonintervention is the norm, bureaucratic
decisions are burdened, and the institution of family can be set up practically
and theoretically as a construct to mediate against the power of the state.
The private family enjoys the noninterventionist norm; the expectations and
claims these favored units can have vis-à-vis the larger society are unavailable
to single mother families.[7]

II. Privacy and Single Mothers

A consideration of existing legal concepts of privacy does not automatically
reveal why single mothers should be excluded from privacy protection. It
seems it should be possible to rework the idea of privacy in a way that,
while compatible with dominant social norms, would nonetheless shield
single mothers from excessive state regulation and supervision. Unfortunately, the legal history of the concept would make that task difficult, if
not impossible. At the constitutional level, notions of privacy are typically
articulated as "rights" belonging to individuals, not family entities, a limitation that actually works to the detriment of single mothers. And the common-
law notion of privacy, which does contain the concept of "family" or "entity" protection, is nonetheless limited by the ideological construction of
the natural-sexual family.

A. The Limits of Privacy—Separate Patrimonies

There are two legal sources for the concept of privacy that are relevant to
delineating the concept of family as a protected space. The first is found in

the common-law doctrines that establish "family privacy," doctrines that have been criticized and largely abandoned by liberals and feminists within contemporary legal academia. These doctrines protect the family as an entity. The second branch of privacy analysis has been developed as a constitutional concept—a protection guaranteed to individuals as part of a constellation of rights to which they are inherently entitled. This particular approach is the one most positively discussed and developed in contemporary scholarship.[8]

Hordes of legal scholars have struggled with defining and refining the doctrinal aspect of a constitutional or individual approach to privacy, adding nuance after nuance. They are vigorous in their attempts to redefine (or confine) the appropriate reach of the doctrine of privacy as a limitation on state regulation of individual decision making about intimate matters. I am not a constitutional theorist. However, I am interested in a more pragmatic inquiry as to why privacy—as a coherent legal concept, derived from either its common law or its constitutional manifestation—seems incapable of attachment to single-mother family units.

1. The Constitution and Individual Privacy

As detailed in numerous constitutional law analyses, the core of the constitutional doctrine of privacy is found in the opinion of Justice William O. Douglas in *Griswold v. Connecticut*.[9] It builds upon the older common-law notions of parental control and family privacy in holding that the state may not criminally punish those who provide contraceptive devices to married couples. Justice Douglas wrote that "various [constitutional] guarantees create zones of privacy"[10] and concluded:

> The present case, then, concerns a relationship lying within the zone of privacy created by several fundamental constitutional guarantees. And it concerns a law which, in forbidding the use of contraceptives . . . seeks to achieve its goals by means having a maximum destructive impact upon that relationship. Such a law cannot stand in light of the familiar principle . . . that a "governmental purpose to control or prevent activities constitutionally subject to state regulation may not be achieved by means which sweep unnecessarily broadly and thereby invade the area of protected freedoms." Would we allow the police to search the sacred precincts of marital bedrooms for telltale signs of the use of contraceptives? The

very idea is repulsive to the notions of privacy surrounding the marriage relationship.[11]

The opinion has been criticized as fashioning a right out of the "penumbras" of explicit constitutional protections. Yet in language reflecting his opinion that the sexual family was (in the terms of this book) both natural and sacred, Justice Douglas saw the issue as transcending mere constitutional guarantees:

> We deal with a right of privacy older than the Bill of Rights—older than our political parties, older than our school system. Marriage is a coming together for better or for worse, hopefully enduring, and intimate to the degree of being sacred. It is an association that promotes a way of life, not causes; a harmony in living, not political faiths; a bilateral loyalty, not commercial or social projects. Yet it is an association for as noble a purpose as any involved in our prior decisions.[12]

While *Griswold* began with an entity focus—the marital *couple* as the unit of constitutional protection—it did not take long to break away from the family-unit model. In a subsequent case, the focus on marriage was modified.[13] *Eisenstadt* involved the dissemination of information about, and samples of, contraceptive devices to unmarried persons. Justice Brennan concluded:

> It is true that in *Griswold* the right of privacy in question inhered in the marital relationship. Yet the marital couple is not an independent entity with a mind and heart of its own, but an association of two individuals each with a separate intellectual and emotional makeup. If the right of privacy means anything, it is the right of the individual, married or single, to be free from unwarranted governmental intrusion into matters so fundamentally affecting a person as the decision whether to bear or beget a child.[14]

While this shift from family entity to individuals has been heralded as "progressive," it is certainly consistent with other doctrinal developments in constitutional law that have the individual as the center of concern and analysis. It is also an unfortunate trend for single mothers.

The possibility of an individualized constitutional limitation is attractive to liberal legal scholars as well as to others who believe in "lifestyle" diversity, the sanctity of choice, and the ultimate folly of using conventional or religious morality as the underpinning of criminal or civil regulation of sexual or intimate behavior. The tendency toward individualization of constitutional principles seems inevitable in our contemporary social and legal cultures. Privacy (or some variant of it) has been the doctrinal mantle under which are collected arguments that all consensual sexual behavior should be free of state regulation, as well as arguments that address a woman's right to make unfettered reproductive decisions.[15] In fact, privacy as construed in *Griswold* and *Eisenstadt* has been used to secure significant rights in regard to reproduction and sexual decision making.[16]

While I support efforts to limit the zealous impulses to regulate intimate behavior that mark many states' criminal and civil rules, I wonder if privacy is the tool with which to do it. Privacy, as a constitutional limitation on state interference with or sanctioning of individual behavior, has some serious conceptual limitations. It is true that the doctrine, which began by protecting the most "sanctified" of intimate relations (marriage), has been expanded to cover other issues in response to various societal pressures (the abortion decision). But what has been the result when the behavior at issue is less "universal" in nature than heterosexuality and reproduction (and, therefore, perhaps less socially acceptable)? It is significant that in the context of homosexuality the doctrine of privacy has not been deemed available for the protective task it performs for more traditional behavior. In *Bowers v. Hardwick*,[17] Justice White, writing for the majority of the Supreme Court of the United States, referenced tradition (or traditional sexuality) and the traditional family in refusing to extend privacy protection to consensual sexual behavior between gay men. Justice White found no connection between the "claimed constitutional right of homosexuals to engage in acts of sodomy"[18] and the traditionally protected "family, marriage or procreation."[19] Relying on a perception that "proscriptions against [consensual sodomy] have ancient roots,"[20] he then rejected as "at best facetious"[21] the claim that "a right to engage in such conduct is 'deeply rooted in this Nation's history and tradition' or 'implicit' in the concept of ordered liberty."[22]

Bowers considered only the constitutionality of Georgia's statute criminalizing sodomy and, therefore, did not directly address the issue of potential privacy claims by single mothers. Its reliance on the "traditional" and "natural" as the basis for constitutional protection, however, raises serious doubts about whether this line of privacy doctrine would be fruitfully pursued by those seeking protection for single mothers.

Also ominous for the same conceptual reasons is a recent case (*Michael H. v. Gerald D.*) decided by the Supreme Court in which the rights of an unwed biological father (which had been so painstakingly constructed in earlier cases)[23] were ignored in favor of the "unitary family."[24] Writing for a plurality of the Court, Justice Scalia upheld the conclusive presumption that a married man was the father of his wife's child in the face of irrefutable evidence to the contrary introduced by the biological father who sought visitation rights. The biological father had been deeply involved in the child's life, even living with her and the mother for some time. In fact, the child's guardian *ad litem* urged that the child's interest would be best served by recognizing the biological father and conferring visitation rights. Quoting *Griswold*, Justice Scalia nonetheless noted:

> The Due Process Clause affords only those protections "so rooted in the traditions and conscience of our people as to be ranked as fundamental." Our cases reflect "continual insistence upon respect for the teachings of history [and] solid recognition of the basic values that underlie our society."[25]

He refused to read the unwed fatherhood cases as establishing a liberty interest created by biological fatherhood plus an established parental relationship:

> As we view them [these cases] rest not upon such isolated factors but upon the historic respect—indeed, sanctity would not be too strong a term—traditionally accorded to the relationships that develop within the unitary family.[26]

As succinctly stated later in the opinion:

> "Our traditions have protected the marital family."[27]

In a footnote, Justice Scalia noted that the marital family only "typified" the unitary family and that the concept "also includes the household of unmarried parents and their children."[28] However, although he conceded that it was possible to expand the notion of the unitary family beyond this presumably heterosexual form, he declined to do so because "it will bear no resemblance to traditionally respected relationships—and will thus cease to have any constitutional significance."[29]

Michael H. represents the intersection and conflict of the two privacy trends—individual and entity. The primacy of the male biological tie (individual), reinforced by subsequent parenting behavior, gave way to the legal preference for traditional marriage (entity).

The several Justices who dissented would have drawn the lines differently, protecting the biological father and not the unitary or marital family. This approach would have limited the role of tradition and resulted in a more fluid notion of paternal and familial practices to be constitutionally protected, but the choice of privacy for protection is a limited one. Privacy as it has developed and been articulated as a constitutional principle is premised on the individual, not on an entity.[30] The individualized nature of the inquiry significantly limits the concept of privacy and makes it less likely to protect the single-mother family as a unit.

In fact, resolving questions of state interference in intimate matters by focusing on the individual seems to inevitably make matters worse for single mothers. This is so because of the assumptions about deviance and pathology that accompany the status. Single mothers are cast as dangerous. And, if the individual is the focus of constitutional concern, it is all too easy for the state to justify increased regulation and supervision of mothering by acting in its "protective" capacity for the child against the mother.[31] Current characterizations of medical decisions women make during the course of pregnancy as "maternal-fetal conflict" are examples of what stark legal configurations result from the tendency to individualize family members: the pitting of one family member's rights against another's.[32] The individualized nature of legal inquiry has also resulted in the development of the discourse of fathers' rights in which, although the child is cast as the rights holder, the right asserted is the entitlement to a relationship with the father regardless of the mother's (or child's) wishes.[33]

Privacy defined primarily in terms of individualized constitutional rights also means that while certain types of monumental but insular types of individual decisions are protected, day-to-day family lives are left susceptible to state regulation and supervision. As an individual right, privacy can be waived or bartered away, for example, as a condition for receiving welfare benefits.[34] Even if that does not occur, privacy offers limited protection for the "routine." For example, while constitutional notions of privacy might protect an individual woman's decision about abortion or contraception, they have not supported her refusal to participate in a demeaning paternity proceeding in which her sexual history is the central focus.[35] Such hearings are now required for single mothers receiving AFDC,[36] and a federally sponsored movement is afoot to require them in all cases of nonmarital births where a father is not listed on the birth certificate.

A Wisconsin law exemplifies this requirement. The mandatory-paternity law, authored by Tom Loftus, then Speaker of the Wisconsin Legislature, provides that a state's attorney "shall commence an action [to establish paternity] on behalf of the state within 6 months after receiving notification . . . that no father is named on the birth certificate of a child who is a resident of the county if paternity had not been adjudicated."[37] This action may be taken by the state regardless of the wishes of the mother and without any consideration for whether the mother and her child are likely to ever be in need of financial assistance from the state.

Such measures are urged not only in the language of economic necessity but also in the rhetoric of individualized "rights"—children have rights to support, to a father, and to a patrimony independent of, and often in opposition to, their mothers' desires.[38] The net gain in this accrual of rights tends to be for the process of state intervention. Loftus clearly echoed this philosophy when referring to the legislation:

> We have now in Wisconsin a law that I authored that will become the model for the nation regarding paternity. It had as its foundation that every child born in Wisconsin has a legal right to a father. Children without legal fathers have started down a slippery slope that leads to poverty. Our new paternity law is a radical departure in that the interests of the child become equal if not paramount to the interests of the natural parents.[39]

This is an example of the legislative perception of single mothers as endangering or depriving their children.

2. The Family as "Entity" and the Common-Law Concept of Privacy

One resolution to the limitation for single mothers associated with the constitutional, individualized notion of privacy would be to return to the idea of privacy as a protection, not only for individuals but also for family units. An "entity" approach to the issue of privacy is found in the common law, recognized in Supreme Court cases, and has theoretical potential for protecting women, particularly poor single mothers, from state supervision and regulation of their mothering.

The common-law concept of privacy as protection for the family unit was a natural outgrowth of the domestic ideology prevalent in the latter part of the nineteenth century in which life was divided between the "public" and "private" spheres. The common-law privacy doctrine is not an individualized concept but is founded on the nature of the protected relationship: theoretically it attaches to the entity of the family, not to the individuals that compose it. Historically, this has meant that, in certain cases, the doctrine operates to shield the family unit from state interference even when the request for intervention comes from one of the family members.[40]

While an individualized notion of privacy has received much positive contemporary attention, family or entity privacy concepts have been criticized and all but abandoned by liberal scholars. This has not occurred without good reasons. The family-unit notion of privacy has strong negative common-law antecedents associated with the exclusion of women from public and economic life. When the world was conceptually divided into separate spheres, the private sphere was designated the "protected" space under the common law. It was the space into which women were placed along with the family and all other domestic concerns.[41] The private was viewed as both subservient to, and supportive of, the public (more important) sphere—the refuge where intimacy and affection were nurtured so heads of households could compete in the wider world.[42]

The doctrine in its strongest form prohibited the state from asserting its protective role even at the behest of one of the spouses in an ongoing relationship who claimed the need for protection.[43] Parent-child interaction was also shielded, sometimes even if it was abusive.[44] The family that stood within the private sphere was traditionally one with a hierarchical organization in which husbands and fathers, by virtue of their public roles, assumed dominance in the family as well.[45]

The notion of separate spheres, and hence family privacy, came under sustained attack by feminists in the second half of the twentieth century.[46] Women historically had been assigned exclusively to the private sphere, at least on a rhetorical level, and discrimination against them in the public sphere was justified by the state's protective role.[47] More recently, feminist scholars have reminded us that the doctrine of family privacy often cloaked the violence against women and children that all too often occurs within families.[48]

The feminist critique of the current state of the common-law family privacy doctrine concludes that the doctrine has been unavailable to protect women and children because as individuals they are undifferentiated, and therefore invisible, within the family as an entity. The reluctance to look beyond entity to individuals within the family has meant that they have been subject to potential dominance and oppression. In fact, feminists assert that privacy has only operated as a mask for male oppression within families and for that reason should be abandoned. The common-law idea of privacy as positive protection for the family *unit* in the context of liberal theory has thus been discredited. As a result, liberal privacy scholarship has tended to concentrate on the promises contained within the *individual* focus of constitutional law doctrine.[49]

But the private sphere ideology, with all its faults, nonetheless has established the concept of the desirability of a family or private space into which the state, absent compelling reasons, is not free to intrude. In this regard, it is important to note that the critiques of entity privacy have not questioned the basic concept of "family" contained in the ideal of family privacy. Feminists, like the originators and contemporary conservative proponents of family privacy, assume a certain type of family as the fixed norm—heterosexual, hierarchical, and patriarchal. The convergence of the traditional notion of family with the concept of entity or family privacy ordains that it cannot be helpful to the women with whom I am concerned.

What would be the result, however, if we refused to accept this imposition of the traditional family as the only unit protected under a common-law concept of entity privacy, arguing that it is an unwarranted ideological limitation on the contemporary use of the concept? The question would then be: Can we move beyond traditional cultural constructs of the family and use the idea of entity privacy to refashion a more fundamental and prevalent protected unit? In other words, can we invoke the common-law notion of family privacy without its patriarchal baggage to protect single-mother families against the presumption of appropriate intervention that now stalks their existence? Is it possible to reimagine the family so that single mothers and poor families are considered entities worthy of privacy— no longer constructed as "public" families, no longer susceptible to supervision as deviant? Given the insights into the designation of single-mother units as deviant in Section 2, it is no surprise that this turns out to be an ideological task not easily accomplished.

B. The Public Family

The development of privacy doctrine has been limited by the same societal assumptions about intimacy, families, and individuality already explored in the context of divorce and poverty discourses. The family remains a concept embedded in social and cultural presuppositions that seems unlikely to be rehabilitated or reworked to include single-mother units as presumptively appropriate functional families.

In fact, given the substantial ideological and doctrinal barriers to social acceptance of single-mother families, any emphasis on entity privacy will probably further reinforce the reification of the natural or normal family. The continued emphasis on privacy, in either entity or individual form, as the primary concept to protect nontraditional families may also deter the development of other legal principles that might help to limit state regulation of poor and single-mother families.

As developed in Section 2, women, merely because they are single mothers, are considered to be not conforming to important cultural and social norms. The fact that some single mothers are also poor further contributes to the process of labeling them as deviant.[50] Poor single mothers not only fail to conform to the nuclear-family model but also do not live up to the norms of "independence" and economic "self-reliance" that underlie our normative images of American families. Occupying either the category of poverty or that of single motherhood places women (along with their children) into the realm of "public" families.

These women potentially can have many aspects of their lives cast as public, and therefore appropriately placed under some form of state supervision. The nuclear-family norm dictates the form "normal" or "natural" families should take. Mothers who fail to conform are "made public"— portrayed as in chronic need of state supervision in making decisions about their families. Divorced mothers are not secure in their custody of children as are mothers in marriages. Custody determinations can be modified.[51] There are proposals that these mothers be made to account for child-support expenditures, and they are threatened with loss of control over decisions affecting their children by courts seeking to involve fathers in the day-to-day operation of functioning custodial mother families.[52] In other words, these single-mother families are subject to public control merely because they experienced a divorce in the past.

For poor women, the supervision is justified because single mothers require economic subsidies from public sources. Consider, for example, the procedures supported by the editorial board of the *Philadelphia Inquirer* several years ago that would have offered AFDC mothers full Norplant (birth control implants) and given "incentives" in the form of increased AFDC stipends.[53] The paper later withdrew its suggestion.[54] In the first such official effort, a Kansas state legislator proposed the state pay $500 to any mother on welfare who uses Norplant. Under the bill, Kansas would also pay for implanting the device, which prevents pregnancy for up to five years by slowly releasing progestin, a female hormone. The state would also pay for annual checkups plus an additional $50 a year as long as the contraceptive remained implanted. In justifying the measure, the sponsor stated:

> By any set of objective criteria, the creation of the program has the potential to save the taxpayers millions of their hard-earned dollars. . . . Something must be done to reduce the number of unwanted pregnancies, and this type of voluntary program, where the public welfare recipient is given a strong financial incentive to use a safe reversible contraceptive device that has a useful life of five years, represents the best way to prevent them.[55]

One must wonder about the use of the term "voluntary" in the context of the inducement of an AFDC recipient, who is already living on a stipend below the poverty level. When confronted with an economic "incentive," the notion she has a "choice" in such circumstances seems illusory. One also wonders about the idea of "unwanted" pregnancies contained in the quote—and the question must be, "Unwanted by whom?"

The public nature of the perceived inadequacies of single mothers justifies their regulation, supervision, and control. "Private" families, by contrast, are protected. They exemplify the "natural" form and fulfill the natural function of families—they are perceived as independent and economically self-sufficient.

There is, of course, a disingenuity about this characterization. "Private" families in fact receive massive public subsidies through a variety of governmental and other programs. They are not considered "public" only because in their basic form and functioning they conform to social norms.

In fact, most middle-class families benefit from extensive entitlement programs, be they FHA or VA loans at below mortgage market rates or employer subsidized health and life insurance. These families receive untaxed benefits as direct subsidies. One welfare rights group in the 1970s described as "marriage relief" programs that allow married couples to file joint income tax returns and therefore pay less taxes than single persons, and characterized as "aid to families with dependent houses" the rules that allow homeowners to deduct from their income tax purposes the interest paid on their mortgages.[56] Private families, by living up to ideological expectations, can be considered to have earned the right to privacy—the right to be free from the state supervision and control that accompanies the designation of deviancy.

It seems that incorporation of single mothers under the protections afforded the natural family is not likely to happen soon. Reconceptualizing these families as just one more form among many equally appropriate alternatives requires of the law and of society more than just minor changes. It requires adjustments more profound than mere manipulation of existing doctrines to cover so-called analogous cases. In an ideological system where the two-parent nuclear model is the paradigm, there are no analogues for our thinking about single-mother families.

Accommodation of single mother families requires radical transformation on ideological and institutional levels. Our emotional understanding of what constitutes "the family" has not changed all that much—this is as true for critics of the traditional family as for those who are traditionalists. It may be that trying to incorporate single mothers and their children into the idea of the "private" family is too threatening to basic cultural and social configurations. Accepting mother/child units as natural or normal ultimately calls into question the role of men within families in our society. Men, we are accustomed to think, are heads of families, or at least they are equal, necessary, and essential parts of the basic core concept of family. Single motherhood also unleashes biases and fears concerning female sexuality unsupervised by the constraints of patriarchal institutions such as marriage.

It is unlikely that the abstract concept of privacy will be successfully employed to limit state regulation of single-mother families. Our social concept of what constitutes a family has not begun to reflect the living redefinitions of intimacy and family that single mothers are practicing every-day. Single motherhood, although increasingly prevalent across all groups within society, deviates too far from traditional norms.

III. Conclusion—The Role of Law in Social Change

The inability of privacy doctrine to expand beyond the confines of a concept of natural family to encompass the circumstances of single mothers supports my assertion that law as an ideological discourse is more "reflective" than "constitutive" of social morality. Furthermore, doctrinal law, considered as either theory or rhetoric, presents a coherent normative system that is not only reflective and passive but also active and useful in the implementation of existing power relationships in society. Law can be, and often is, an essential part of the overall imposition and perpetuation of societal norms.

To the extent that legal discourse is integral to enforcing socially and culturally defined norms, it is a concrete force in confining the lives of real people. However effective, the normative regulation of people's lives, at least in a heterogenous society such as the United States, cannot be accomplished on just a cultural level. To an individual, law is a reminder that there is a direct and potentially coercive societal interest in areas of presumed individual and family decision making. Law and legal institutions thus become exemplars of the public institutionalization of social coercion.

That the development of any specific doctrine may be limited by the existence of cultural and social norms may seem obvious. The more interesting issue, which is of both theoretical and practical significance, is to try to understand in what circumstances law could be used to counter those norms—to redistribute power. For example, many attorneys involved in public-interest work employ existing legal concepts in order to empower disempowered groups of people in our society. Quite often results are obtained for individuals. But all too often existing law operates as a limitation, distorting the aspirational nature of reform. Sometimes the supposed "beneficiaries" of such efforts often find their lives overly regulated and controlled by legal definitions that fail to reflect their circumstances.

Thus, while the law can sometimes be the originating or initiating source of social change, if reforms fail to reference some more generally held norms, the law cannot be used effectively to transform. The law is a limited conceptual or ideological tool when used to attempt to alter widely shared basic assumptions that are at the core of our cultural ideology.

Privacy protection of single-mother families does not seem imminent. The concept of privacy as developed in constitutional doctrine is too focused on the rights of individuals to accomplish this end; it focuses on sexual and reproductive choices in a classless paradigm that assumes an individual's freedom to act outside of state enmeshment. The traditional concept of the nuclear family that underlies the common-law idea of "family privacy" seems so embedded in our collective culture that doctrine will not be easily adapted to accommodate and protect contemporary single-mother family situations.

Notes

1. Married persons receive significantly favorable treatment under the estate and gift tax law, enabling them to give gifts and to pass on estates of unlimited value to a spouse without the grantor having to pay taxes on the gift or estate transferred. *See* 26 U.S.C. §§2056, 2523 (West Supp. 1993). *But see* David J. Roberts and Mark J. Sullivan, "The Federal Income Tax: Where are the Family Values?" 57 *Tax Notes* (Oct. 26, 1992): pp. 547, 549 (arguing that tax provisions for filing joint returns may unevenly impact married couples so that some receive a benefit while others pay a penalty). Another significant benefit, which has recently been expanded to nonmarried partners, is insurance or other employment-related health-care coverage.

2. For a critique of this test on the basis of its indeterminacy *see*, Fineman, *Illusion* [chapter 2, note 8] chapters 5–9.

3. Olsen [chapter 2, note 2].

4. *Ibid.*, p. 839.

5. *Ibid.*, p. 843.

6. *Ibid.*, p. 858.

7. Privacy as a constitutional concept means the state cannot enact criminal penalties or establish punitive regulations as to certain behaviors between adults. *See*

generally, Griswold v. Connecticut, 381 U.S. 479 (1965) (holding state cannot regulate contraception between married partners); *Bowers v. Hardwick,* 478 U.S. 186 (1986) (by implication, sodomy within the traditional family would be protected).

8. This position can be seen in the current privacy debates surrounding the protection of homosexual relationships, *see* Chapter 6, note 36, and abortion rights, *see* Chapter 7, note 16.

9. 381 U.S. 479 (1965).

10. *Ibid.,* p. 484 (citation omitted).

11. *Ibid.,* pp. 485–86 (citation omitted).

12. *Ibid.,* p. 465. Many other Justices wrote concurring opinions that also focused on the nature of the marriage relationship and the sacred aspects of that institution.

13. *Eisenstadt v. Baird,* 405 U.S. 438 (1972).

14. *Ibid.,* p. 453.

15. *See Planned Parenthood of Missouri v. Danforth,* 428 U.S. 52 (1976) (a woman's right to privacy prevents the state from requiring written consent from her husband before she may legally obtain an abortion); *Roe v. Wade,* 410 U.S. 113 (1973) (the constitutional right to privacy prevents that state from unduly interfering with a woman's choice to obtain an abortion); *Eisenstadt v. Baird* [chapter 7, note 13].

16. *See* Colb [chapter 3, note 3] at 122 (discussing an appellate court's equation of forced paternity with forced maternity, and observing that when the court protects men against forced fatherhood by likening it to forced motherhood, "the court abstracts the pain and vulnerability that women alone endure out of the definition of human experience. It mandates gender-blindness even though reality makes greater demands of women than of men"). *Id.*

17. [Chapter 7, note 7] (upholding a Georgia statute that criminalized the practice of sodomy between consenting adults and rejected the argument that such governmental intrusion was prohibited by respondent's constitutional right to privacy).

18. *Id.* at 191.

19. *Id.*

20. *Id.* at 192.

21. *Id.* at 193.

22. *Id.*

23. *See* discussion in chapter 4.

24. *Michael H. v. Gerald D.,* 491 U.S. 110 (1989).

25. *Ibid.*, p. 122–23, for an analysis of how the California presumption of paternity as well as Justice Scalia's description of it as "natural" serves to deny what power women have to thwart paternal certainty about their offspring, *see* Colb [chapter 3, note 3] pp. 109–111.

26. *Ibid.*, p. 123.

27. *Ibid.*, p. 124.

28. *Ibid.*

29. There are exceptions to this, but they tend to reflect the common-law privacy concept attaching to the family unit. Thus, for example, the "grandmother" cases decided on a constitutional privacy basis rely on the unique nature of certain relationships. *See Pierce v. Society of Sisters,* 268 U.S. 510, 534 (1925) (holding invalid state restrictions that "unreasonably interfere with the ability of parents and guardians to direct the upbringing and education of children"); *Meyer v. Nebraska,* 262 U.S. 390, 399 (1923) (stating that the "right . . . to marry, establish a home and bring up children" strictly limits government action in that area).

30. This has already occurred in the context of ADFC. *See Wyman v. James,* 400 U.S. 309 (1971). In *Wyman,* the Supreme Court relied on the rights of the child against the mother to uphold the state's power to send social workers into the homes of benefits recipients, unannounced and without consent. Writing for the majority, Justice Blackmun held, "The dependent child's needs are paramount, and only with hesitancy could we relegate those needs . . . to a position secondary to what the mother claims as her rights." *Id.* at 318.

31. John Hart Ely critically analyzes the potential constitutional sources for a woman's right to an abortion. John Hart Ely, "The Wages of Crying Wolf: A Comment on Roe v. Wade," 82 *Yale Law Journal* 920, 933–35 (1973). Professor Ely couches his discussion almost exclusively in terms of maternal/fetal conflict. At one point, for example, he states, "Compared with men, very few women sit in our legislatures, a fact I believe should bear some relevance . . . to the appropriate standard of review for legislation that favors men over women. But *no* fetuses sit in our legislatures." *Id.* at 933. *See also* Donald H. Regan, "Rewriting Roe v. Wade," 77 *Michigan Law Review* 1569 (1979), where the author proposes that abortion is an omission, not an act, and thus a woman's right to an abortion is protected under the "good samaritan" doctrine (which provides the mother has no affirmative duty to the fetus); Judith Jarvis Thomson, "A Defense of Abortion," 1 *Philosophy and Public Affairs* 47 (1971), where the author defends abortion on the grounds that it is an act of self-defense on the part of the mother against the fetus.

32. *See* Chapter 8 for examples of this discourse.

33. *See Wyman v. James* [chapter 7, note 30] pp. 317–19 (because they receive benefits, some families cannot prohibit state workers from visiting their homes).

34. *See* Chapter 5, notes 39 and 40. Women receiving benefits are required to undergo mandatory paternity proceedings as a condition of receiving their bene- fits. Women who have named men later excluded by blood test or who have said they do not know the name or location of the father have been subjected to severe scrutiny and questioning by the state agencies. *See, e.g., Allen v. Eichler,* No. 89A-FE-4, 1990 WL 58223 (Del. Super. Ct. 1990) (where the plaintiff named several men as possible fathers, but they were excluded by blood tests or could not be located. The agency required her to turn over a calendar on which she supposedly had written the names of her sexual partners; when she refused, her benefits were cut).

    The woman receiving benefits is not, however, required to establish paternity if, considering the best interests of the child, she has "good cause." 42 U.S.C. §602(a)(26)(B)(1988). "Good cause" is determined according to the child's need only when the child will suffer physical or emotional harm or if the mother will suffer such harm such that she cannot "care for the child adequately." 45 C.F.R. §§232.42 (a)(1)(i)-.42(a)(1)(iii)(1990).

    "Good cause" has been denied to a mother in such extreme situations as when she alleged rape and, because she anticipated harm to herself and her child, did not report the rape to the police. *Waller v. Carlton County Human Servs. Dep't.,* No. 06-89-1116, 1989 WL 145393 (Minn. App. 1989).

35. *See* Chapter 5, notes 39 and 40.

36. *See Wis. Stat.* §767.45(6m) (1993).

37. Tom Loftus, *Remarks at the National Child Support Enforcement Association Annual Conference,* New Orleans, LA (August 23, 1988): pp. 427–28 (transcript on file with author).

    This theme is also reflected in the modern trend in custody and visitation determination proceedings, where courts are substituting for the "best interest of the child" standard one that emphasizes the child's right to continue relationships with both parents. *See Egle v. Egle* [chapter 4, note 32] at 1017, ("the preserva- tion of relationships with both parents is normally in the best interests of the children"); *Kemp v. Kemp,* 42 Md. App. 90, 98, 399 A.2d 923, 928 (1979) ("Absent any other evidence here that visitation would adversely affect the child's welfare, the father's visitation with his son must be reinstated"); *Devita v. Devita,* 145 N.J. Super. 120, 130, 366 A.2d 1350, 1356 (App. Div. 1976) (Antell, J., dissenting) (the court's "first obligation" is "to 'strain every effort to attain for the child the affection of both parents rather than one' " [quoting *Turney v. Nooney,* 5 N.J. Super. 392, 397, 69 A.2d 342, 344 (App. Div. 1949)]).

38. Loftus [chapter 7, note 37].

39. *See State v. Black,* 60 N.C. 274, 275 (1864) (where the court wrote in response to a wife's claim against her husband for assault: "[The law] prefers to leave the parties to themselves, as the best mode of inducing them to make the matter up and live together as man and wife should."). For further discussion and examples, see Beirne Stedman, "Right of Husband to Chastise Wife," 3 *Virginia Law Reg.* (New Series) 241, 244–48 (1917).

40. *See* Demos [chapter 6, note 28] pp. 49–55.

41. *See* Olsen [chapter 4, note 29].

42. *See State* v. Black [chapter 7, note 39].

43. *See* Eva R. Rubin, *The Supreme Court and the American Family* (New York: Greer, 1986): p. 165.

44. *Ibid.,* pp. 16–17, 19.

45. *See, e.g.,* Chapter 3, note 6.

46. Such "protective" treatment of women was expressed by Blackstone when, after noting that a married woman had no right to hold property, contract, or bring suit and may be subject to certain "correction" by her husband, he states, "The disabilities which the wife lies under are for the most part intended for her protection and benefit: so great a favorite is the female sex of the laws of England." W. Blackstone, *Commentaries* (3d ed. 1768): p. 445. This notion was echoed in *Bradwell* [chapter 3, note 7], when the Supreme Court upheld a woman's denial to the Illinois Bar simply because she was a woman. Justice Bradley noted in his concurrence:

    > The civil law, as well as nature herself, has always recognized a wide difference in the respective spheres and destinies of man and woman. Man is, or should be, woman's protector and defender. The natural and proper timidity and delicacy which belongs to the female sex evidently unfits it for many of the occupations of civil life. *Id.* at 141.

    For more modern examples of the Court's adherence to this view, see *United States v. Yazell,* 382 U.S. 341 (1966) (upholding summary judgment in favor of a married woman who had entered into and defaulted on a contract with plaintiff/appellant on the grounds that under the state law of coverture she had no capacity to enter into the contract in question); *Goesaert v. Cleary,* 335 U.S. 464 (1948) (upholding Michigan law that provided no woman could obtain a bartender's license unless she was the wife or daughter of a male owner of a licensed liquor establishment).

47. *See, e.g.,* Schneider [chapter 6, note 39].

48. *See* June Aline Eichbaum, "Towards an Autonomy-Based Theory of Constitutional Privacy: Beyond the Ideology of Familial Privacy," 14 *Harvard Civil Rights Civil Liberties Law Review* 361 (1979).

49. *See* discussion in chapter 5.

50. Joan Wexler argues this should be unconstitutional under an idea of family autonomy. Joan G. Wexler, "Rethinking the Modification of Child Custody," 94 *Yale Law Journal* 257, 803–818 (1985).

51. This is especially striking in the area of religion. With the increase in interfaith and interdenominational marriages, questions frequently arise regarding the religious training of the children. Sometimes the decision is left to the custodial parent, *see, e.g., Reace v. Reace,* 350 N.E. 2d 143 (1976); but sometimes the noncustodial parent is given control of religious decisions affecting the children, *see, e.g., Stern v. Stern,* 188 N.E. 2d 97 (1963). For a review of this issue, *see* Jordan C. Paul, Note, "'You Get the House, I Get the Car, You Get the Kids, I Get Their Souls.' The Impact of Spiritual Custody Awards on the Free Exercise Rights of Custodial Parents," 138 *Univ. Pennsylvania Law Review* 583 (1990).

52. *Philadelphia Inquirer* (December 12, 1990), p. A18.

53. *Philadelphia Inquirer* (December 23, 1990), p. C4,

54. Lewin, "A Plan to Pay Welfare Mother for Birth Control," *New York Times,* February 9, 1991, p. 9A. *See also* discussion, Chapter 4, note 3 of PCS/HB 1451 filed by two Florida state legislators for the 1994 session.

55. *Id.*

56. Milwaukee County Welfare Rights Organization, *The Real Welfare Crisis.* In *Welfare Mothers Speak Out* (Thomas Howard Tarantino and Dismas Becker eds. New York: Norton, 1972): pp. 17–19. The programs provided benefits in the fiscal year 1970 of $1.6 and $2.6 billion, respectively. *Id.* at 17.

PART 4

Other Tragedies and Utopian Visions

THIS SECTION EXAMINES some further difficulties that result from the ways in which we conceptualize the family and motherhood. Chapter 8 begins with a consideration of the tensions within fathers'-rights rhetoric about goals and aspirations. Certainly one significant tragedy is that the opportunity to reconceptualize fatherhood as part of the evolving family debates has produced more rights rhetoric than re-visioning. Rights attach to individuals, and the overriding tragedy is the fact that children, cast in opposition to Mother as a by-product of the individualization process, are also financially and emotionally abandoned by fathers and by the state. Individual rights and individual responsibility impede the development of a concept of collective responsibility for children who increasingly are relegated to lives of poverty in this country. The question of fathers' responsibility for children is addressed in a consideration of proposals to provide incentives for fathers to use birth control. This is an attempt to institute "responsible reproduction", but such proposals quite often work to the disadvantage of women, who are most likely to become targets of state policy when incentive systems fail.

Chapter 9 concludes the book. In it I recommend a utopian re-visioning of the legal relationship between family and state that builds on the critique of the neutered Mother and the sexual family. I argue for the abolition of marriage with its special family law rules. I urge leaving adults who are sexually affiliated free to use traditional means, such as contract or property, to forge desired legal relationships. They would be given the option of resorting to tort or criminal law if they were harmed or abused by each other. Children and other "dependents" need special protection, however, and are not so easily set free of the "protective" confines of the family and the constrictions of family law. To insure that there is a "family" for them, I build on the cultural power of the Mother/Child dyad as the appropriate metaphor with which to refashion our concepts of family and intimacy. I argue that the core family relationship is nurturing, and it is that connection rather than the sexual one that should be pivotal. It is this unit that I urge be considered our "core" family unit—the entity that defines "natural" and is protected as "private"; the unit around which policy should be structured.

8

Other Tragedies

IN THIS CHAPTER I want to return to some of the ideas developed in previous sections in order to highlight some of the other tragedies inherent in the trend toward deterioration, individualization, and competition in societal expressions of intimacy. One aspect of the overall tragedy is that even in a climate of reconsideration generated by social changes and the women's movement culminating in the neutering of Mother, there has been no corollary reconstruction or reconsideration of the institution of fatherhood.

Mother is neutered and fatherhood ascends. "Authorities," including medical and other professional personnel, operate without substantial opposition within the context of historically male institutions. They are the "default" experts in regard to children, reproduction, and families. Revised laws ensure that men as fathers maintain their social and economic advantages under the law with little change in behavior. Mothers are structurally set up in opposition to fathers and, ultimately, in opposition to their own children, whose newly articulated "rights" typically are cast as coinciding with the interests of the father. Children are placed at the vortex of backlash energy. In struggles over control, they become the objects of privilege within patriarchal families.

I. The Discourse of Fathers' Rights

A. Three Strains

The rhetoric of fathers' rights and fathers' responsibilities reflects the tendency to reduce family policy to mere discussions of individual rights. Three strains of fathers'-rights rhetoric appear in contemporary discussions about mothers, children, and families. A perceived loss of paternal power or privilege is the focus of both the middle class and the emerging African-American fathers' rights discourses. Much less vocal (and visible) are the men who call for a transformation of the whole notion of "father," moving toward a redefinition that is neither hierarchical nor patriarchal. Unfortunately, most prevalent is the discourse in which the primary concern seems to be a perceived and generalized loss of male privilege: Many men no longer feel secure within the traditional family.

In this society, the roles men historically have occupied in the patriarchal family are theoretically threatened by the re-visioning of gender equality. In response, punitive and harsh rhetoric is directed at mothers, and proposals surface that are designed to shore up or reinstate male control even after separation or divorce. The rules propose supervision and/or punishment for women who live outside the confines of the nuclear family. These proposals are provoked by and often accompany fathers'-rights discourse replete with allegations of maternal abuse and abandonment of responsibility for children. For example, there are arguments that mothers' disbursement of (measly) child-support awards should be monitored because women are stealing from their children to support new lovers or vile habits. Custodial mothers are the subject of reform proposals that would have them submitting to yearly accounting, a ludicrous suggestion given the typically minuscule amount of money involved and the nature of the bureaucratic mechanism that would be required for such a procedure.[1]

A sense of crisis is generated in fathers'-rights discourse on visitation. The assertion is that mothers, as a group, persist in interfering with access to children and, therefore, should be subject to fines and/or imprisonment on a father's complaint. In the same category as the horror stories about visitation and misuse of child support are concerns that women receiving public assistance are engaged in irresponsible consumption of public (tax) funds. There is a great deal of concern with such women's sexuality, which is operating outside of male supervision and control. Mothers receiving such support are portrayed as irresponsibly reproducing, as well as consuming, and their actions must be contained. Selfish mothers monopolize reproduction, refusing to have children and choosing abortion, or, when they do have children, keeping them from their fathers. This strain of fathers'-rights rhetoric assumes that mothers can "win" rights only at the expense of others—fathers or society at large. The perception is that every small step to protect women in general and mothers in particular comes at someone else's expense.

In a recent column William Safire spoke for these men and told us "what fathers want":

> Let me tell you what fathers want. We want our intrinsic authority back.
> This essential prerogative of fatherhood has been stolen from us by children who want us to be their friends and by those children's mothers who insist on shared parentalism.[2]

Safire is clear about his reaction to the idea of parental equality:

> What about the new parental equality? Mother now often brings home the bacon, or at least her fair share of it; why shouldn't she expect Father to share child-nurturing duties along with other household tasks?
> That's for parents to work out between themselves, but as far as most kids are concerned, the sources of parental power are not the same. Motherpower is rooted in love, fatherpower in authority. The ultimate maternal sanction is "This would break your Mom's heart." The ultimate paternal guilt-implanter is "Dad will be disappointed in you."[3]

In eulogizing fathers as uniquely good at "laying down the law," Safire casts about for a way to make men more responsible as fathers:

> What psychological incentive can we give young fathers to do their duty? With all its trials—the nights awake, the worries about not spending quality time, adolescent rebellion, the money for college—fatherhood is tough enough; we don't have to strip away its unique mystique of lifelong respect.
> Beyond the pleasures of watching their seed miraculously develop, fathers who make the family effort need recognition as "head" of a household. Frequent challenges to that authority are affirmations, not denials, of its existence; occasional obedience also helps. The expectation of paternal authority—freely, if grudgingly, given—goes with the family territory.[4]

A second strain of fathers'-rights rhetoric, not overtly hostile to mothers, doesn't conceptualize the problem as a loss of men's historically privileged position. Nonetheless, in this discourse it is imperative to restore fathers to their mythic position as "head" of the household. Men historically excluded from many of society's rewards, specifically African-American and Hispanic fathers, are the reference points in this discourse. Quite often in making the concerns of these fathers central, the arguments resort to images of traditional patriarchy in an attempt to persuade dominant culture of the need for economic justice.[5]

In this discourse, fatherhood is a window into the "real" or hard issues of unemployment. Fathers must have access to jobs and training programs in order to "be" fathers, but their status as fathers remains unexplored. The concerns are still economic and the competitive focus is still the relationship between the sexes in the arena of the family. The emphasis is different and the solutions proposed typically less explicitly harsh and punitive toward women and children, but often the same implications are evident.[6] Some of the rhetoric may be understood as suggesting that Black women, particularly as single mothers, emasculate Black men and that women in general are incapable of raising sons. Even if women are sympathetically perceived, the discourse is decidedly paternalistic and patriarchal with well-defined idealized places for women and men. The focus is on the male, the father who must be economically and socially empowered to assume his traditional responsibilities.

I am more sympathetic to the second discourse, but both the fathers'-rights arguments based on loss of privilege and those based on notions of economic justice symbolically hold the child-to-be-fathered hostage until either women or the larger society treat men right. The individual mother and child unit on the one hand, and the larger political, industrial and market orders on the other hand, must give men their due as the actual or potential heads of families. Men's claims are based on their status as father—the status is a claim to entitlement.

A third type of fathers'-rights rhetoric might be more grounded in genuine concern for the circumstances of mothers and children; it might even evidence a respect for what real-life single mothers have been doing in raising children in the face of major social and economic disadvantages. In fact, this discourse, which is more imaginary than real, resists adopting a primarily punitive and retaliatory attitude toward women. The focus is on refashioning fatherhood—teaching men (and boys) how to be responsible and responsive fathers. In other words, the target for "reform" is not the mothers, who have been shouldering the burdens all along, but the inadequacy of the definition of fatherhood in our culture.

We must reconceive the role of father within contemporary society. The focus should not be on control but on the assumption of responsibility, including the responsibility for self-definition. This third type of discourse (which is not really about rights but about redefinition) rejects the casting of fatherhood as primarily an economic or disciplinary relationship. It attempts to move beyond these traditional hierarchical meanings of fatherhood to forge social and political meanings that are corollaries to the challenges presented by single mothers. To be a nurturing father is to raise questions about, perhaps challenge the whole conceptual basis of the "private" family and to recognize the need for systemic societal reform to address inevitable dependencies. To be a nurturing father is to concede the importance of mothering.

This third strain of fathers' rhetoric acknowledges the crucial fact that mothers have been the "present" parent—the parent providing for the child, taking on the inevitable dependencies in our society. Mothers may have been doing so in less than ideal circumstances, producing uneven results, but at least they have been present. In fact, given the current situation and the impediments that daunt single mothers, it is surprising that they succeed at all. Mothers should not be subjected to negative comments or punitive responses if they "fail" when welfare payments and/or child-support orders are set at a mere fraction of what is necessary to raise a child.[7] In fact, quite often the resources transferred to her from either father or state do no more than place the single mother and her child below the poverty level. Women supplement or supplant these payments by working, but when they do, they encounter a work place with institutions and policies that do not accommodate their responsibilities as mothers.

B. Submerged Symbolism—Father and the Masculine

There is a tendency to use "fatherhood" in fathers'-rights discourses as interchangeable with traditional notions of masculinity. Fathers' rights in a broad sense, therefore, become a defense of culturally dominant images and practices of masculinity. This is certainly a subtext to much of the rhetoric, although it is a point seldom engaged directly. Fatherhood is, after all, an "essential" form of *male* behavior and, as male behavior, it is profoundly affected, defined, even confined, by societal representations. On that level, control, dominance, and independence are quintessentially masculine. The success of single mothers would be a blow to traditional masculinity.

Related to this point is the observation that, as males within this culture, fathers' attitudes about a wide range of activities are overdetermined. The culture is a male culture, violent (or at least competitive), confrontational, and individualistic. Socially "appropriate" male gender behavior is often characterized by feminists and others as punitive, repressive, and dismissive of women. Men, either as fathers or as sons, might more appropriately be concerned with how we might act as a society to change this dominant imagery of masculinity. If fathers fail to challenge the violent and misogynist aspects of the culture, a question might arise as to what is the purpose or point of providing them access to children? Will fathers, as men complacent with the dominant images, model this kind of behavior, perpetuating the distorted masculinist components of the culture? If that is the case, perhaps the best social policy would be a moratorium on fatherhood so as to break the chain of indoctrination into masculinist culture.[8]

This last point, offered more as a rhetorical device than a serious policy proposal, highlights the fact that even the most virulent fathers'-rights discourse does not really seem to be talking much about fathering. What does it mean to be a father from an aspirational perspective, recognizing that access isn't the same as nurturing, and that economic contributions are qualitatively different from sacrificing career and other individual pursuits to care for a child on a day-to-day basis? Fatherhood, like motherhood, should be more than a biological connection that carries with it all sorts of abstract legal rights.

In this regard, the Supreme Court Justices in the cases considering the rights of unwed fathers (see chapter 5) have been right to insist on something more than mere biology as the basis for the recognition of fathers' rights. Biology alone should not be considered a sufficient connection. Furthermore, marriage alone should not be sufficient to confer paternal privilege. Marriage is appropriately understood as forming a legal relationship to a woman, not as the basis for a claim to her child. Biology *plus* should be the prerequisite for all paternal-rights claims. The nurturing or caretaking connection should be a requirement for all fathers, married as well as unwed. Unfortunately, this is not the dominant perception, and notions of fathers' rights based only on biological connection are beginning to dominate discussions of access and claims to children.

Furthermore, while fathers' responsibility may be a corollary to such discussions, rights claims are typically premised on the presumption that fathers satisfy their responsibilities through economic contributions. Paternal responsibility is coterminous with economic transfer. When policy discussions turn to fathers' "responsibilities," therefore, the issue is not whether fathers are unconnected from or uninvolved with their children (i.e., whether they are exercising visitation rights and nurturing them), but whether they are keeping up with child support payments. The policy proposals directed at fathers are thus too often punitive and judgmental attempts to forge only enforceable economic ties.

Assuring paternal affection is not the object of social policy. Fathers'-rights groups were correct to pick up on and criticize this tendency to focus on the economic issue, but unfortunately, instead of challenging the primacy of the economic emphasis, they manipulated it to their rhetorical advantage in demonizing mothers. The overblown rhetoric about "evil" and "vindictive" mothers depriving fathers of their children provides the explanation and justification for the well-documented economic irresponsibility of many single and divorced fathers. Casting men primarily in economic roles in regard to their children obscures other connections between fathers and children and fosters the notion that children are objects over which one can buy control.

Of course, child support and paternal claims are not really a *quid pro quo* relationship. And there are fathers who do not want to maintain contact or assume responsibility for their children. These fathers do not seek to assert rights but are nonetheless targeted in the attempts by the state to impose financial responsibility on all fathers for their children.

The "problems" presented by fathers who do not make economic contributions tend to dominate contemporary policy discussions, which focus on how to provide "incentives" for these absent fathers. Often these discussions regress into mother blaming and single-mother bashing, with women targeted for punitive measures. There is a tendency for most discussions about fathers to sooner or later get around to blaming mothers. This tendency, and the policies that emanate from giving it vent, hamper the ability of women to perform the tasks associated with child rearing that are culturally and socially assigned to them. The extent to which mothers are not represented in these policy discussions is striking—mothers are typically objects but seldom participants.[9]

Significant in this rhetoric is the degree to which simplistic and unwarranted assumptions substitute for sound social policy. Pundits and politicians assume, for example, that coerced paternal visitation after divorce means automatic assumption of economic responsibility. Mothers might dispute that assumption, or at least point out that access can also mean abuse in the worst cases and attempts to control and dominate in many more.

II. Differentiating Fathers

An essential part of the never-married or newly single mother's story has become the failure of biological fathers to assume any kind of responsibility for their offspring. Currently, there are considerations of the potential role of the law in creating incentives for men to use contraception, pay child support, and marry their children's mothers. Given that feminists and liberal policy makers have long sought to distribute more evenly the burdens associated with reproduction and child rearing, one might inquire, "What is wrong with that goal?" I want to examine the implications of the search for ways to provide legal incentives for male use of birth control and the resultant potential for adding even more burdens to the load mothers carry.

My basic concern with proposals for using law to encourage male responsibility for birth control is that the question of how to provide incentives inevitably will slip into a discussion of how to create disincentives— a debate about the appropriate form of punishment for irresponsible reproduction. Furthermore, in reproductive issues, typically it is women who are punished, even in those cases in which men were the initial focus of the incentive-disincentive system. Perhaps this is due to an implicit realization that, because of their "unique" position regarding reproduction, women are likely to be more effective targets for coercive social policy reforms.

The focus on incentives for men is shaped by, and reflective of, society's values and norms about reproduction. Regarding the question of existing incentives, for example, the fundamental premise of the reproduction story seems to be that women have a natural incentive to use birth control because their decision is influenced by the potential for pregnancy and the resulting social role they will play as mothers. For men, however, the incentive must be artificially manufactured through the creation of economic consequences using the legal system.

A. The "Responsible" Reproducer

The conclusion that legal changes are necessary to provide incentives for all men to use birth control is not an obvious one for someone familiar with existing family law and policy. Because of the existing, well-established set of legal obligations that goes with marriages, a careful consideration reveals that men are more appropriately divided into two distinct categories. Some men are conclusively presumed to be responsible potential reproducers, others are not. It is the legal institution of marriage that provides the cloak of responsibility for some men.

Men who are neatly and securely tied to the nuclear family by marriage have plenty of legal and economic incentives to plan families—to engage in "responsible" reproduction. The incentives that married men experience in regard to reproduction are derivatively, not biologically, compelled: derivative, because being married ties the economic future of husbands to their wives' reproductive fortunes. Married men are legally responsible for child support, an obligation that extends beyond the marital tie should there be a divorce. Therefore, from a policy perspective, married men can be comfortably presumed to be "responsible" reproducers, not in need of further incentives regarding birth control. Married men's reproductive potential is contained and contextualized within an institution that has well-defined legal expectations and obligations for them and their relationship to their children.

Of course, it could be that, as a policy matter, we are not satisfied by the incentive for male participation in decision making about contraception that marriage provides. Some policy makers may want to use law to *enhance* male control over reproduction in the nuclear-family context. Perhaps some people feel that men would make better, more responsible decisions about reproduction than women do. A few men have expressed dismay about their perception that men have lost control (or perhaps never had control) over reproduction. These men believe that women unfairly exercise a monopoly over the reproductive decision. This attitude is reflected in the rhetoric of spokesmen for several men's-rights groups who strongly endorsed the idea of an oral male contraceptive because, as Dan Logan, Executive Director of Free Men, stated:

> We always treat reproductive rights as a women's subject and something
> they control[.] I think the fact that women carry a womb in their body
> is an accident of biology. It could just as easily have been men. We have
> just as much at stake in reproductive subjects as women do.[10]

In addition, Fredric Hayward, Executive Director of Men's Rights, Inc.,
believes it is important for men to get equal access to better contraceptive
options because, under the current system of reproductive roles, men have
been excluded from full parenthood. He stated that a woman's "idea that,
'It's my body, I'm bearing the risk, therefore I'm the one who will make
the decisions,' [is] the female chauvinism version of men who think women
shouldn't have the vote because they weren't the ones who fought in the
fields to get democracy."[11]

It is interesting to note that one of the issues in an abortion case recently
decided by the Supreme Court was spousal notification.[12] The Third Circuit
had recognized that existing Supreme Court doctrine precluded finding that
a requirement for spousal notification reflected a legitimate state concern
in protecting a husband's interest in a previable fetus. Therefore, the judges
reasoned, what the Pennsylvania legislature must have sought to preserve
was something considerably more modest—the preservation for the husband
of "the possibility of participating in a decision his wife is constitutionally
privileged to make on her own for her own reasons."[13] However, even this
possibility did not constitute the kind of compelling state interest that could
justify substantial burdens on the wife's right to abortion.[14]

A majority of the Supreme Court ultimately agreed that the requirement
of spousal notification was impermissible.[15] Nonetheless, it remains apparent
that other segments of society remain very concerned with protecting a role
for married men regarding abortion, a concern that may be gaining adher-
ents. In the words of one of the Third Circuit judges in *Casey:*

> A man has a fundamental interest in preserving his ability to father a
> child. . . . . [A] husband who is willing to participate in raising a child
> has a fundamental interest in the child's welfare. . . . It follows that a
> husband has a "legitimate" interest in the welfare of a fetus he has
> conceived with his wife. . . .
>
> This interest may be legitimately furthered by state legislation. . . .
>
> The Pennsylvania legislature could have rationally believed that some
> married women are initially inclined to obtain an abortion without their

husband's knowledge because of perceived problems—such as economic constraints, future plans, or the husbands' previously expressed opposition—that may be obviated by discussion prior to the abortion.[16]

B. The Irresponsible Reproducer

While furthering male control over reproductive decisions made in the context of marriage may be one element of concern, most law-reform efforts have focused on controlling the conduct of the unmarried man, presumed to be not only an irresponsible potential reproducer but also a likely repeat offender. It is with regard to this group of men that the reason for the use of law in the search for incentives becomes clear. Recent changes in the law are attempts to replicate the derivative incentives for reproductive responsibility that marriage provides—to tie legally the father to the mother and the child. While the paternity proceeding, the particular device to accomplish this goal, has been with us a long time, recent measures greatly increase its use and direct its consequences.

Theoretically, through the paternity proceeding, irresponsible reproducers are burdened with the same economic and legal consequences that men within traditional marriage relationships have. The reasoning is that the unmarried men will then have the same incentive to be responsible. The use of the term "incentive" in this context, however, is disingenuous. To a great extent, the social policy is really a search for an effective deterrent for irresponsible potential reproducers. In this case, therefore, the legal response should be viewed as creating disincentives or punishment—punitive responses to socially unacceptable behavior and its consequences.

A punitive model is consistent with history. At common law, disincentives for irresponsible reproduction included bastardy proceedings and criminal sanctions for fornication or nonmarital cohabitation.[17] Such starkly punitive responses seem out of date in our more sexually permissive era.[18] But while some states have abolished criminal regulation of nonmarital heterosexual relations, noncriminal consequences exist that are still enforced by the legal system. The criminal process has been replaced with civil proceedings that assign financial responsibility for nonmarital children, thereby coupling the single mothers' economic needs with presumed economically viable fathers. Theoretically these fathers will assume the financial obligations for their nonmarital children.

C. The Paternity Proceeding—
Transforming Irresponsible Reproduction

The paternity proceeding is typically classified as civil in nature, yet it is viewed by many public-interest advocates as akin to a criminal trial. The imposition of a child-support award is considered to be the equivalent of an eighteen-year sentence (the typical length of time before children legally reach "adulthood"). There are constant efforts to secure criminal-process-type protections for putative fathers in these proceedings, such as the right to counsel, the imposition of higher burdens of proof, and other reforms. From a state's perspective, however, paternity proceedings are far more remedial than punitive in nature. Perhaps most significant is their restitutive purpose—restoration to the state of the public funds expended on the non-marital child.

The frequency of paternity proceedings prompted by state and federal reforms has greatly increased during the past several years. Reliance on this process is an essential step in assuring private or family responsibility for children, and it has been a mainstay of recent welfare reforms. These reforms seek to ensure that children are firmly anchored financially, morally, and legally to a father by creating a legal tie between the single father and the dependent single mother and child. Unlike the consensual nature of the relationship between a married couple, however, neither the mother's nor the father's wishes regarding the establishment of such a tie are considered relevant.[19] This tie is essential for the incentive or sanction of child support to apply in a nonmarital situation.[20]

There is another issue involved, however, in exploring the potential of the law to provide economic incentives for male use of birth control. Even if incentives or reforms are conceived of as exclusively aimed at fathers, they will inevitably affect mothers negatively. It is the mothers, and ultimately the children, who are now, and will continue to be, sanctioned in pursuit of incentives for male responsibility for birth control. For instance, aspects of the paternity process itself are objectionable. First, single mothers lose their privacy, they are asked questions about their intimate lives and potentially are subject to penalties, including incarceration. Benefits may be withheld if they refuse to cooperate. In addition, many may also find themselves exposed to possible violence and abuse as a result of the establishment of an unwanted paternity tie. Furthermore, there may be other long-term implications because with paternity obligations come visitation rights and, perhaps, claims for custody.

The story of responsible reproduction and the role of incentives has significant social consequences that are perhaps even more potent than the potential for individual harm. The focus on paternity proceedings designed to tie together financially men and single mothers and their children obscures the magnitude and dimensions of the economic deprivations that make it difficult for women who make decisions to reproduce or to raise their children. Rather than addressing the needs of existing single mothers, disincentive reforms take the form of either punishing them for reproducing or pushing them into a nuclear family form—a model of family life increasingly discredited, even in the middle class from which it arose.

A legal anthropologist might view the paternity proceeding as a ritual. The state, in its orchestration and performance of the proceeding, reinforces, recreates, and reiterates several fundamental societal values. Paramount among these is, of course, the strong preference for formally celebrated heterosexual marriage as the core social unit upon which all else is founded. This preference places responsible reproduction within the context of the traditional family—a context in which the legal consequences are clear and the decisions will be considered and controlled.

III. Single Mothers and the "Costs" of Responsibility

The connection between irresponsibility and reproduction is even more explicit in the stories told by the recently enacted state welfare reforms. The New Jersey reform, for example, has two basic thrusts. First, it encourages marriage formation by creating economic incentives, thereby demonstrating a preference for responsible family formation. Married couples would be allowed to live together without losing a portion of their welfare benefits, as would have happened under the earlier law.[21]

Second, the reform both escalates and defuses the punishment or sanctions for irresponsible reproduction. The sanctions are justified by the rhetorical linking of reforms in public assistance with the assumption of personal responsibility. The punitive paternity proceeding is present, of course, but the legislation goes further than this in its imposition of sanctions. Mothers and children are directly punished by the removal of economic incentives for irresponsible reproduction. The new statute denies a monthly increase of $64 for each additional child born into a welfare family.[22]

As the New Jersey reforms indicate, the logic behind economic incentives in conjunction with reproduction ultimately leads to sanctions (disguised as incentives) on the single mother and her child. Justification for the escalation and expansion of disincentives is couched in terms of incentives—translated into an attempt at weaning people off welfare by forcing them to "be responsible for their actions."

In fact, it may be that even if fathers are also a source of concern, the mothers' behavior is more easily brought within the incentives conceptualization, simply because they are the ones who actually give birth and assume care for the children. Maryland recently announced welfare reforms designed to reduce benefits for welfare mothers who fail to exhibit responsible behavior regarding their children's school attendance and health care.[23] In California, Governor Wilson's Secretary of Health and Welfare commented on reforms to limit or deny aid if welfare mothers engaged in a variety of behaviors, including having additional children or failing to find employment: "Clearly what we are trying to do is promote personal responsibility and get people back into employment."[24]

If it is, in fact, easier to structure arguments for incentives directed at mothers as potentially more effective, more states are likely to produce such mean-spirited and parsimonious reforms like those in New Jersey.[25] Early signs from the Clinton administration indicate that federal reforms will follow in the punitive footsteps that beat the well-worn path to the door of the single mother. As a political matter, these women and their children are the weakest members of society, the most dependent, and the least immediately dangerous. Yet if contraception fails, punishment seems to be ideologically justified in contemporary welfare rhetoric.

The real tragedy, of course, is that the relationship between family and state is *not* central in the rhetoric. In the debates about the "responsibilities" of mothers and fathers, the inevitable nature of dependency is denied, childrens' needs are rendered invisible, the legitimacy of the claims of the needy and the disadvantaged on society is never addressed, and the concept of social or collective responsibility is ignored.

Also obscured is the politically forced intersection of morality with economics. Individual responsibility rhetoric neatly sidesteps the devastating impact of forces beyond individual control such as the global recession, the withdrawal of many businesses from the urban communities, and the restructuring or "downsizing" resulting in lost employment and downward mobility that is occurring in our contemporary economy. These forces, which have been particularly devastating to working-class and African-American communities, are what responsible (and responsive) fathers'-rights rhetoric should have brought in and made central to the policy discussion. Instead, fathers'-rights activists continue to engage in a misguided nostalgia for patriarchy.

For far too long and far too extensively, family policy in this country has been fashioned and formulated by patriarchal ideology. The nuclear-family ideal and the policy based on it foster the assumption that the maintenance of the family, from contraception to responsibility for the day-to-day care of children, is exclusively a private task. The costs of reproducing the next generation of citizens are assigned to the family—a unit that is assumed to be self-sufficient and independent, and in which traditional gender roles have functioned to assure reproduction and nurturing. This fetish with the private family has become more pronounced over the past decade and has precipitated the withdrawal of governmental assistance from all families, not only those of the poor.

Another basic problem with a consideration of incentives is that the wrong issues are often addressed due to the inherent limitations of law and the process of lawmaking. Law is a very crude instrument with which to fashion and further social policy. For one thing, law is much better at fashioning prohibitions and determining punishments for certain behavior; law is most effective when it tracks societal norms and values about which there is strong agreement. Using law to transform society by imposing norms on an unreceptive population, however, is seldom successful. Asking the wrong questions regarding incentives and reproduction in areas other than contraception has meant that the issue of how best to support women and children in society is relatively neglected. The concern with child poverty in welfare debates is subsumed into the debate on nonmarital reproduction and how to curtail it.

For these reasons, the idea of using law to provide incentives for male responsibility seems doomed to fail. The logic of a privatized reproductive story will inevitably contribute to the creation and furtherance of associated myths about the idealized private family and its relationships that instead should be challenged. The stories we are telling about our families, whether traditional or reconfigured, continue to justify sanctions and punitive reforms that create disadvantages for women and children.

Rather than seeking to punish Mother, we should be devising ways to enable her to provide effective mothering. With this in mind, Richard T. Gill and T. Grandon Gill have proposed a change in how we structure our working lives.[26] Noting the increasing numbers of women in the labor force and the increasingly early retirement of men, they suggest that we should delay entry into the labor force for parents, coupled with later retirement. Gill and Gill propose a Parental Bill of Rights modeled on the GI Bill of Rights that would allow one parent to stay home and care for the children without losing career prospects. This would "encourage parents to provide primary care for their own children, at least for the first five years of life."[27] This, of course, would require some form of state subsidy to the parents.

While this program appears most easily adaptable to intact families in which one spouse could stay home and care for the children without penalty, the authors believe it could work for poor single mothers as well. They propose three public policy alternatives: (1) encourage poor women on welfare to work and have others rear their preschool children; (2) encourage them to rear their own preschool children and then later get training and education; or (3) maintain a strictly neutral position with regard to these options. Their position is that the second alternative is the best policy, and they suggest that we might, at least, try experimenting with alternatives (1) and (3).[28] Numerous other positive approaches have been suggested.[29] Certainly some of our European neighbor states provide good models. Family allowances and other social supports facilitate caretaking in single-mother families, allowing these mothers to raise their children *without* the resulting social chaos. As noted by Angel and Angel,

> [I]t is clear that father absence is not a single phenomenon and that the rise in the number of female-headed families is the result of a complex set of factors. The consequences of father absence depend on the social and political context in which it occurs. In an affluent and progressive country like Sweden, where nearly half of all births occur outside of marriage, father absence has no serious social or economic consequences.

In Sweden, out-of-wedlock births are not stigmatized, and the extensive family support system of the Swedish welfare state insures fatherless families an adequate level of material well-being. In contrast, in the United States, which does not have a formal family support policy, the consequences of father absence depend on a woman's social class.[30]

IV. The Further Separation of Mother from Child

The focus on sexual affiliation has operated to deflect serious social attention away from children. At the same time, the individualization of the family has had the effect of separating Mother from Child—breaking apart the historic cohesiveness of that unit. While it is not possible to detail all the ways in which these trends manifest themselves in contemporary society, a few brief examples will give some idea of the nature of the problem.

The attention to biology in the fathers'-rights discourse and the struggle over reproductive power in the context of discussing paternal responsibility have pitted men against Mother in competition for the Child. These struggles make a fetish of children who are increasingly cast as victims of parental (particularly, maternal) excesses. This is certainly true in the context of the expanding definitions of what constitutes child abuse,[31] and patently evident in the whole concept of child neglect. There is a contemporary fascination with ideas such as those expressed by Alice Miller that virtually all children are abused—abuse is an inevitable condition of childhood.[32] Of course, since it is typically mothers who care for children, these perceptions support professional constraints on and supervision of mothering.

Furthermore, as women are alienated in their mothering, they are, at least theoretically, increasingly marginalized in the reproductive rhetoric. Legal and technological innovations such as surrogacy, frozen sperm, embryos, and egg donation make it abstractly feasible to speak as though we can "replace" Mother. It is possible for eggs to be taken from one woman, fertilized in vitro, and then implanted in another woman.[33] The conceptual separation of Mother from Child in this sort of technology, which commodifies both women and children, facilitates the separation of all mothers from their children. Women can be reduced to wombs, to surrogates, called "fetal containers" whose social worth is found in breeding healthy infants for society.

These procreational technologies fragment the reproductive process, separating conception from gestation and raising serious questions about parentage of children.[34] As John Hill says:

> We now live in an era where a child may have as many as five different "parents." These include a sperm donor, an egg donor, a surrogate or gestational host, and two nonbiologically related individuals who intend to raise the child.[35]

Some women welcome these innovations as giving them more reproductive choices; others feel that they represent greater control of the process of reproduction by patriarchal societies.[36] Janice G. Raymond presents an extremely strong critique of this phenomenon.[37] She notes that the western concern with infertility (a primarily white concern, I might add)[38] was a "script," written after the corrective technology was available.[39] She quotes Erwin Chargaff, molecular biologist: "The demand [for the technologies] was less overwhelming than the desire on the part of the scientist to test their newly developed techniques. The experimental babies produced were more of a by-product."[40] Raymond notes further "that over 200,000 embryos have been stockpiled in European IVF centers that have been specifically created for research."[41] She concludes:

> In this process, [w]omen's experiences of self, of reproduction, and of pregnancy are subsumed or negated. . . . Women are not present in the medical language, which speaks only of "maternal environments" and "alternative reproductive vehicles." . . . Worse still, women are not present to themselves. One women [receiving] in vitro fertilization . . . describes herself in the third person:
> "Here she is . . . debased and degraded, embarrassed and humbled, shamed and subdued. Their guinea-pig, their hatching-hen, hormone cow, their willing victim. And why? Because, fifteen years ago, when all she willed was sex and not babies, the doctor put an IUD in her almost virgin womb."[42]

When Mother loses her ability to assume her "rightful" place in a unit with her child, the vacuum created by her absence will be filled. History has already demonstrated that governments will step in to control the reproductive power of women when they believe Mothers incapable of making the "correct" choices. For example, when the government of Rumania decided that it needed to increase the population, it prohibited the use of contraception and made abortion illegal.[43] In contrast, when China determined that overpopulation was a problem, women were forbidden to have more than one child.[44]

Increasingly in the United States as Mother is marginalized, reproduction seems to be cast as of public concern (and, therefore potentially subject to public control). We see warring societal factions seeking to codify their world view in the debates about abortion, birth control, and sexual intimacy, thereby giving legitimacy to their version of what are appropriate ideals and values. The lawmaking process has become a highly charged, symbolic endeavor in these areas. Quite often the weaker, underrepresented members of society—women, children, and the poor—are those whose interests are sacrificed to the symbolic.

Notes

1. *See* Chapter 7, note 6.

2. William Safire, "What Fathers Want," *New York Times* (June 16, 1994): p. A27.

3. *Ibid.*

4. *Ibid.*

5. In this regard, *see* Wilson [chapter 5, note 19] discussing the work prospects for black men.

6. This is not always the case. The New Jersey legislator who proposed no new funds for new babies was African-American, and this fact was fully exploited by the press and other conservative politicians and by the presumptively punitive fathers' righters. *See, e.g.,* Lally Weymouth, "Building Self-Sufficiency," *Washington Post* (March 27, 1992): p. A21.

7. Lenore Weitzman's work is instructive. Weitzman reviewed child-support and alimony awards in California in the late 1970s and discovered some startling facts. Contrary to popular belief, alimony has never been awarded in a majority of cases, and in 1977 only 17 percent of women in California received it. Although most of these women were in marriages of long-term duration, over 54 percent of those married for more than fifteen years were not awarded support. The median award was $210 per month; the median duration, 25 months. Child-support awards were similarly meager: the mean child-support award was $126 per child with a total family average of $195. Rarely were men required to pay more than one-third of income. Reviewing the impact of these awards on men and women, Weitzman found that almost three-fourths of the fathers could pay the amount ordered without a substantial change in

their standard of living, but 93 percent of women and children would fall below poverty level.

Child-support awards have been affected by federal legislation mandating child-support guidelines, which have a limiting effect on judges' discretion. However, the equality rhetoric and no-fault divorce have combined to diminish the award of permanent alimony even further. When alimony is awarded, it is generally short term to help the wife acquire marketable job skills. Nor are these low child-support awards offset by property disposition, in large part because there is no property to be disposed of. Weitzman's study revealed that most couples have little or no joint or separate property. Those with family incomes of $10,000–$20,000 had a net worth of less than $5,000; those with incomes between $20,000 and $30,000 had an average net worth of $22,000; and those earning $30,000–$50,000 had a $30,000 net worth. For those who owned one, the family home was the most valuable asset with a 1977–78 median value of $33,000. However, only 31 percent of those married fewer than ten years owned their homes; for those married twenty years or more, the figure was 83 percent. Lenore J. Weitzman, "Examination of Divorce: Social and Economic Consequences of Property, Alimony and Child Support Awards," 28 *U.C.L.A. Law Review* 1181 (1981).

Eleanore E. Maccoby and Robert H. Mnookin have also conducted a more recent study of the consequences of divorce. Also in California, their study surveyed 1,100 families who were divorced during 1984–1985. Some of the families were followed through 1989 for postdivorce analysis. About a third of the parents had a high-school education or less; one-fifth of the mothers and one-third of the fathers had a college education; but the majority fell somewhere between, with two-year college degrees or technical training postsecondary school. Income for the fathers ranged from zero to more than $100,000 annually, with the most common amount being around $35,000. More women than men were not employed in a salaried job or were working part-time, and the most common level of earnings for those who were working full-time was $15,000–$16,000 annually. Substantial numbers were earning less than $10,000, a few in excess of $40,000. Family income was not reported. Most couples had been married four to eight years; half had only one child, and most of the rest had only two.

The study also looked at child-care responsibilities and found that 84 percent of mothers reported themselves as being more involved, whereas 42 percent of fathers reported mothers as more involved. Thirteen percent of mothers and 30 percent of fathers reported equal involvement; and 3 percent of mothers and 28 percent of fathers reported fathers as being more involved.

With regard to the economic consequences of divorce, the Maccoby/Mnookin study findings were similar to those of Weitzman. The couples had little net worth and the family home was the major asset, if any. When the mother had both physical and legal custody of the child, 89 percent of the fathers were ordered to pay support; when she had physical custody and shared legal custody with the father, 96 percent were ordered to pay. Most strikingly, however, when parents shared both physical and joint custody, only 67 percent of the fathers were required to pay child support. This is especially noteworthy for two reasons. The fathers in this category earned more than other fathers, and the mothers, who had to maintain a household large enough for the child, earned significantly less than these fathers.

The amount of the child support was affected by the number of children but not by whether the mother had both physical and legal custody or shared legal custody with the father. In both instances, the father was ordered to pay 10 percent of his gross income as child support for one child. The award for two children was more than two-thirds higher. In the joint physical (and legal) custody cases, the difference for one and two children was less and the average for two children was 8 percent of the father's income.

Spousal support was awarded in only 30 percent of the cases and was affected by the duration of the marriage and the incomes of both spouses, which are statutory standards. In those cases where spousal support were awarded, the parties had been married an average of twelve years, two years longer than the group average. Other factors affecting the awarding and amount of support were home ownership, education of the husband, who wanted to end the marriage, and whether or not the mother was employed prior to the separation. The difference in spousal income explains 30 percent of the variation in the amount awarded; addition of the other variables explains 50 percent of the variation.

Immediately after the separation or divorce, more of the women went to work, but their husbands were still earning almost twice as much as they were. Child support raised the income of those who received it to almost two-thirds that of the fathers, but for the less than one-third of the mothers receiving spousal support, the economic disparity was still great because usually she was supporting herself and any child(ren). Postdivorce follow-up indicated that fathers paid an average of two-thirds or three-fourths of the support owed and that compliance decreased over time. At the time of the final follow-up, approximately four years later, the rate of mothers working had increased from 73 percent to 82 percent. The employment rate for fathers (95 percent), although it fluctuated and dropped slightly immediately post-divorce (90 percent), remained fairly constant and was at 92 percent at final contact. Median income for mothers had increased by about a third—from $15,535 to $21,596 (1985 dollars); the median income of the fathers had increased by about 20 percent from $32,106 to $37,887. Thus, the median income of the mothers was still only about 60 percent of the median income of the fathers. The discrepancy is heightened when one recalls that fewer mothers were employed. When child support was factored in, the disparity was reduced only slightly, even assuming full payment. Overall, the immediate drop from preseparation income for mothers was almost twice that of fathers and did not change significantly through the three-year period of the survey. *See generally* MacCoby and Mnookin [chapter 5, note 58].

With evidence like this, one wonders what reality convinces policy makers that mandatory establishment of paternity and child-support awards, especially from those in low-income, dead-end jobs, is going to resolve the problems attributed to single mothers.

8. I realize that this is impossible and that it is not only individual fathers who transmit these values (or lack of values), but I use this argument polemically to make a point that the questions that are never asked in broad societal terms are: Give fathers access to children for what purpose? What do we hope to accomplish by this other than just validating an individual right? Shouldn't more be required when access is punitively secured?

9. A related issue is that of grandmothers, who are often the functional mothers in many poor homes and increasingly in middle-class situations. No one speaks for them in fathers'-rights discourses and the consequent public policy, which characterize the issue in the context of the sexually affiliated pair—mother and father in competition. *See* Karen Czapanskiy, *Grandparents, Parents and Grandchildren: Making a Case for Interdependency in Law* (on file with author).

10. Jean Marbella, "Men Offer Mixed Opinions on Male Birth Control Pill Contraception: Men's Rights Activists Applaud Option, but Others raise Concerns Over Side Effects," *Baltimore Sun* (May 14, 1990): p. 3E.

11. *Ibid.*

12. *Planned Parenthood of Southeastern Pennsylvania v. Casey,* 112 S.Ct. 2791 (1992).

13. *Planned Parenthood of Southeastern Pennsylvania v. Casey,* 947 F.2d 682, 715 (1991).

14. *Id.*

15. *Casey* [chapter 7, note 12].

16. *Casey* [chapter 7, note 13] at 725–26 (Alito, J., dissenting).

17. *See* Chapter 4, notes 6 and 7.

18. Nonetheless, adultery remains a crime in many jurisdictions in the United States. *See generally* Yolanda Woodlee, "Adultery Law is Rewritten: Council Aims to End Bias against Men," *Washington Post* (March 10, 1994): p. J1 (reporting that the D.C. Council, rather than repeal the law against adultery, extended its coverage to women); LynNell Hancock, "New York Forum About Adultery:

No Whoopie in New York," *Newsday* (May 16, 1991, Viewpoints): p. 118 (noting New York's and other states' continuing criminalization of adultery).

19. *See* Chapter 8.

20. Child support as a sanction for irresponsible reproduction (i.e., reproduction outside of marriage) is part of the structure of the Family Support Act of 1988 (FSA). The FSA reflects the belief that welfare dependency is a significant problem requiring dramatic reorientation of welfare policy. Provisions of the FSA mandate stricter enforcement of child-support orders, including wage withholding.

    While federal provisions help collect support from divorced fathers, thereby insuring continuation of responsible reproduction, it is in relation to unmarried men that major efforts were undertaken. States are required to meet federal standards for establishing paternity for children born out of wedlock as a means of obtaining child support from absent fathers. The provisions mandating paternity proceedings reflect the idea of responsible reproduction and, by legally tying the father to the mother-child unit, reinforce traditional norms of male economic responsibility for children that are typically expressed in the context of the nuclear family.

21. *See* Robert B. Gunnison, "Clinton Tells Governors Experiment With Welfare: President says Federal Rules Will be Relaxed," *San Francisco Chronicle,* February 3, 1993, p. A1; N.J. Statute Annotated §44:10-3.8.

22. *See* Chapter 4, note 8.

23. *See* Sevilla [chapter 5, note 52].

24. Vlae Kershner, "Wilson Plan Puts Welfare in Spotlight Across U.S., Other States Move to Trim Benefits," *San Francisco Chronicle,* December 16, 1991, p. A1. These and other welfare reforms proposed by Wilson were intended to help reduce California's budget deficit. Under Wilson's plan, California's wealthiest 1 percent would experience a one-half of 1 percent reduction in purchasing power. Most AFDC families, by contrast, would suffer a 10 percent reduction in purchasing power. Carla Javits, "Social Services Net State Budget Plan Puts Double Burden on the Poor," *San Francisco Chronicle* (June 11, 1991), p. A19.

25. This appears to be happening. It's as if the states are in a contest to see which one can be the first to abolish "welfare as we know it." *See, e.g.,* Schram [chapter 5, note 38]; Mann [chapter 5, note 51]; and Baker [chapter 4, note 4].

26. Richard T. Gill and T. Grandon Gill, "A New Plan for the Family," 111 *The Public Interest* 86 (1993).

27. *Ibid.,* p. 91.

28. *Ibid.,* p. 94.

29. For an excellent discussion of family support policies in other countries and suggestions for the United States, *see* Nancy E. Dowd, "Envisioning Work and

Family: A Critical Perspective on International Models," 26 *Harvard Journal on Legislation* 311 (1989); and Nancy E. Dowd, "Family Values and Valuing Family: A Blueprint for Family Leave," 30 *Harvard Journal on Legislation* 335 (1993).

30. Angel and Angel [chapter 5, note 5] at 9.

31. J. Dennis Semler, Note: "A Child's Emotional Health—The Need for Legal Protection," 15 *Tulsa Law Review* 299 (1989).

32. *See, e.g.,* Alice Miller, *Thou Shalt Not Be Aware: Society's Betrayal of the Child* (Hildegarde Hannum and Hunger Hannum trans., New York: Farrar, Straus, Giroux, 1984). For some of the difficulties associated with the "democratization" of abuse allegations, *see* Jane Gross, "'Memory Therapy' on Trial: Healing or Hokum?" *New York Times* (April 8, 1994): p. A1; Sandra G. Boodman, "Kathy O'Connor of Arlington Says She Remembered That Her Father Raped Her. She Sued Him and Lost. Are Delayed Memories Like This True or False?" *Washington Post* (April 12, 1994): p. Z12.

33. *See, e.g.,* John A Robertson, "Technology and Motherhood: Legal and Ethical Issues in Human Egg Donation," 39 *Case Western Reserve Law Review* 1 (1988).

34. *See generally* John L. Hill, "What Does It Mean to be A "Parent"? The Claims of Biology as the Basis for Parental Rights," 66 *New York Univ. Law Review* 353 (1991).

35. *Ibid.,* p. 355.

36. *See generally,* Nadine Taub, "Feminist Tensions: Concepts of Motherhood and Reproduction," in *Gender in Transition: A New Frontier* Joan Offerman—Zuckerberg, ed. (New York: Plenum, 1989).

37. Janice G. Raymond, *Women as Wombs: Reproductive Technologies and the Battle Over Women's Freedom* (San Francisco: Harper, 1993).

38. For a discussion of the greater concern with biology and genetics among white people, *see* Dorothy E. Roberts, *"The Genetic Tie," University of Chicago Law Review* (forthcoming, Winter 1994).

39. Raymond [chapter 8, note 37] at xiii. Critiquing the *Baby M* case, Raymond notes that Bill Stern, who had a "drive to procreate", had no corresponding " 'drive' to rear the child." The child would have been (and presumedly is being) reared by his wife, Betsy Stern, M.D., a full-time pediatrician, who planned to stay home to do this. "Surrogacy is about two women, both of whom provide mere maternal environments, doing for one man. It is a reproductive *menage a trois,* as always with the man at the center." (35–36.)

40. *Ibid.,* p. xiii.

41. *Ibid.*

42. *Ibid.*, p. xv.

43. Renate Duelli Klien, "What's 'New' About the 'New' Reproductive Technologies," in *Man-Made Women: How New Reproductive Technologies Affect Women* G. Corea, R.D. Klein, J. Hanmer, H.B. Holmes, B. Hoskins, M. Kishwar, J. Raymond, R. Rowland, and R. Steinbacher (Hutchinson, London 1985).

44. Robyn Rowland, "Motherhood, Alienation and the Issue of 'Choice' in Sex Preselection," in *Man-Made Women, Id.*

9

Re-Visioning

THE FAMILY IN AMERICA serves an important ideological and functional relationship to the state. It is not surprising, therefore, that the institutional or official representation of the contemporary family reflects the class and supports the socioeconomic position of those who hold formal and economic power. It is these people who are most involved with the formulation and implementation of family law and policy and who therefore control the content of the family.

As developed in previous chapters, the family operates as a complementary institution to the state on an ideological and a functional level. In our individualistic society, the state relies on the family—allocating to it the care and protection of society's weaker members and the production and education of its future citizens. To facilitate its performing of these social roles, the functioning of the traditional family is idealized and romanticized. The institution is conceptually positioned outside of the state—in its traditional form entitled to protection from intervention and control by external forces. State power and control, however, are implemented in the processes of legally defining the family, in delineating the functions it is to perform, and in creating the standards by which to measure the performance of any specific family.

Given the historic role of the family within the state, it is realistic to expect that decisions reinforcing the traditional family are perceived as necessary and, therefore, "neutral" and "just." Many of these decisions, however, represent unequal allocations of major societal resources—ideological and economic capital—to subsidize existing nuclear families. Tax rules, probate and inheritance laws, zoning ordinances, insurance and benefit regulations, are just some examples of the hidden subsidies that aid middle-class and wealthy family units. Although any individual provision may be called into question during political debates, the interdependency of state and the traditional family is ignored. The family as a societal structure is rendered invisible at the same time it is accommodated.

Thus, the subsidized nuclear family unit, mischaracterized as "self-sufficient" and "independent," is held out as the idealized norm. The rhetorical recounting of the presumed successful performance of this family contributes to a mythology in which the construct of the "independent" family masks the universal and inevitable nature of dependency. Thus, we formulate and implement state family policy around a paradigm that does not conform either to the ways in which a majority of Americans live their lives or to the dictates of the rhetoric used to valorize it.

The current normative system defines some families as deviant, subject to special regulation and control or to a separate, stigmatized set of social subsidies, increasingly punitive in nature. The "public" family is unjustly vilified in public policy discourse and provided with "incentives" to replicate the ideal model. These families suffer regulation through a variety of legal schemes from welfare regulations to the laws of abuse and neglect. "Private" families, by contrast have a gentle, supportive set of rules designed to govern them.

I. Re-Visioning Family Law

Property, contract, and (private) family law have been called the "three pillars of the civil law."[1] Family law differs from the other pillars, however, in that it has been formulated to regulate idealized families—those units that are the sites of socially condoned intimate associational relations. Family rules are most often based on the assumption that individuals interacting in the context of family do not interact with the same independence and distance as strangers dealing with property and contract issues. In fact, the traditional family is considered so "special" that the state is a necessary partner in the formation and dissolution of its traditional foundational relationship, marriage, and is thereafter actively involved in determining the contractual terms and property consequences of "the family."

Family law orders the interactions of individuals, creates rights and obligations, interests and expectations, entitlements and options, as does the law of either contract or property, but it does so within the context of assumptions about the family as an institution and its place within society.

Concurrently (and complementarily), the legal roles of Husband-Father, Wife-Mother, and Child-Adult are formulated in the context of the relationship that resides in the contrived institution of the official family, which is entitled to privacy and protection from intervention, regulation, and the state. Dependency is naturally assigned to this private family by the state. Within the family, this dependency is further directed by continued gendered role division.

Because we are concerned with this institution from a functional perspective, as a complement to the state designated to care for dependencies, we must consider the natural family a failure. In its historic form it is not adequate to handle both the demands for equality and the contemporary manifestations of inevitable and derivative dependency. It is essential that we begin to reconceptualize the relationship between law and the family in regard to these dependencies. In doing so, we should keep a few basic principles in mind. First, we must abandon the pretense that we can achieve gender equality through family-law reform. The egalitarian family myth remains largely unassisted by other ideological and structural changes in the larger society and is belied by the statistics reflecting the ways women and men live.

We also should recognize that family policy is a form of state regulation. We must therefore, be explicit about the norms and values motivating public and legal decisions about what should be protected or encouraged through social and economic subsidies. Furthermore, family policy must be secular, not based on a religious model. It should reference the functional aspirations we have for families in our society and be supportive of those aspirations. I therefore propose two recommendations for legal reform: the abolition of the legal supports for the sexual family and the construction of protections for the nurturing unit of caretaker and dependant exemplified by the Mother/Child dyad. These proposals are intended to direct policy discussions toward support for caretaking.

A. Ending Marriage as a Legal Category

Consistent with the first goal, we should abolish marriage as a legal category and with it any privilege based on sexual affiliation. I want to emphasize I am addressing only the *legal* significance of marriage. There would be no special legal rules governing the relationships between husband and wife or defining the consequences of the status of marriage as now exist in family law. In fact, these categories would no longer have any legal meaning at all. Instead, the interactions of female and male sexual affiliates would be governed by the same rules that regulate other interactions in our society— specifically those of contract and property, as well as tort and criminal law. The illusive equality between adults in sexual and all other areas would thus be asserted and assumed, a result that to many will be symbolically appealing. Women and men would operate outside of the confines of marriage, transacting and interacting without the fetters of legalities they did not voluntarily choose. Of course, people would be free to engage in "ceremonious" marriage; such an event would, however, have no *legal* (enforceable in court) consequences. If they didn't execute a separate contract, there would be no imposed terms as now operate in the context of marriage.[2] Any legal consequences would have to be the result of a separate negotiation. Mere agreement to form a live-in sexual relationship would not suffice.

This proposal is actually not very farfetched. We already encourage antenuptual agreements that are contractual deviations from state-imposed marriage consequences. No-fault divorce makes marriage a "tenuous" relationship. Opportunities for individual bargaining about economic and other aspects of sexual relations typically now occur at the termination of the relationship. Separation agreements (contracts) are the norm, not judicial decrees. My proposal would merely mandate that such bargaining occur *prior* to the termination of the relationship, ideally before the couple becomes too "serious." This is what occurs in some nonmarital cohabitation cases. Many states have begun to recognize such contractual commitments (promises) about sharing assets or providing compensation for "services" in "marriage-like" arrangements. Even if promises are not explicit, equity sometimes intervenes to protect "expectations" or to reimburse and compensate contributions to the accumulation of property.

One benefit of abolishing marriage as a legal category (upon which a whole system of public and private subsidies and protections is based) is that the state interest in bolstering the institution would dissolve. Adult, voluntary sexual interactions would be of no concern to the state since there would no longer be a state-preferred model of family intimacy to protect and support. Therefore, all such sexual relationships would be permitted—

nothing prohibited, nothing privileged. Of course, children would continue to be protected by incest and other laws, and rape would continue to be subject to criminal sanctions. *Voluntary* sexual relationships between adults would be unregulated, however.

Ending legal marriage would have other diverse beneficial implications. For example, it would remove the justification for the defense of marriage to a charge of rape; it would render indefensible the differential treatment of children based on their parents' marital status; it would obliterate the whole idea of "marital property" and end obligations for spousal support during and after termination of the relationship.

I realize that relying on other areas of law to regulate long-term sexual relationships is likely to have an effect on the development of doctrine. The ideas of "arms-length" transaction or the "autonomous" individual "voluntarily consenting" that are the basis of current contract law may have to be rethought and revised. Such a task is not the purpose of this book, however. If contract law were to become more reflective of "reality," in that it incorporated an awareness of differential power in bargaining relationships, this would be an improvement for contract law in general. The point is that the rules that developed would be applied to *all* contracts, sexually-based or otherwise.

This proposal to abolish marriage as a legal category, which I realize may be viewed as quite radical, is necessary given the ideological position of the sexual family and its role in maintaining inequality. This very position, however, forces the conclusion that the institution is incapable of reform. As long as it exists, it will continue to occupy a privileged status and be posited as the ideal, defining other intimate entities as deviant. Instead of seeking to eliminate this stigma by analogizing more and more relationships to marriage, why not just abolish the category as a legal status and, in that way, render all sexual relationships equal with each other and all relationships equal with the sexual?

B. Mother/Child Dyad

The second objective—securing protections for the nurturing units—reflects concern for the "weaker" members of society, the dependents who need protection. If marriage has no legal significance and the traditional family is not state subsidized and supported, these dependencies will be more visible. Hopefully, they will also become the object of generalized societal concern. One solution to inevitable dependencies unanchored by the private family would be the direct assumption of responsibility by the state through public institutions. I am uncomfortable with such unmediated state power, and would therefore want to maintain the concept of family privacy, merely drawing the line around a non-traditional configuration of family. It is necessary to give new content to the concept of family in order to provide 'a protected space for nurturing and caretaking. As Lawrence Tribe has noted:

> Once the State, whether acting through its courts or otherwise, has "liberated" the child—and the adult—from the shackles of such intermediate groups as family, what is to defend the individual against the combined tyranny of the state and her own alienation?
>
> Certainly the whole answer cannot lie in the municipalities and other political subdivisions that are euphemistically portrayed as tight-knit, cohesive communities. . . . Whatever the elusive ideal of community might require, one is entitled at least to be skeptical that it can be found in America's governmental units. . . . The polis of ancient Greece simply is not ours to re-create. Nor is a rebirth of religious community a realistic prospect for more than a handful of moderns. . . .
>
> What all of this has to do with constitutional law should be clear enough. The dilemma of contemporary individuals—isolated and made vulnerable to the state's distant majorities at the very moment that they are liberated from domination by those closest to them—cannot be ignored by those seeking to give meaning to the terms "life" and "liberty" or to the "privileges" or "immunities" of citizenship. If there is any answer, it is to be found in facilitating the emergence of relationships that meet the human need for closeness, trust, and love in ways that may jar some conventional sensibilities but without which there can be no hope of solving the persistent problem of autonomy and community.[3]

In my newly redefined legal category of family, I would place inevitable dependents along with their caregivers. The caregiving family would be a protected space, entitled to special, preferred treatment by the state.

The new family line, drawn around dependency, would mark the boundaries of the concept of family privacy. The unit would also have legitimate claims on the resources of society. Specifically, I envision a redistribution or reallocation of social and economic subsidies now given to the natural family that allow it to function "independently" within society. Family and welfare law would be reconceived so as to support caretaking as the family intimacy norm.

This re-envisioning reflects current empirical and social reality as to evolving family form. Instead of being a society where our ideals and our ideology (the private, natural family) are out of sync with the real lives of many of our citizens, we would become a society that recognized and accepted the inevitability of dependency. We would face, value, and therefore subsidize, caretaking and caretakers.

Of course, as this book demonstrates, rethinking on this scale is a quite grandiose objective, requiring massive reconsideration of many assumed roles and institutions on an ideological level as well as a structural one. It is certainly utopian to assume that such an endeavor would be undertaken, or, even if it were, that it would result in a significant shift in the way we, as a society, order intimacy. We can be sure that change will not occur any time soon (if at all).

The production of practical suggestions is not the only justification for theory, however. Sometimes re-visioning, even if utopian, is valuable simply because it forces us to look at old relationships in new lights and thereby understand some things about how we perceive the natural or normal, as well as how we create the deviant. I have argued in this book that law is a weak tool with which to attempt societal transformation. Nonetheless, when behaviors are changing, there appear some possibilities for social and cultural, and therefore legal, adjustment. Changing behaviors may present the opportunity for the creation of new theoretical paradigms or the occasion for the resurrection and rehabilitation of old ideals.

In using the term "utopian" to refer to the speculations in this chapter. I am characterizing the prospects for ideological change. Utopian is not the label to apply to the growing reality of single-parent families at the center of existing punitive and parsimonious social policies. It is utopian, however, to suppose that our ideology of the family will accommodate the need for change they represent.

Unmediated motherhood—motherhood outside of patriarchal controls—is threatening. Chapters 4 and 5 addressed the way single mothers are stigmatized and blamed for social ills as well as for the failure of their own family members. Homophobic fears for the sexual identification of male children raised by single mothers is also prevalent. On a grander scale, there are concerns about the "feminization" of society. Caretaking may be women's work, but only if it is safely confined within the structures of patriarchy—in the presence of men, be they represented in the natural family or in the state bureaucracy. Perhaps it is this fear that produces policies destined to ensure that unsupervised motherhood fails. Certainly the welfare and divorce rules seek to tie mothers to men. Abuse and neglect schemes introduce the state into single-mother families. Women may transmit and reproduce the culture, but men produce it—define the terms, control the structures.

What would unsubjugated motherhood look like? Unsupervised mother-hood, as a social institution, recognized as performing a valuable societal role, would be given privacy (without paternity), subsidy (without strings), space (to make mistakes). In thinking about this vision, it would not be enough merely to have laws that protected motherhood. In fact, the existence of law itself mandates negotiation with the state. Unsubjugated motherhood requires a social vision. It is this that will confirm the spaces where the state may not go—spaces protected and unsupervised.

C. Mother and Metaphor

As a concluding matter, I want to explicitly address my device of the Mother/Child metaphor. Abandoning myself to ideological utopianism, I have con-cluded that what is necessary in order to confront the hegemony of the sexual-natural family is an equally powerful cultural symbol. The most vivid and shared image of connection is the Mother/Child dyad. This is the prototypical nurturing unit, a fitting substitute for the Husband/Wife dyad that forms the basic unit of the sexual family. I propose Mother/Child as the substitute core of the basic family paradigm. Our laws and policies would be compelled to focus on the needs of this unit. Mother/Child would provide the structural and ideological basis for the transfer of current societal subsidies (both material and ideological) away from the sexual family to nurturing units.

The need for a positive societal vision is the reason the Mother/Child metaphor is appropriate. In excavating the image, I want to pull in the powerful resonances it has across a variety of discourses. Sara Ruddick combines positive images of Mother in arguing for "peace politics" based on maternal practices: "Preservative love, singularity in connection, the promise of birth and the resilience of hope, the irreplaceable treasure of vulnerable bodily being—these cliches of maternal work are enacted in public, by women."[4] Mother is an embodied concept with biological, anthropological, theological, and social implications that give it strength in the public sphere. It is also a concept that embodies the dependency that is inevitable in the form of the Child. The Child is part of the Mother—the embodiment of the idea of derivative dependency now hidden in the private family. Mother is a metaphor with power to make the private visible.

I have deliberately (even defiantly) chosen not to make my alternative vision gender neutral by substituting terms such as "caretaker" and "dependent" for "Mother" and "Child," although that is the interrelationship in all its forms that I seek to address. Historically, and in terms of its cultural cachet, mothering is a gendered concept and, partly for that reason, is qualitatively different from terms currently (incorrectly) substituted for it such as "caretaker."

I realize that affirmatively introducing Mother into a feminist debate will be considered by many to be too dangerous, but I believe it is essential that we reclaim the term. Motherhood has unrealized power—the power to challenge the hold of sexuality on our thinking about intimacy; the power to redefine our concept of the family, which may be why men have tried for so long to control its meaning. The Mother/Child metaphor represents a specific practice of social and emotional responsibility. The strength of the image is in its redistributive potential, grounded on empirical evidence ("reality") about the need for and the assumption of caretaking.

I realize that there are mothers who abuse, neglect, and abandon children. I realize that there are women who do not want to mother and men who do. The goal I have is to shift our perspective and expectations about family, and to do so it is necessary to rely on a social vision. Establishing Mother/Child as the symbolic embodiment of the nurturing ideal does not mandate that all women become mothers or that the "bad" mothers would not be punished or deprived of their children.

Two additional theoretical caveats are necessary. First, I believe that men can and should be Mothers. In fact, if men are interested in acquiring legal rights of access to children (or other dependents), I argue they *must* be Mothers in the stereotypical nurturing sense of that term—that is, engaged in caretaking. Second, the Child in my dyad stands for all forms of inevitable dependency—the dependency of the ill, the elderly, the disabled, as well as actual children. The child is an embodied concept, exemplifying the need for physical caretaking.

The more amorphous, socially encouraged, emotional dependency, so widely discussed in pop-psychology books, and socially constructed and maintained economic dependency are not included in the concept of "Child." I realize that these types of dependency may accompany the embodied, physical dependency that is the focus of my concern. It is imperative to limit the reach of the concept of dependency so that it can retain some coherence as a useful theoretical device. Emotional and economic dependency may be handled by resorting to "private" contract, but the social or "public" concern would be with more concrete and immediate types of needs.

Mothering should be thought of as an ethical practice, as embodying an ideal of social "goodness." As an idealized notion, motherhood should not be confined to women but be a societal aspiration for *all* members of the community. Mother/Child would combat the grip on our collective imaginations of the private, natural family with its centrality of sexual affiliation. This unit, graced as the new family norm, would provide the structural and ideological base for societal subsidies and policy. Our special family-law rules, no longer oriented to protecting sexual families, would bolster nurturing units.

On an ideological level, our understandings of justice are inseparable from our concepts of appropriateness or naturalness when discussing the family. Our appreciation of the implications of grand theoretical concepts, such as justice, is dependent upon our understanding of the effects and influences of power. Our societal sense of what constitutes justice for families as social entities, as well as our conclusions about what is just when conflicts must be resolved within families, are formulated in the context of existing, historically legitimated relations of power. Our definition and acceptance of the family as a legal and, perhaps to a somewhat lesser extent, social institution, and the acceptance of assigned roles to individual family members reflect the contemporary (and temporal) resolution of struggles of power and dominance.

Conversely, our experience of power is filtered through our perception of justice. Justice is the societal conclusion legitimating and condoning what might otherwise be viewed as inappropriate coercive maintenance of certain traditional family forms and expressions of individual power within families. Society's sense of justice allows the state to condemn alternatives to the preferred family arrangement as "deviant" and to subject them to exercises of state power that would not typically be condoned if directed toward traditional entities. The process of securing and maintaining state norms in regard to families reveals an interesting interaction between appeals to dominant cultural and social stereotypes and the process of law making and reform.

To be a "just" society, we must treat "all" families with respect and concern at the same time that we realize that the traditional family is not a panacea for the problems society faces. Our approach to the question of inevitable and derivative dependencies is crucial to the project of societal definition. The family can no longer be an assumed institution in policy discussions, but must be an explicitly self-conscious, constantly reconsidered configuration that reflects both existing reality and collective responsibility.

Notes

1. Mary Ann Glendon uses this characterization by French sociologist Jean Carbonnier to develop her ideas of "new property" in which the lines between these three areas are blurred and developments in one understood to reference and relate to developments in the other areas. *See* Mary Ann Glendon, *The New Family and the New Property,* (Toronto: Butterworths, 1981).

2. Special state laws and rules define the terms of the state marriage contract with regard to such legal issues as support, property division, debts, and responsibility for necessities.

3. Lawrence Tribe, *American Constitutional Law,* 2d ed., (Mineola, NY: Foundation, 1988): p. 1428.

4. Sara Ruddick, *Maternal Thinking* (Boston: Beacon, 1989): p. 229.

Index

Aid to Families With Dependent Children (AFDC), 107, 112, 116, 178, 186, 190; Wisconsin reforms, 112; Florida reforms, 112
American Bar Foundation, 121
American Enterprise Institute, 108
Angel and Angel, 104–05, 216–17
anthropology, 153, 213
Ashe, Marie, 123–24
Association of Family and Conciliation Courts, 120

Bartlett, Katharine, 66 (note 65)
battered woman's syndrome, 39
Becker, Gary, 153
Beezer, Judge; opinion in *Ellison v. Brady*, 49–51
Bowers v. Hardwick, 183–84
Bradley, Justice, 36, 48; opinion in *Bradwell v. Illinois,* 36, 38, 48
Brennan, Justice, 182
Butler, Stuart, 116

Caban v Mohammed, 86
Campbell, Emily, 123
caretaker/caretaking, 9
categories; colonized categories, 38; "mother" as, 51; in general, 18, 45, 125; in law, 38, 41, 125
Chargaff, Irwin, 220
child/children, 25, 84, 119, 147, 152–53, 203, 219–20; as an abstraction, 9 (note 1); child abuse, 119–21, 122–24, 180, 219; child custody, 77–80, 83, 118–20; child support, 212; children, in poverty, 113
Chodorow, Nancy, 155
classification, 18–19, 29–30 (notes 7–8)
Clinton, President Bill, 114

Cockburn, Alexander, 114–15
cross-over discourses, 102–03
Crenshaw, Kimberle, 31 (note 18)

Davidson, Nicholas, 122
de Beauvoir, Simone, 73
Delorey Ann Marie, 83
dependency, 2, 72, 158, 161–66, 231–33, 235–36; inevitable dependency, 161–63, 233; derivative dependency, 162–63, 236
deviance/deviancy, 6, 103–04, 118–19, 122, 146–48
divorce, 117, 118–19, 123, 148–49, 158–59
domestic violence, 156
dominant discourse, 21–22
dominant ideology, 21–22, 125
Douglas, Justice William O., 181, 183

Eagleton, Terry, 21
Eisenstadt v. Baird, 182–83
Eberstadt, Nicholas, 122–23
Edelman, Murray, 19, 52
Equal Rights Amendment, 37
equality, 148, 157–61, 164–66; formal, 37
essentialism, 43–44

family, 23, 25–27, 124, 143, 147, 156–57, 160, 163–66, 181–82, 191–92, 227–28, 231–32; alternative 1, 147; "broken" (as cause of poverty), 113–14; core unit 4–5, 200, 233–34; deviant family, 5, 144, 146–47; natural family, 5, 23, 85, 145, 147, 150–51, 157, 161, 163, 177, 189–91; nuclear family, 15, 27, 85–86, 113, 143, 146–47, 150–55, 157, 163, 189, 193, 215, 227; private family, 190–91, 205, 227; public family, 189–90, 227; sexual family, 143–45, 147–51, 161,

230; traditional family, 113, 146–47, 156–57, 163–64, 177–78
family values, 104, 106
Family Security Act, 116
Family Support Act of 1988, 110–13, 117
Family Transition Program, 112
fatherhood, 113, 119; new conceptions of, 55–57 (note 3)
fathers—77, 81, 113, 119, 123, 148, 186, 199, 201–08
female standard, 38
feminist legal theory, 12, 23–24, 26–27, 34, 36–44, 52–53, 155–56, 159, 188–89; acceptance, 42; accommodation, 42, 44; post egalitarian, 41–42, 52–53; post-modern, 43; sameness-of-treatment feminism, 37, 40–41, 67
feminist theory, 39, 154–55
Florida Employment Opportunity Act, 112
Frankfurter, Justice Felix, 38–39
Freud, Sigmund, 152

Gardner, Dr. Richard A., 119–20
Garfinkel, Irwin, 124
gender, 26, 148–49, 159, 164; gender difference, 34–39, 149; gender neutrality, 37–40, 67, 70–71, 75, 82, 88, 158
gendered life, 12–13, 47–48, 50–54
Gill Richard T., 216
Gill, T. Grandon, 216
Griswold v. Connecticut, 181–84
Grossberg, Michael, 80–81

Hamilton, John, 86
Harris, Angela, 66 (note 65)
Hayward, Fredric, 210
heterosexual unions, 4, 143, 145, 150–51, 160
Hill Anita, 63–64 (note 50)
Hill, John, 218
history, 154

illegitimacy, 79–80, 84, 114, 122, 148
International Union, UAW v. Johnson Controls, Inc., 64–65 (note 56)
intimacy, 147–48, 155, 162–63; burdens of, 25–26; organization of, 8, 26, 143, 145–46; as a vertical tie, 109, 145; as a horizontal tie, 109, 145–46

Jacobs, Joanne, 122–23
Jobs Opportunities and Basic Skills Program (JOBS), 110

Katz Michael, 107–08
Kay, Herma Hill, 40–41
Kelly, Florence, 38
Kondratas, Anna, 116–17
Kristeva, Julia, 65 (note 57)

Lacan, Jacques, 152–53
law, 15–18, 25, 144, 148–49, 152, 155–59; and categories, 18, 24; and coercion, 211–16; and societal change, 11, 19–20, 35–36, 155–60, 192–93, 208–11, 215–16; family law, 147, 150, 157–159, 227–32; custody law, 76–79
learnfare, 112
legal realism, 24
Lerner, Girda, 22–23, 65 (note 60)
Levi-Strauss, Claude, 153
Littleton, Christine, 42
Loftus, Tom, 186
Logan, Dan, 209–10

Maccoby and Mnookin, 220–22 (note 7)
MacKinnon, Catharine, 42–43
Madison Equal Opportunities Commission, 1–2
marriage, 3, 143–44, 146, 149–50, 157–58, 206, 209, 211, 228–30; as the solution to poverty, 108–09, 113–14, 116; contrasted with parent-child ties, 3
Michael H. v. Gerald D., 184–85
Miller, Alice, 217
Morris, Sandra, 120–21
Mother, 25–26, 70–78, 83, 87–88, 103, 148, 152–53, 155, 216–19; as metaphor, 235–37; as symbol, 71–72, 78, 89
mothers/motherhood, 24, 38, 51, 74, 78, 124–25, 148, 205; bad mothers, 117–18, 123, 234; deviant motherhood, 101–02, 106–08; divorced motherhood, 117–18, 123, 178, 190; married mothers, 148; natural motherhood, 5–6; single motherhood, 75–76, 80, 101–02, 114–18, 122–25, 147–48, 166, 178, 180–87, 189–93
Moynihan, Senator Daniel Patrick, 113–14, 116

Munchausen syndrome, 121; by proxy, 121; Munchausen moms, 121–22
Murray, Charles, 114

neutered mother, 67–70, 201
neutrality; of law, 25–26, 42

Oedipal complex, 152, 172 (note 32)
Olsen, Frances, 28 (note 2), 178–80
Okin, Susan Moller, 154–55

parenthood, 71
parents, 85
paternity proceeding, 196 (note 34) 211–13
patriarchy, 24, 103, 125, 146–47, 150, 202, 215, 232–33; as ideology, 11, 22–24
perspective scholarship, 11–12, 24–25
Planned Parenthood v. Casey, 210–11
post-egalitarian feminists, 41
poverty, 15; "deserving" verses "undeserving poor", 115–17
pregnancy 40–41, 57–58 (note 9)
privacy, 177–89, 192–93, 212; entity privacy, 187–89; individual privacy, 185–89
private sphere, 15, 24, 187–88
psychoanalysis, 152–53, 155
public sphere, 24, 188

Quayle, Dan, 104

racism, 102, 116
Raymond, Janice G., 218
reproductive roles, 35, 37, 208–11
rights, 180, 183–86; children's rights, 185–86; father's rights, 79, 82–87, 119, 184–85, 199, 201–08, 217
Rothman, Barbara, 73–74
Roukema, Marge, 117
Rubin, Nancy, 73
Ruddick, Sara, 233–34

Safire, William, 203
same sex relationships, 4, 143
Scalia, Justice, 184–85
Schreirer, Dr., 121–22
sexual affiliation, 1–2, 4–5, 143–48, 159, 217
sexual harassment, 49
sexuality, 202
Snitow, Ann, 74
sociobiology, 154
Stacey, Judith, 105–06
Stanley v Illinois, 84–85
Stevens, Justice, 85–86
Stewart, Justice, 86

teenage births/pregnancy, 115
Tribe, Lawrence, 231

Vogel, Lise, 54–55 (note 1)

Waite, Chief Justice, 146
Washington Post, 114
Weitzman, Lenore, 219–20 (note 7)
welfare, 114–118, 124, 185, 213–17; reform proposals, 113–14
White, Justice, 183
wife, 26, 68, 148
Williams, Wendy, 40, 57–58 (note 9), 59 (note 20)
Wilson, Pete, 146
Wilson, William Julius, 109
Woman, 43–44, 51–52; reasonable woman standard 49–50
women, 217–19; as members of gendered categories, 25–26; representation of women, 44 46–47
Work Incentives Program, 110
Workfare, 112

Young, Iris Marion, 54